CW00661370

infrastructure
at crossroads

infrastructure
at crossroads

The Challenges of Governance

GAJENDRA HALDEA

OXFORD
UNIVERSITY PRESS

OXFORD
UNIVERSITY PRESS

Oxford University Press is a department of the University of Oxford.
It furthers the University's objective of excellence in research, scholarship,
and education by publishing worldwide. Oxford is a registered trademark of
Oxford University Press in the UK and in certain other countries

Published in India by
Oxford University Press
YMCA Library Building, 1 Jai Singh Road, New Delhi 110 001, India

© Oxford University Press 2011

The moral rights of the author have been asserted

First Edition published in 2011
Second impression 2012

All rights reserved. No part of this publication may be reproduced, stored in
a retrieval system, or transmitted, in any form or by any means, without the
prior permission in writing of Oxford University Press, or as expressly permitted
by law, by licence, or under terms agreed with the appropriate reprographics
rights organization. Enquiries concerning reproduction outside the scope of the
above should be sent to the Rights Department, Oxford University Press, at the
address above

You must not circulate this book in any other form
and you must impose this same condition on any acquirer

ISBN-13: 978-0-19-807119-8   ⋅
ISBN-10: 0-19-807119-1

Typeset in 11.5/14.4 Perpetua Std
By Excellent Laser Typesetters, Pitampura, Delhi 110 034
Printed in India by Artxel, New Delhi 110 020

Dedicated to the nation

On the Author

In the eight or nine so called fast track projects, which were initiated around 1993, and which were still under discussion in 1996 when I took over as Cabinet Secretary, I tried hard to coordinate the forward movement; by bringing the various agencies and parties together, and coaxing them to find mutually accepted positions. Despite the endless hours that were spent, I could not make much headway. Various junior officials, including those from the finance ministry, saw it as a game to constantly throw a spanner in the works, to impede any forward movement. They would demonstrate authority without accountability...There used to be one officer who on first sight at a coordination meeting, I valued as worth a billion dollars. The Indian nation would have been better off paying him a billion dollars and retiring him from its services. Towards the end of my tenure, I found that he was in fact worth five billion dollars!

—**T.S.R. Subramanian**
Former Cabinet Secretary, Government of India
Journeys through Babudom and Netaland: Governance in India (2004)

The man a lot of IPPs apparently love to hate has also been nominated. Gajendra Haldea, joint secretary, Department of Economic Affairs, is the man who decides who will and will not get counter-guarantees. It's a tricky job that makes for unpopularity but people in some quarters feel he has acquitted himself superbly. He was praised for withstanding 'his ground against enormous pressures from the PMO and other influential people when it comes to making sure that no private company or MNC takes the country for a ride. A person of very high caliber.'

—Heroes of the Power Sector (1997)
Power Line, February 1998

Frankly, I have not come across such a clause in any guarantee. During conferences held in the matter, I was keen to know how this expression came to be incorporated in the GOI's counter-guarantee and I found that it was owing to the efforts and good work done by Shri Gajendra Haldea, a former officer of your Ministry, that the exposure of GOI under the counter-guarantee was substantially reduced. During negotiations with DPC, Shri Haldea insisted on the inclusion of this expression and modified the draft of the GOI's counter-guarantee which was submitted by Enron. He also capped the termination liability of GOI to a maximum of $300 million compared to a possible $1400 million under the State guarantee and made other significant modifications.

Shri Haldea's contribution becomes all the more remarkable in view of the considerable clout that Enron wielded at that time. It would have taken exceptional brilliance, skill, integrity and courage of conviction to be able to modify the draft of the counter-guarantee proposed by Enron ... I would humbly commend Shri Haldea for the recognition that is legitimately due to him.

—**Soli Sorabjee**
Then Attorney General of India
Letter dated 14 February 2004 to the Union Finance Minister

I was also against the counter-guarantee by the central government. When we came to power in 1998, many of these schemes were still pending. Rangarajan Kumaramangalam, the minister for power in our government, was very keen to implement the pending projects. We had innumerable meetings in the finance ministry to work out the details. Gajendra Haldea, the joint secretary dealing with this matter in my ministry, was an extremely efficient officer with a flair for detail. He was also a hard nut to crack. Ranga often complained to me about Haldea's tough and uncompromising attitude.

—**Yashwant Sinha**
Former Union Finance Minister
Confessions of a Swadeshi Reformer: My Years as Finance Minister (2008)

Gajendra Haldea, ranked at No. 5 in the list of 'Top 10 Bureaucrats'
—*Indian Express*, 22 February 2009

Haldea, who has been leading the dissent war on the process (of privatisation of Delhi and Mumbai airports), is backed by his boss, Montek Singh Ahluwalia ...

In the first round of pre-qualification (after 10 bidders submitted their expressions of interest), only one bidder was eliminated. But after the second round, only two bidders remain. 'A process that rejects a majority of such pre-qualified bidders must be viewed with concern. It suggests that either the first round was far too lax or the second round far too stringent', he argues in his dissent note ...

As a result of all these developments, the UPA-led coalition finds itself in one of the hottest soups since it took charge. Just as Haldea describes the entire process as 'untenable' ...

—**Anjuli Bhargava**
Contributing Editor
'An Unholy Mess', *Business World*, 30 January 2006

What makes the Jaipur–Kishangarh section of the golden quadrilateral special is that it is a true public–private partnership based on transparent legal contracts that might be a model for the world ... Such contracts have created a new level of trust and are enabling India to access funds, skills, and technologies from the best companies in the world, who will build and operate our roads, ports, bridges, airports, and container trains, and transfer them to the state in 15 to 30 years.

Gajendra Haldea, an unusual economist-lawyer of integrity and conviction, drew up these model contracts at the Planning Commission. As a result, he is the most hated man in Delhi's infrastructure ministries. He has demolished opportunities for corruption.

Soon we shall have 20,000 km of highways, hundreds of private container trains, and many private ports and airports—all in public–private partnership. These quiet steps teach us that reforms are not about 'what' but the 'how'. They are less about economics and more about law.

—**Gurcharan Das**
Author and Columnist
'Men and Ideas', *The Times of India*, 28 January 2007

The Haldea 'issues paper' on 'sub-prime highways' is important precisely because it deals with both these issues simultaneously. It talks of the NHAI promoting high-cost projects while, at the same time, trying to restrict competition. You don't have to agree with Haldea on everything, but the issues he flags are serious enough to warrant detailed investigation, certainly not the slanging match that Kamal Nath reduced it to.

—**Sunil Jain**
Columnist and Editor, *Business Standard*
'The Great Highway Robbery', *Business Standard*, 19 July 2010

Gajendra Haldea's essay, 'Infrastructure at Crossroads', is a valuable piece, which reflects the courage, the knowledge and the wisdom of the author.'

—**Dr Y.V.Reddy**
Former Governor, Reserve Bank of India
Book review of *India's Economy: Performance and Challenges*,
in *EPW*, 10 July 2010

For over a decade and a half, he has been leaving his distinctive imprint in sector after sector—ports, airports, highways, power and now railways. And leaving many gnashing their teeth and foaming at the mouth. As a wag remarked, the recent history of infrastructure in India is divided into two periods—BH and AH. That is, Before Haldea and After Haldea.

At the request of the Union Power Ministry, he drafted the Electricity Bill 2001 as part of the restructuring and modernisation of the electricity sector ... His book *Indian Highways: A Framework for Commercialisation* was released in 2000 by the finance minister ... In November 2004, he was handpicked ... with particular responsibilities relating to infrastructure reform.

In doing all this path-breaking work, Gajendra Haldea has been considered insufferable by many ... as the nation's conscience-keeper for infrastructure projects ... It is often said that you should count the impact a person has made on society by the number of detractors he has. Gajendra Haldea's detractors are legion.

—**Vinayak Chatterjee**
Chairman of CII's National Council on Infrastructure
'Who's Upset with Gajendra Haldea', *Business Standard*,
15 September 2008

At times, he reminds me of Rana Sanga, the famous warrior, who wore innumerable scars from the battles he fought for a cause.

—**Montek Singh Ahluwalia**
Deputy Chairman, Planning Commission
Introducing Gajendra Haldea in a meeting at
the Planning Commission, 16 August 2004

There are few persons about whose ability and integrity I have greater respect than I have for Shri Haldea.

—**Dr Manmohan Singh**
Then Leader of Opposition in Rajya Sabha,
Speech at Conference on Power Reforms in Chandigarh, 9 June 2003

Contents

Prologue

This volume attempts a narration of the principal challenges of governance that constrain the development of infrastructure in India. Comprising articles written by me during the past decade, the volume engages with various aspects of infrastructure policy and governance. At the end of each article, I have added a postscript that briefly explains how the events have actually unfolded. A striking conclusion that emerges from these articles is that the outcomes of flawed policy are usually predictable with a fair degree of precision, a conclusion that holds important lessons for the future. Of course, flawless governance is never attainable and it must be remembered that when change is pursued, it is often necessary to be guided by the consideration that the best must not become enemy of the good. However, while acknowledging this balance, one must also strive to ensure that the good is at least good enough.

From 1993 onwards, I have had the privilege of being associated with the evolution of policy and regulation relating to various infrastructure sectors. Since I have been directly involved in many an episode, I must acknowledge that my perceptions may at times be subjective. However, to the extent possible, I have tried to rely more on facts than on perceptions and preconceptions. It has been a long, challenging, and yet rewarding journey that needs to be shared with policymakers, researchers, and general readers alike.

This volume should be read in the context of growing awareness that India's growth momentum is being constrained by the government's inability to provide the requisite infrastructure. It is widely recognised that physical infrastructure has a significant impact on economic growth, quality of life, and poverty reduction. Yet, the infrastructure deficit in India has continued to rise over the years, primarily because of failures of governance leading to inadequate investments in capacity addition as well as inefficient utilisation of available resources. The Eleventh Five Year Plan, therefore, recognised the need to ramp up investment in infrastructure to a level of about 9 per cent of gross domestic product (GDP), at par with East Asian economies, as compared to an average of about 5 per cent of GDP in the past.

During the Eleventh Plan period (2007–12), the total investment in infrastructure is projected to rise 2.2 times in real terms as compared to the Tenth Plan period (2002–07). This ambitious programme has led to a spurt of activity, but it may still fall short of the targets due to inadequate reforms in governance coupled with the global financial crisis. Since the economic liberalisation of the early 1990s, many initiatives have been taken in the infrastructure sector, but only with limited success. It is necessary to draw lessons from the past for carving out the way forward, as transformation of the Indian economy cannot be achieved without modernising its infrastructure.

Private participation in infrastructure was one of the important planks of the economic reforms unleashed by the government in the early 1990s. This was so for two reasons. One, it was obvious that inadequate infrastructure was one of the main causes for India's slow economic growth over the past four decades. The other more pressing reason, from the point of view of the severe balance of payments crisis, was the need to restore the fiscal balance by containing public expenditure. It was inevitable that the government had to seek private investment in infrastructure to make up for the increasing shortfall in public investment.

Call it conflict of interest or unwillingness to cede turf, the incumbent players in the government were reluctant to facilitate the entry of competing private players on a level playing field. Both the government and the private sector courted each other assiduously, as anyone in government at that time—and I was lucky enough to have had a ringside seat—will tell you. The courtship lasted a few years, and even got solemnised in some cases—like the Enron power project in Maharashtra—but most of these did not last long. The parting was often acrimonious, and ended in the courts in the case of Enron. At the end of the five years of the Narasimha Rao government in 1996, there was not much to show by way of private investment in infrastructure, including the power sector where overseas private investors had evinced keen interest. As a result, the country remained starved of power, perhaps more so because public investment in capacity creation had gone down significantly.

In the absence of well-defined rules and norms, the initial years of private participation led to sub-optimal outcomes in several cases, some of which were exposed while many others went unnoticed or were contained. Besides, there were tussles between various wings of the government pursuing diverse objectives. The power companies, not surprisingly, wanted all types of concessions on their gold-plated projects and many powerful people in the government were keen to grant these concessions which, if allowed, would have bankrupted several state governments and even caused considerable financial distress to the Central Government.

Some men stood between India and financial disaster. Dr Manmohan Singh, the then Finance Minister, was at the forefront, supported ably by Finance Secretary Montek Singh Ahluwalia. I was fortunate to be in the team that put together a policy framework to ensure that private participation in infrastructure did not result in an unfair burden on the country. In particular, a clear policy framework was laid down way back in 1995 for eliminating Enron-like projects, while in several other countries, such as Pakistan and Indonesia, many high-cost power projects continued to be contracted. Considering the large number of sponsors that were seeking investment approvals in India, a great deal of potential damage was thus averted.

The efforts to create a fair and transparent policy framework met with limited success mainly because of the challenge from the vested interests. The politicians had their obvious reasons, though some genuinely could not even comprehend the issues. The bureaucrats, despite the Constitutional protection against being fired, and even though better equipped to assess the consequences, often chose not to stand up. Those who did, like me, were at times fortunate to receive political support, but only up to a point. After that, the entrenched interests took over, as indeed they continue to take over.

One of the ways to rein in biased umpires and incumbent players is to get independent regulators who would do a fair job, taking into account the need for infrastructure, the legitimate concerns of those willing to invest hundreds of crores in providing this infrastructure, and the need for not overburdening the consumers with exorbitant bills. Once appointed by the government, the regulators are expected to function fearlessly and impartially, and there are examples like T.N. Seshan in the Election Commission and Justice Sodhi in the first Telecom Regulatory Authority of India that come to mind. Unfortunately, Justice Sodhi was removed in 2000 for exercising his independence, suggesting a lack of appetite within the government to allow regulators any significant autonomy. Over the years, the hope of independent regulation has been substantially belied and the experience relating to the selection and performance of regulators has been far from positive. Though the United Progressive Alliance (UPA) government of 2004–09 was committed to regulatory reforms, the initiative to enact reform legislation could not fructify and continues to languish during its second term in office.

In this situation, there is a danger of getting the worst of the public and the private sectors. And since the people meant to protect the country from this mal-governance have by and large been silent spectators, the 'licence-permit raj' is still flourishing in the guise of a 'contract raj' where flawed concessions and contracts are granted by the government to provide opportunities for much rent-seeking.

There are plenty of instances that suggest how fragile and vulnerable the governance framework is when it deals with large contracts and concessions. In a recent case relating to the award of two of the largest infrastructure projects in India—Delhi and Mumbai airports—it became evident that the concerned officials and advisers had manipulated the evaluation process leading to elimination of competition. As a participant in the Inter-Ministerial Committee that processed these projects, I was unwilling to endorse this flawed outcome of the evaluation process and recorded my reasoned dissent. As a result, I was widely accused in the media and elsewhere of being an obstructionist and anti-development. Ultimately, the entire process was examined, reviewed and rectified. The outcome of the flawed process was thus altered. It also withstood legal scrutiny right up to the Supreme Court. In the process, some very influential interests were deeply annoyed. Indeed, philosopher–statesman Machiavelli had said, 'Hatred is gained as much by good works as by evil.' There is no dearth of similar incidents that expose the underbelly of our governance.

I was lucky to have been able to effect many a change, thanks in no small measure to the backing I have got from top political leaders, including Dr Manmohan Singh. I have also benefited from the support I got from Shri Montek Singh Ahluwalia, who has always encouraged a frank and honest expression of views and never suppressed a viewpoint even if it was politically inconvenient. Thanks to the confidence they reposed in me, I got the opportunity to write many policies, model documents, and frameworks that reflect best practices and have been adopted in several infrastructure sectors. I must admit that I did not succeed in many cases, though not always because of my shortcomings. However, the essays and articles in this book are not meant to tell my story; they tell the story of India's infrastructure sector: of where it is, where it should be, and what is stopping it from getting there.

My overall assessment is that a remarkable beginning has been made but a great deal of unfinished agenda remains to be pursued if the Indian economy is to be placed on a trajectory of high growth. It will require a leadership with resolve and foresight, as the reforms needed would face an enormous challenge from entrenched interests. Clearly, good governance should be regarded as a pre-requisite for growth and development. Notwithstanding the alleged illegalities in the allocation of spectrum in 2008, an interesting example of the impact of governance lies in the telecom sector, where introduction of competition did the trick.

After much trial and error that went on between 1994 and 1999—much of it arising from the telecom operators declaring their inability to pay the licence fee that was determined by competitive bidding—the NDA government finally set up a Group of Ministers under the chairmanship of External Affairs Minister Jaswant Singh for resolving the stalemate, with the Prime Minister's Office playing a proactive role. The outcome was a National Telecom Policy (NTP) 1999 which restructured the payment obligations of licencees on the basis of revenue sharing. The NTP 1999 spurred a very impressive growth in mobile telephony. While the annual growth rate during the past decade has almost matched China's, call charges have been much lower compared to those in China, or for that matter any developed country, thanks to intense competition in the market. Though the NTP 1999 laid down a sound industry structure to promote competition, growth, and welfare, it was not without its share of controversies. Allowing the existing licensees to migrate to the new regime without an appropriate charge or penalty was cause for severe criticism in some quarters. Condoning some blatant violations that were committed by a particular licensee in 2003 also led to criticism of the regulator and the government.

The telecom revolution is an extraordinary example of what decisive action in a framework of good governance can do. Private investment in 2008–09 was an impressive Rs 51,000 crore, which represented an increase of 8.6 times over a span of just seven years, and constituted over 80 per cent of the total investment in this sector. The achievement of targets for teledensity is three years ahead of schedule; over 10 million subscribers are added every month; and the total subscribers have crossed 700 million. This success is clearly unparalleled.

This extraordinary track record of the telecom sector was swamped by the award of fresh licences and spectrum in 2008, which has led to a controversy of unprecedented proportions. The report of the Comptroller and Auditor General, tabled in the Parliament in November

2010, caused a furore that forced the resignation of the incumbent Telecom Minister, followed by his arrest. This issue is currently *sub judice*, but the stark governance failures that have been revealed need to be addressed forthwith.

In contrast with the telecom sector, reform of the power sector never really took off. Even today, the incumbent state-owned monopolies continue to rule the roost and the introduction of competition in the supply of electricity to consumers remains a pipe dream. As a result, power shortages have only increased during the past decade, compromising growth and welfare. For example, the peak shortage of power increased from 12.2 per cent in 2002–03 to 16.6 per cent in 2007–08, though it declined thereafter to 13.3 per cent in 2009–10. Among other reasons, the telecom revolution occurred because there was vacant space in mobile telephony where the incumbents had little presence. In the case of the power sector, however, public sector incumbents are firmly entrenched in every segment of the industry structure and they are unwilling to yield to any reform that would challenge their monopoly.

Among the experiences that I treasure most, the opportunity to draft the Electricity Bill was indeed a rare privilege in the pursuit of reform. In 1999, I was able to convince late P.R. Kumarmangalam, the then Union Minister for Power, to enact a new law for modernising the electricity industry, as the 1910 and 1948 enactments had become obsolete, especially when compared to the industry restructuring in developed countries. When he insisted that I take on the responsibility of drafting the new law, I accepted the challenge and took long leave to be able to devote myself to what I regarded as a complex task of great national importance.

The Herculean effort involved in writing a new law for the electricity sector began with the presentation of the first draft of the Electricity Bill at the Chief Ministers' Conference held in February 2000 under the PM's chairmanship. The Conference gave a mandate to engage in a consultative process with a view to evolving consensus for the proposed legislation. In the 18 months that followed, 41 seminars and conferences were held and 234 written interventions were received.

The Bill was revised through eight successive versions that were circulated for an open debate. When the Bill was introduced in Parliament in 2001, another 18 months of consultation followed. The Bill was finally enacted in April 2003. This was perhaps the only legislation in independent India that followed such an extensive, broad-based, and open consultative process. What emerged was a comprehensive legislation that provided the framework for modernising and invigorating India's power sector to bring it at par with the developed world.

Yet again, the failures of governance have withheld the fruits of reform that the Electricity Act promised. At the heart of the new law was the introduction of competition and open access that would enable producers to access consumers in the market—as in the case of telecom. It is regrettable that the power sector is still far from this objective, as the entrenched interests have erected barriers that have prevented any competition and open access for the consumers. While a household consumer in London can choose from among 12 competing suppliers, this is not even recognised by the Central and state governments as an objective worth pursuing. Even today, all producers and traders must sell their produce solely to near-bankrupt state utilities. As a result, investment continues to shy away and shortages persist. This represents an extraordinary example of subversion of an important legislation that affects the lives of virtually all citizens.

Manipulation of the new electricity law has also led to unintended outcomes that threaten the very viability of the power sector. Through a convoluted form of trading that is confined to bulk purchases by state-owned monopolies, trading prices have been jacked up during the past few years. In 2009–10 alone, 6,590 crore units of bulk power were sold for about Rs 33,000 crore at an average price of Rs 5 per unit (about 11 cents per unit). This has led to unearned profits of about Rs 20,000 crore for the sellers and corresponding losses for the state-owned distribution companies. The situation was no different in 2008–09. As a result, the losses of distribution companies have increased from Rs 27,101 crore in 2006–07 to about Rs 58,285 crore in 2009–10. The only comparable event is the infamous California power crisis of 2001 when traders pushed up the bulk prices relentlessly. Since these high prices could not be passed on to the consumers, the entire power industry in California suffered a collapse, compelling the state to make costly interventions. Unfortunately, there are no signs yet of any resolve to deal with this growing menace in India. Perhaps, the government would intervene only after this problem assumes crisis proportions.

In the case of ports owned and operated by the Central Government through the respective port trusts, good governance remains equally elusive, both in the operation of the existing capacity as well as in its expansion. Concessions for six new terminals have been awarded in recent years on the basis of a prevailing structure that blatantly violated the interests of the users as well as the government. For example, a case study published by the Planning Commission showed that at a terminal in the Nava Sheva port at Mumbai, the concessionaire was allowed by the regulator to get over 80 per cent returns on its equity by overcharging the users. In Tuticorin, the concessionaire has been charging almost double the tariff s compared to what is due.

Of the 46 port terminals that were to be awarded during 2006–11 at the major ports run by the Central Government, not even one had been awarded until March 2009. After much delay and resistance, some order was restored and 13 concessions were awarded in 2009–10 through a fairly transparent framework. However, it would take about three years for the new capacity to be constructed. Thanks to the rapid expansion of private ports in the state sector, the adverse effect of the lack of capacity addition by the port trusts has been substantially mitigated for the time being. It is a different matter that the selection of project sponsors for private ports in the state sector has often been less than transparent because it has rarely followed a competitive bidding route which should normally have been a key requirement.

Coming to the national highways sector, the Congress government (1991–6) did place the highway programme on the national agenda, but it could not show tangible results, especially in its efforts to get private investment in toll roads. In 1999, the NDA government announced the four-laning of the national highway network comprising the North—South and East—West corridors as its flagship project.

This alignment did not carry much traffic and when this became evident the initiative was restructured to give primacy to the well-established Golden Quadrilateral (GQ) connecting Delhi, Mumbai, Kolkata, and Chennai. The GQ project was implemented efficiently and is generally regarded as a success story. However, it was almost entirely funded by public expenditure with little private investment through public–private partnership (PPP). In that sense, the GQ programme was based on a conventional approach which was constrained by the limitations of budgetary resources and did not, therefore, have much scope for exploiting new potential. As the programme got underway, it also suffered from the usual time and cost overruns associated with conventional contracts.

The maintenance of highways constructed by the National Highways Authority of India (NHAI) through cash contracts has also begun to pose serious issues while pilferage of toll revenues is eating into the much-needed resources. A notable exception in the GQ is the 95 km section between Jaipur and Kishangarh that was undertaken through private participation; a drive from Delhi to Mumbai, which includes this stretch, would at once reveal the comparative advantages of private participation in highway development.

The story of national highways is indeed one of missed opportunities. The UPA Government (2004–09) did emphasise the role of PPP in highway development but progress was patchy at best. The politician–contractor–engineer trio operates with full force in this sector. Projects are routinely over-engineered and implemented in a manner where public interest is the casualty. This trio typically shuns a fair and transparent concession framework for PPP projects and, as a result, it has prevented large volumes of competitive private investment that would have ensured rapid development of the highway sector. The NHAI is the statutory entity charged with the task of developing national highways. Over the years, it has not been able to come up to expectations in the crucial areas of ensuring transparency and enforcing accountability. Scores of contracts suffer from large time and cost overruns, often involving double the anticipated time and costs, yet neither the engineer nor the contractor is ever penalised.

While the NHAI has always been quick to award cash contracts for road construction, it has only awarded an average of about 20 per cent of its own targets for PPP concessions, year after year. While the efficacy of PPP concessions has been well recognised in the highways sector, it has nevertheless been difficult to wean away NHAI from its cash contracts and move to a transparent and competitive award of PPP concessions. As a result, not only has the road sector suffered immensely, its ability to provide a stimulus for economic growth has also been severely compromised. Of late, progress in the award of PPP projects has picked up, but this seems to be accompanied by growing concerns about the credibility and sustainability of the modified approach, which seems to be accompanied by gold-plating of costs and cartelisation in bidding. In effect, the costs to be borne by the government have been rising significantly, especially because the user charges are not being adjusted to off-set these increased costs. The prevailing budgetary constraints are bound to slow down this loss-making approach by curtailing the programme size in the same way that crippled the state electricity boards. A fresh dose of reforms in the highway sector, therefore, seems necessary.

The airport sector has in some ways done exceptionally well in creating two greenfield airports at Bengaluru and Hyderabad, and in redeveloping the airports at Delhi and Mumbai to world-class standards. From the perspective of good governance, however, there were several infirmities. The terms of the concession agreements for the Bengaluru and Hyderabad airports were negotiated after the preferred sponsor was selected. As such, there was no competitive bidding worth the name. The case of Delhi and Mumbai airports shows a much superior process. Their concession agreements were settled prior to bidding, representing a significant improvement compared to earlier projects. However, some of the terms were relaxed after the award of concessions, which has been criticised in the media. During the course of implementation, it is possible that some of these changes may compromise both the government and the user interests with possible perceptions of partisan decision-making. Moreover, besides PPP in these four metro airports, there is little else to show by way of reform in the airport sector.

The railways had turned around for a few years in terms of their profitability—largely on account of an increase in freight traffic, propelled by the robust growth of the Indian economy coupled with some re-engineering of commercial policies. Predictably, these turned out to be short-term gains because the basic flaws in the structure of Indian Railways continue to persist. Unlike the railways in other countries, Indian Railways are still run as a government department with an archaic structure, outmoded policies, and outdated technology. Compared to China, where the railways carry over 48 per cent of the total freight, the Indian Railways carry just about 36 per cent. The need for fundamental reform in railway structures and policies has been emphasised in many Five Year Plans, but the Indian Railways have thus far avoided any substantive reform even while all other sectors of the economy have undergone significant liberalisation. There is hardly any private investment in the railway sector, while public resources continue to be grossly insufficient. Without a major shake-up, the railways will continue to be a significant constraint on economic growth.

In the case of metro rail projects, there have been several new initiatives but not conforming to a single model. For example, the Delhi Metro Rail Corporation (DMRC) and its counterparts in Bengaluru, Chennai, and Kolkata are owned by the Centre and the respective states in a ratio of 50:50. As a result, these companies are neither under the control of the Central Government nor under their respective state governments. This model is seen to have worked well in DMRC, but that is because it gives an unusual freedom to the CEO of DMRC, which can be found neither in the public sector nor even the private sector. The CEO's tenure is also unparalleled as it has already exceeded 14 years. It is clearly not a model that can be replicated.

It needs to be mentioned that DMRC received government funding of about Rs 10,000 crore at an average annual cost of only about 1 per cent for meeting the entire capital cost of its Phase I, which was completed in 2006. Further, about half of its annual operational costs are met out of revenues from the real estate so generously provided by the government. Such hidden subsidies must be costed and accounted for in an open and transparent manner, and evaluated in the context of competing demands for allocation of public resources. If Delhi Metro were a lone project, the aforementioned issues would have been contained. However, the proposal to follow a similar approach for Bengaluru, Kolkata, Chennai, and other cities would throw up significant issues of financing, sustainability, and governance in the years to come. On the other hand, two metro rail projects in Mumbai and one in Hyderabad are coming up in the PPP mode. They have relied on private investment for funding bulk of the capital costs and no subsidies or losses would be borne by the government during the period of operation. For example, the Hyderabad metro project would require an investment of about Rs 14,000 crore, of which only Rs 1,458 crore will be provided by the Central Government as a capital grant. These projects are also expected to be more efficient compared to the public sector metro projects.

While choosing the high-cost metro rail option, some consideration must be given to the fact that far more economical options like augmentation of bus services have languished in neglect while the government seems to be bending over backwards to sanction capital-intensive metro projects that will serve a limited segment of urban commuters. External assistance from Japan has helped finance these projects but this assistance is effectively a claim on the limited borrowing capacity of the government. It is time to intensify the search for sustainable options that can meet the challenges posed by the accelerated growth of urbanisation in India.

It is clear that the public sector does not have the resources or the implementation capacity to sustain a rapid growth in infrastructure development. The financial viability of its projects is often compromised on account of time and cost overruns while users face the consequent delays in provision of services. Furthermore, the expenditure culture encourages public sector entities to over-engineer and build ever costlier projects. For example, the manner in which specifications and costs have been increased sharply for the national highway projects would only lead to fewer projects, which in turn would leave the bulk of the network in continued neglect. Similarly, the opulent and high-cost air terminals being built by the Airports Authority of India (AAI) at several non-metro airports would only push the respective airports into further losses, leading to an inevitable hike in user charges. That corruption is rampant in construction contracts is an open secret. In sum, the prevalent corruption, inefficiency, and gold-plating in public sector projects raise the capital costs that inevitably reduce the programme size and compromise the delivery of services across sectors. As a result, user feedback in respect of services provided by the public sector is rarely positive.

The solution obviously lies in attracting more private investment in infrastructure, but this will not be easy to mobilise if the incumbent ministries and organisations are not willing to cede turf to the private sector. They use all possible means to expand their own contracting options instead of allowing the private sector to move in. Wherever the private sector is allowed to enter, it is not unusual to find a bidding and contractual framework that enables favoured entities to gain undue advantages based on not-so-holy alliances between the government entity concerned and the preferred bidder. User interests are routinely compromised and user charges go up frequently, making such reforms unpopular and self-defeating. Another serious fallout is that the public exchequer loses heavily in terms of lower revenues, costlier bids, and other liabilities. The fact that several foreign investors have shown keen interest in infrastructure but have actually refrained from bidding for projects suggests that the framework in some of the sectors is not credible enough for providing the assurance of fair and transparent transactions.

Fear of the avarice of private entrepreneurs is often cited as the reason for limiting the role of the private sector in providing public services. There should be little doubt that the private sector works for profit, not charity. It may cut corners where it can and may also short-change the consumers in pursuit of its profit motive. That is where the role of governance assumes significance. It is for the government to enforce the rules that protect the ordinary citizen. For example, if fair competition is enabled and performance standards relating to the quality of services are enforced, then the private sector can hardly exploit the common man. Unless the greed of a private entity is accompanied by corruption or negligence in the government, rent-seeking cannot normally occur. Crony capitalism is a phenomenon that essentially involves the government and the private sector acting in concert. Whichever way you look at it, the fundamental issue is that of governance.

One of the central problems of governance is the lack of accountability which allows policy to be manipulated by vested interests. Over the years, the bureaucracy has evolved systems and processes that virtually absolve the bureaucrats and their political masters of the consequences of their acts of commission and omission. The intent of their actions and the outcomes thereof are rarely attributed to them; nor do failures affect their career progression. There is neither any compulsion nor any incentive to perform in a professional manner or in public interest. In this 'free-for-all' environment, what seems to keep the government moving is perhaps the sheer momentum of past traditions, procedures, and processes. Without comprehensive reforms in governance, the pace of deterioration will only accelerate and inflict further damage to the fabric that sustains India's economy.

The aforementioned examples clearly suggest that the most critical issues facing infrastructure development relate to governance. There is a huge demand for infrastructure; users are willing to pay economic charges for improved services; and there is enormous interest among domestic and foreign investors. Yet, the barriers erected by incumbent government entities have constrained progress, and the annual investment in infrastructure continued to hover around 5 per cent of GDP during the decade of the Ninth and Tenth Five Year Plans (1997–2007).

I have often been told that my stance is substantially negative. After all, no one can deny that many projects have indeed attracted private investment and that economic growth too has stepped up considerably. But the key question arises: can we do better? Why is a quarter-full glass good enough? The huge power shortages and the consequent loss in jobs and productivity are enough of an answer to this.

Imagine the jobs that would be created and incomes generated if the investment in infrastructure were to rise from 5 per cent of GDP to about 9 per cent or so, implying an additional investment of over Rs 2,00,000 crore every year in absolute terms. This will not just create jobs in building roads, ports, or airports, but also provide more jobs in factories that will start humming once there is power. Besides causing the loss of potential employment and incomes, a low level of investment in infrastructure is also unsustainable on several other counts. For example, if the users of port terminals keep paying steep charges and also face delays, they lose out in global competitiveness; if air travellers face twice the airport charges, they could choose other modes of travel; if the best infrastructure firms shy away because they are unable to compete with corrupt and inefficient firms, the infrastructure services would be compromised. If all this continues to lead to sub-optimal services and rising tariffs, the users will rebel at some point while manufacturing and services will become uncompetitive. This chain of events would, of course, slow down economic growth itself.

In response to my critics, I would only say that I have tried to do my best and I believe that I have been able to make a difference. As noted earlier, I had the privilege of drafting the Electricity Bill that was enacted by the Parliament in 2003 and is generally regarded by sector experts as a modern piece of legislation for reform of the power sector. It took an enormous effort to create this draft legislation and build consensus among diverse stakeholders. I was also fortunate in being able to introduce the concept of model concession agreements in 1997, and then went on to author 12 model concession agreements that have already tied up private investment in different sectors in excess of Rs 2,00,000 crore. Such documents do not exist elsewhere in the world and are widely regarded as a pioneering effort towards building infrastructure in a fair, transparent, and efficient manner. It was also my good fortune to have been able to draft the standard bidding documents and processes that have vastly improved and accelerated the process of private participation in infrastructure sectors. A notable example is the Rs 14,000 crore Hyderabad Metro

Rail project that has relied completely on these model documents for delivering a fair, transparent, and economic outcome. It is not surprising that the vested interests feel constrained by these transparent and fair systems. They often lead a fairly vocal charge that seems personal rather than issue-based. On my part, I do recognise that it might take several years for the dust to settle down and for an objective picture to emerge.

Evidently, the objective of public policy should be to strike an equitable balance among multiple stakeholders who may be pursuing divergent interests, which are often in conflict with one another. However, the relatively influential stakeholder groups tend to lobby for a greater share of the pie even though it comes at the cost of others and may render the policy unfair or unacceptable to other stakeholders. Any policymaker who resists such demands and tries to balance the conflicting interests of different stakeholders is seen as unsympathetic to the respective pressure groups and risks unpopularity in several quarters, especially among those who wield greater influence. On the other hand, none of the stakeholders would extend tangible support to the policymaker as most of them would tend to believe that the policy did not address what they considered as some of their 'legitimate' demands. Pursuit of equitable and fair governance clearly has its own hazards and can often be a lonely venture. Over the years, I have drawn much flak for trying to formulate policies that would optimise general welfare. A young and very capable officer who had watched my predicament in the effort to bring about change read out the following quote from Machiavelli (*The Prince*), which aptly sums up the challenges of reform:

It must be considered that there is nothing more difficult to carry out, nor more doubtful of success, nor more dangerous to handle, than to initiate a new order to things. For the reformer has enemies in all those who profit by the old order, and only lukewarm defenders in all those who would profit from the new order. This lukewarmness arises partly from the fear of their adversaries, who have the laws in their favour; and partly from the incredulity of mankind, who do not truly believe in anything new until they have the experience of it. Thus it arises that on every opportunity for attacking the reformer, his opponents do so with the zeal of partisans, the others only defend him half-heartedly, so that between them he runs a great danger.

It could be argued that a political system which is financed through opaque sources may lack the capacity to deliver good governance. That would amount to giving up and conceding defeat. The towel that is thrown in has never deserved any applause. Indeed, the Government has recognised this malady and a high-powered Group of Ministers has been set up to suggest the possible modalities for state funding of elections. A comprehensive reform of the prevailing procurement practices is also under way. When implemented, these initiatives will help liberate governance from the shackles of corruption and vested interests. The good news is that no less than the President of the ruling UPA coalition has given a call for combating these challenges and there seems a growing groundswell of support to cleanse the system. That so much positive has happened and the glass seems half-full is evidence of the fact that much is possible and more can be achieved.

This volume demonstrates that there is no escape from the consequences of poor governance. They visit us without fail. Predicting these outcomes requires no rocket science. If only unencumbered debate and robust common sense could prevail, it would be possible to predict the consequences of bad governance and avert them by affirmative action. Each essay tells a story of missed opportunities and short-changing of the common man. Some of the essays relating to the power sector may appear repetitive to a reader unfamiliar with the complexities of this sector. However, the focus of each essay is somewhat different from the rest. Moreover, these essays also demonstrate that despite repeated attempts to raise issues in the public domain, the government has not been inclined to respond. As the reader will see, these essays raise issues that are as relevant today as they were when written about, and much of what was anticipated years ago has actually taken place. Each article is, therefore, followed by a postscript to let readers know where we stand today on particular issues.

If poverty is to be eliminated, quality of life improved, inclusive growth and welfare promoted, and access to public goods assured, the government has to play a key role in improving the infrastructure services, without which the economy and the individual would be severely constrained. In order to achieve these outcomes, the government needs to distance itself from the ownership of infrastructure sectors that clouds its judgement in creating a progressive and equitable order. The key mantra, as we all know, is good governance, be it for reviving the public sector or attracting competitive private investment. This volume provides several illustrations and suggestions that will hopefully help pave the way ahead.

In conclusion, the government can be congratulated for placing infrastructure at the top of the national agenda. It has also done well in shaping policies and creating an enabling framework, some of which can compete with the best in the world. However, it has not yet succeeded in implementing many of these policies, largely on account of the failures of governance. It has, nevertheless, succeeded in creating a huge volume of low hanging fruits that can enable successive governments to accelerate the growth and development of India.

New Delhi   GAJENDRA HALDEA
1 August 2011

I
The Infrastructure Challenge

1 The Infrastructure Challenge*

Infrastructure deficit in India is widely recognised as a constraint on growth. Be it airports or rural roads, a mega power station or a rural supply line, the wheels of growth require well-oiled infrastructure in every segment of the economy. It is also a critical input for broad-based and inclusive growth aimed at improving the quality of life, generating employment, and reducing poverty across regions. China and other East Asian economies have been investing over 10 per cent of their gross domestic product (GDP) in infrastructure as compared to about 4–5 per cent in India. The Eleventh Five Year Plan (2007–12), therefore, aims at ramping up the investment levels to about 9 per cent of GDP by 2012. In absolute terms, the investment of about Rs 9,19,225 crore ($230 billion) during the Tenth Five Year Plan would have to rise to Rs 20,60,193 crore ($515 billion, at an exchange rate of Rs 40 per dollar) during the Eleventh Plan. It is indeed a tall order—but one that needs to be delivered if the GDP growth rate of 9 per cent is to be sustained.

DEFICIT IN INFRASTRUCTURE

Inadequate investment has been responsible for the inability of the infrastructure sector to keep pace with the enhanced requirements

* Originally published in *Business Standard India 2008*, New Delhi: Business Standard Books, 2008.

of accelerating growth. As a result, congestion on highways, ports, airports, and railways has increased, as have power shortages. This infrastructure deficit imposes additional costs and constraints, which in turn compromise the competitiveness of the agriculture, manufacturing, and service sectors in the domestic as well as global markets. As a result, growth and employment suffer. Table 1.1 provides an overview of the infrastructure deficit.

TABLE 1.1   Infrastructure Deficit

Sector	Deficit
Highways	65,569 km of national highways carry 40% of the traffic; but only 12% of these highways are four-laned; 50% are two-laned; and 38% are single-laned.
Ports	Inadequate berths, low drafts, and bottlenecks in rail/road connectivity adding to costs and delays.
Airports	Inadequate runways, aircraft handling capacity, and terminal buildings causing congestion and delays.
Railways	Old technology, saturated routes, slow speeds, and low payload imposing constraints on operations and growth.
Power	13% peaking deficit; 9% energy shortage; 40% transmission and distribution losses; and absence of competition.
Irrigation	There are 1,123 billion cubic metres of utilisable water resources, yet per capita availability and storage are low; only 43% of the net sown area is irrigated.
Telecom	Only 18% of the market accessed; obsolete hardware; acute human resource shortages.

The widening deficit is characterised by the facts that (a) the demand has grown beyond the anticipated levels and (b) the creation of infrastructure fell short of targets. For example, the growing demand for electricity led to an increase in peak deficit from 12.6 per cent in 2001–02 to 13.8 per cent in 2006–07. At the same time, the Tenth Plan target for capacity addition of 41,110 MW fell short by no less than 49 per cent while the expenditure outlays fell short by 42 per cent. In the ports sector, cargo traffic grew by

120 per cent compared to the anticipated growth of 95 per cent in the Tenth Plan, while expenditure on capacity addition in major ports fell short by 54 per cent. In civil aviation, traffic grew by 141 per cent during the Tenth Plan period compared to the anticipated growth of 43.42 per cent, while expenditure on capacity addition fell short by 43 per cent. Similarly in the roads sector, expenditure in the central sector fell short by 29 per cent. The story that clearly emerges is that while the actual demand far exceeded the projections, the government could not create capacity even at the levels it had planned for. As a result, the infrastructure deficit at the beginning of the Eleventh Plan was significantly larger than that at the beginning of the Tenth Plan.

INVESTMENT REQUIRED

There is consensus that infrastructure inadequacies would constitute a significant constraint in realising the growth potential. An ambitious programme of infrastructure investment has, therefore, been evolved for strengthening and consolidating recent infrastructure-related initiatives. As part of the Eleventh Plan, the Planning Commission has recently projected the investments that need to be made by the Central and state governments as well as the private sector in each major infrastructure sector. These projections have been made in two ways. First, rough top–down ('order-of-magnitude') estimates of investment have been derived from the government's GDP growth targets and estimates of the likely evolution of the share of gross capital formation (GCF) in infrastructure as a proportion of the GDP. Second, a bottom-up exercise has been undertaken based on a detailed analysis of past trends in combination with financing plans for various infrastructure sectors.

Projection of GCF based on Growth Targets

India's GDP is projected to grow annually at an average rate of 9 per cent over the Eleventh Plan period. Based on analyses of fast-growing Asian economies, it can be argued that GCF in infrastructure may need to be increased to around 11 per cent of GDP by the terminal year of the Eleventh Plan to achieve the targeted annual growth rate. In the Indian context, starting from a level of less than 5 per cent of GDP in 2004–05, such a rapid change in the structure of investments may not be feasible. Moreover, it may not be a necessary condition for achieving the growth target since many East Asian countries seem to have invested more than is essential. Taking these factors into account, a top–down target of around 9 per cent of GDP to be invested in infrastructure by the last year of the Eleventh Plan seems reasonable. The total GCF in infrastructure during the Eleventh Plan is thus projected at Rs 20,01,776 crore (at 2006–07 prices) or $500 billion (at an exchange rate of Rs 40 per dollar). This would amount to an annual average of 7.44 per cent of GDP over the plan period.

To supplement these estimates of GCF in infrastructure, the Planning Commission has made projections of public and private investment in each sector, basing these on a detailed review of sectoral trends and projected expenditures. This exercise yields a total investment of Rs 20,60,193 crore ($515 billion) in infrastructure during the Eleventh Plan, which is about 2.2 times the investment of Rs 9,19,225 crore ($230 billion) during the Tenth Plan. This would amount to an annual average of 7.65 per cent of GDP. The physical targets broadly corresponding to these investment projections are presented in Box 1.1.

Private Sector Investment

Table 1.2 compares projections for the Eleventh Plan with investment levels anticipated to be achieved during the Tenth Plan. It also categorises this investment into public and private components. The private sector category includes public–private partnership (PPP) projects as well as pure private sector projects. While the former must be based on a concession agreement with the government (such as for toll roads, ports, and airports), the latter are market-based (as in telephony and merchant power stations). Investment in irrigation, rural roads, other

**Box 1.1   Some Physical Targets for Infrastructure
in the Eleventh Plan**

- Power
  - Additional power generation capacity of about 78,000 MW
  - Reaching electricity to all un-electrified hamlets and providing access to all rural households through the Rajiv Gandhi Grameen Vidyutikaran Yojna (RGGVY)

- National Highways
  - Six-laning 6,500 km of Golden Quadrilateral and selected national highways
  - Four-laning of about 20,000 km of national highways
  - Widening 20,000 km of national highways to two lanes
  - Developing 1,000 km of Expressways
  - Constructing 8,737 km of roads, including 3,846 km of national highways in the North-East

- Rural Roads
  - Constructing 1,65,244 km of new roads, and upgrading an existing 1,92,464 km covering 78,304 rural habitations

- Railways
  - Constructing the Eastern and Western Dedicated Freight Corridors on trunk routes
  - 10,300 km of new railway lines; gauge conversion of over 10,000 km
  - Modernisation and redevelopment of 21 railway stations
  - Introduction of private entities in container trains for rapid augmentation of capacity

- Ports
  - Capacity addition of 485 million MT in major ports, 345 million MT in minor ports

- Airports
  - Modernisation and redevelopment of 4 metro and 35 non-metro airports
  - Constructing 7 greenfield airports
  - Constructing 3 greenfield airports in the North-East
  - Upgrading CNS/ATM facilities

contd...

Box 1.1 contd...

- Telecom and IT
  - Achieving a telecom subscriber base of 600 million, with 200 million rural telephone connections
  - Achieving a broadband coverage of 20 million and 40 million internet connections
- Irrigation
  - Developing 16 million hectares through major, medium, and minor irrigation works

TABLE 1.2 Public and Private Investment: Projections
for the Eleventh Plan

(Rs crore at 2006–07 prices)

Sector	Tenth Plan (anticipated expenditure)	Projected for the Eleventh Plan	Share (%)
Electricity (including NCE)	3,40,237	6,66,525	
Centre	1,02,665	2,55,316	38.31
States	1,00,738	2,25,697	33.86
Private	1,36,834	1,85,512	27.83
Roads	1,27,107	3,14,151	
Centre	50,468	1,07,359	34.17
States	67,416	1,00,000	31.83
Private	9,223	1,06,792	33.99
Telecom	1,01,889	2,58,439	
Centre	48,213	80,753	31.25
Private	53,676	1,77,686	68.75
Railways (including MRTS)	1,02,091	2,61,807	
Centre	98,914	2,01,453	76.95
States (MRTS)	2,508	10,000	3.82
Private	669	50,354	19.23
Irrigation (including watershed)	1,19,894	2,57,344	
Centre	8,597	24,759	9.62
States	1,11,296	2,32,585	90.38

Water Supply & Sanitation	60,108	1,43,730	
Centre	20,261	42,003	29.22
States	38,830	96,306	67.00
Private	1,018	5,421	3.77
Ports	22,997	87,995	
Centre	4,051	29,889	33.97
States	619	3,627	4.12
Private	18,327	54,479	61.91
Airports	6,893	30,968	
Centre	3,811	9,288	29.99
States	712	50	0.16
Private	2,370	21,630	69.85
Storage	5,643	22,378	
Centre	1,416	4,476	20.00
States	2,124	6,713	30.00
Private	2,104	11,189	50.00
Oil & Gas Pipelines	32,367	16,855	
Centre	31,367	10,327	61.27
Private	1,000	6,528	38.73
Total (Rs crore)	9,19,225	20,60,192	
Centre	3,69,763	7,65,623	37.16
States	3,24,242	6,74,978	32.76
Private	2,25,220	6,19,591	30.07
Total ($ billion) (at Rs 40 per dollar)	229.81	515.05	
Centre	92.44	191.41	37.16
States	81.06	168.74	32.76
Private	56.31	154.90	30.07
Total (Rs crore)	9,19,225	20,60,192	
Public	6,94,006	14,40,601	69.93
Private	2,25,220	6,19,591	30.07
Total ($ billion) (at Rs 40 per dollar)	229.81	515.05	
Public	173.50	360.15	69.93
Private	56.31	154.90	30.07

Note: NCE—Non-conventional Energy; MRTS—Mass Rapid Transit System. The percentages in the 'Share' column do not add up to 100 in all cases because they have been rounded off.

roads in backward and remote areas, and in the water supply and sanitation sectors will almost entirely be undertaken by the public sector. Private investment is expected to constitute more than 61 per cent of total investment in telecom, ports, and airports sectors during the Eleventh Plan. For the power sector, it would rise to 28 per cent and for the road sector to 34 per cent. The ratio of public to private investment in infrastructure during the Eleventh Plan has been projected at 70:30, as against 80:20 during the Tenth Plan period. In absolute terms, private investment would have to increase from Rs 2,25,220 crore ($56.31 billion) during the Tenth Plan to Rs 6,19,591 crore ($154.9 billion) during the Eleventh Plan.

Central and States' Shares of Public Investment

Projections for the Eleventh Plan period envisage a spending of Rs 7,65,623 crore (53 per cent of public investment) by the Centre and Rs 6,74,978 crore (47 per cent of public investment) by the states, aggregating a total public sector investment of Rs 14,40,601 crore. Investment by the private sector makes up the balance of Rs 6,19,591 crore.

Investment in Rural Infrastructure

Improvement in rural infrastructure is one of the key indicators of economic progress, and the government launched the Bharat Nirman Yojna in 2005 for upgrading rural infrastructure—to provide electricity to the remaining 1,25,000 villages and to 23 million households; connect the remaining 66,802 habitations with all-weather roads and construct 1,46,185 km of new rural roads; provide drinking water to 55,067 uncovered habitations; provide irrigation to an additional 10 million hectares; and connect the remaining 66,822 villages with telephones. It is estimated that out of the total projected public investment of Rs 14,40,602 crore during the Eleventh Plan, Rs 4,39,392 crore would be spent exclusively towards improving rural infrastructure (see Table 1.3).

TABLE 1.3 Investment in Rural Infrastructure: Projections for the
Eleventh Five Year Plan

(Rs crore at 2006–07 prices)

Sector	Projected Investment
Electricity	34,000
Roads	41,347
Telecommunications	16,000
Irrigation (including watershed)	2,57,344
Water Supply and Sanitation	90,701
Total	4,39,392

Business as Usual Scenario

To demonstrate the level of investment that can be expected if the
policy environment remains in its present form, the Planning
Commission has made an assessment of the 'business as usual' scenario
at constant 2006–07 prices, based on log-linear projections of public
and private investment in some sectors. 'Business as usual' projection
of total investment in infrastructure during the Eleventh Plan is
Rs 14,05,059 crore or $351 billion. The share of private and public
investment in total investment would be 27 per cent and 73 per cent,
respectively.

TEN-YEAR VISION

If India is to maintain the growth path established in recent years,
infrastructure development must remain a core concern even beyond
the Eleventh Plan period. Projections for the Twelfth Plan have been
made by the Planning Commission, assuming that GCF in infrastructure
as percentage of GDP would rise from 9 per cent in the terminal year
of the Eleventh Plan (2011–12) to 10.25 per cent by the terminal
year of the Twelfth Plan (2016–17), and that GDP would continue
to grow at an average of 9 per cent per annum during this entire period.
On the basis of this assumption, the projected GCF in infrastructure

during the Twelfth Plan would be about Rs 40,55,235 crore ($1,014 billion). As an aggregate of the two plan periods, the 10-year projection for investment in infrastructure would be Rs 60,57,011 crore ($1,514 billion).

FINANCING THE PROJECTED INVESTMENT

Financing the proposed investment of Rs 20,60,193 crore over the Eleventh Plan relies on budgetary support only to the extent of Rs 6,48,713 crore (32 per cent). The remaining Rs 14,11,480 crore is expected from the private sector and from internal and extra-budgetary resources (IEBR) of the public sector. IEBR would typically consist of internal savings of the public sector and the market borrowings raised by it. The allocation of budgetary support is limited because of pre-emption of larger allocations in favour of agriculture, health, and education. What is available for infrastructure will be directed largely towards rural infrastructure and the North-East, leaving little room for funding other infrastructure projects.

The ability to raise resources for large infrastructure projects would depend critically on a regime that would enable recovery of economic user charges where risk allocation is clearly defined. Investment in large infrastructure projects would, therefore, need to be structured on sound commercial principles and legal structures that rely on competition and credible regulatory practices—thus enabling financially viable projects that deliver efficient and affordable services to users.

The projected private sector investment of Rs 6,19,591 crore ($154.9 billion), when coupled with estimates of the Centre's IEBR of Rs 5,65,622 crore and the states' IEBR of Rs 2,26,266 crore, aggregate to Rs 14,11,479 crore ($353 billion). This represents the total funding required to be raised from sources other than the Central and state budgets. Assuming that about 30 per cent of these funds would be sourced from equity, internal resources, and other non-debt sources, the debt component of the total investment would be around Rs 9,96,291 crore ($249 billion).

THE EMERGING SCENARIO

The challenge is to create enabling conditions for raising and sustaining these large investments, keeping in mind that budgetary outlays would not be available for meeting the shortfalls. In the case of public sector projects, the focus would have to shift to efficiency improvements, cost reduction, and rationalisation of user charges. Inadequate attention to these aspects would seriously restrict the ability of the public sector to fund the requisite investments.

Assuming that the public sector would achieve its ambitious targets, a substantial expansion in private investment would still be necessary for meeting the aggregate demand. The share of the private sector in total infrastructure investment would have to rise to around 30 per cent ($154.9 billion) compared to the present 20 per cent ($43.05 billion). In some sectors—telecom, ports, and airports—this contribution would need to be far higher, over 60 per cent of the total investment. If these initiatives succeed, India would deliver a large programme of PPPs, even by international standards.

KEY CHALLENGES

This section of the essay identifies the key challenges that the government needs to address for its ambitious plans to fructify.

The Governance Challenge

The single most important challenge is the governance of infrastructure services. The robust economic growth that India has been able to log for over a decade was largely the result of economic liberalisation that demolished the 'licence raj'. The same story did not repeat itself in infrastructure sectors where the command and control era was perpetuated by the 'contract raj'. Large fiefdoms and lucrative contracts associated with infrastructure projects have increasingly become the mainstay of political and bureaucratic patronage. As a result, the slow-moving infrastructure sector stands in stark contrast to the rapidly advancing manufacturing and services sectors. The only exceptions have been telephony and aviation, both of which have shown remarkable progress simply because they were thrown open to competition.

There is an acute demand for better highways, ports, airports, railways, and power. Users are willing to pay the economic price for these services and there seems no dearth of private investment for building the requisite infrastructure. Quite clearly, the supply and demand can address each other, but only if incumbent government entities, widely perceived as unwilling to yield what they regard as their rightful turf, remove barriers to growth and open up the sector to competition. By and large, state-owned monopolies continue to dominate different infrastructure sectors and the main resistance to change comes from their 'contract raj'. This would change if the projected 30 per cent of the total investment in infrastructure comes from competing private entities. However, private investment would be attracted only if (a) the government is able to deal with the incumbents' resistance and create an enabling environment for private participation on a competitive basis, and (b) the government is able to roll out enough projects—a factor that has been the single biggest constraint on private investment.

Economic Regulation and Competition

It should be recognised that competition is the best safeguard for consumer interests. Regulation should aim at removing barriers to competition and eliminating abuse of market power. In those segments of infrastructure services where competition is feasible, regulation should be light-handed and tariff-setting could be left to competitive markets, whereas segments that have elements of monopoly need to be subjected to close regulation. In all cases, performance standards should be regulated for ensuring the quality of service.

Infrastructure sectors can be broadly divided into carriage and content segments. Content normally refers to electricity, gas, data, or voice; carriage refers to transmission lines, networks, exchanges, airports, ports, highways, and other fixed assets. While the carriage segment is typically regarded as a natural monopoly, the content part is eminently amenable to competition. In order to enable competition in the content segment, the carriage part should be subjected to non-discriminatory open access under close regulatory oversight, including determination of tariffs.

While the aforementioned overarching principles are well recognised, many of them have been followed in their breach. For example, open access and competition in the supply of electricity have been kept at bay by the electricity regulators acting in tandem with incumbent state monopolies. In the ports sector, the regulator has watched while private operators have charged 50–100 per cent in excess of what was due to them. While the concept of independent regulation has become quite fashionable in India, its evolution has been severely compromised by the selection process of regulators as also by their accountability. In an environment that is widely perceived as encumbered by corruption and patronage, the notion of independent regulation sans accountability can offer little hope. A comprehensive review of the regulatory framework is essential for recognising and adopting global best practices.

STRUCTURING PPP PROJECTS

The way PPP projects are structured and bid out holds the key to their outcome. While public sector projects are infamous for their time and cost overruns, PPP projects can cause far greater damage to users by manipulating the large revenue streams spanning over long periods. Though the rationale for adopting the PPP approach lies in efficiency improvements and lower costs, their track record in India has been far from convincing. The Dabhol power project had to be terminated as its tariffs turned out to be exceptionally high; the NOIDA Toll Bridge Company has claimed an extension of its 30-year concession to 70 years, besides grant of real estate rights; private terminal operators at major ports such as the Jawaharlal Nehru Port and Tuticorin have been charging tariffs that can be regarded as almost twice their entitlement.

This list can go on. Such experience leads to a negative perception of PPP and privatisation, leading to public opposition that deters policymakers from expanding the scope of private participation.

Since PPPs in infrastructure are a recent phenomenon, the rules of the game are still evolving. In this transition, public and private stakeholders would pursue their individual objectives, which may not necessarily optimise social welfare. These distortions could, perhaps, be absorbed if they were restricted to a few projects. But if PPPs are to be a significant source of infrastructure delivery, then they must be structured so as to optimise on efficiency and user charges. As noted in the Approach Paper to the Eleventh plan, the key to making PPPs widely acceptable is to create an environment where they are seen to be a way of attracting private money into public projects, not putting public resources into private projects.

Standardisation of Documents and Processes

The structure of PPP projects is largely determined by concession agreements and the bidding process. For example, the bidding process for the Delhi and Mumbai airports raised a huge controversy that went right up to the Supreme Court; the privatisation of electricity distribution in Delhi attracted adverse comments from several official and non-official fora; and the construction of the Bengaluru–Mysore expressway has been embroiled in controversies for over a decade. Interestingly, concession agreements for a majority of infrastructure projects have been initially drafted by the potential concessionaires. Predictably, these projects have raised many an eyebrow and can hardly be regarded as replicable. What is needed urgently is the standardisation of documents and processes.

The government has put in place model concession agreements (MCA) and other bidding documents to reduce transaction costs and ensure that sponsor selection and project terms are fair and transparent. Though the policy intent is loud and clear, incumbent government entities have been slow in evolving and accepting standardised documents and processes. Clearly, the roll out of PPP projects and the quality of investors would depend on the government's ability to evolve and enforce transparent and standardised arrangements consistent with global best practices.

PUBLIC SECTOR OPERATIONS

In the case of public sector enterprises, the key issues relate to their operational and commercial efficiency. For example, if the railways continue to improve on their efficiency and generate internal resources, their ability to fund expansion and modernisation of the railway system will be greatly enhanced. Similarly, unless the state power utilities are able to cut their excessive transmission and distribution (T&D) losses, besides rationalising their tariff structure, they will continue to make inadequate investments in their distribution networks, thus perpetuating a vicious cycle of low investment in system improvements leading to higher losses. Reform of water supply and sanitation is long overdue, while delivery of rural infrastructure continues to be hugely deficient in quality and quantity. Some of the key challenges in the selected sectors are now discussed.

Highways

The issue of financial viability is equally relevant for the highways sector where the viability of a toll road is mainly determined by its capital cost, volume of traffic, and the level of user charges. While traffic growth would be largely determined by macroeconomic considerations, the viability of individual projects can be improved by adjusting the level of capital costs and user charges. In practice, however, governments are often unable to levy economic user charges. The current policy of the Central Government relies on modest toll rates which are applied uniformly across the country, to be subsidised by up-front capital grants where necessary. The present structure of toll rates is calibrated primarily for servicing the additional investments required for upgrading of existing highways. In effect, this implies that all past investments in land and road construction are treated as a subsidy.

Ideally, such projects should require no further cash support from the government. However, the present policy allows up to 40 per cent of the capital costs to be provided as capital subsidy, to be determined by bidding for the least grant required.

The model concession agreement for PPP in national highways, coupled with the aforesaid financing framework, should therefore be able to attract large private investments. Yet, a bulk of the contracts continue to be in the public sector mode where the average construction time is easily twice that compared to PPP projects while cost overruns are endemic. The collection of toll revenues by public agencies has also turned out to be significantly lower compared to their PPP counterparts, possibly due to significant leakages and poor enforcement.

Besides slower than expected adoption of PPP, one of the key challenges that seems to have emerged in the highways sector is the escalation in capital costs on account of over-engineering, besides the usual time and cost overruns. The highways sector, unlike power, railways, ports, and airports, does not have a commercial outlook and the connection between costs and returns is, therefore, virtually missing. A typical highway functionary is accustomed to tailoring his expenditure to the size of the budget made available. As a result, the higher the budget allocation, the greater is the tendency to over-engineer. This mindset needs to be addressed so that costs can be contained in order to expand the highway programme on a self-sustaining basis. Since the highways sector requires a massive infusion of investment, the orientation of policymakers would need to shift from budgetary expenditure to self-sustaining and financially viable operations.

Ports

The ports sector poses a different set of issues, and a holistic review and restructuring of this sector is long overdue. About 74 per cent of cargo is currently handled at major ports that are controlled by the Central Government. Typically, the world over, ports are controlled either by state governments or by the local governments. The structure followed in India is quite unique and poses several limitations. In particular, the major ports have not been able to keep pace with the rising volumes of cargo. As a result, they have become very congested, besides being inefficient. Being monopoly entities with active trade unions, archaic procedures, and old equipment, they stand in urgent need of restructuring and modernisation. Though PPPs have been adopted as the preferred mode of constructing and operating new port terminals, the award of such projects has moved at a snail's pace. As a result, we have semi-monopolistic conditions. Clearly, the port trusts have been singularly unsuccessful in augmenting the capacity needed for increased cargo movement.

With an overall increase in the size of ships in the industry as a whole, there is an urgent need to increase the drafts (water depth) of the respective ports. This requires the respective port trusts to make significant investments for deepening the drafts in a commercially sustainable manner. So far, the pace of capital dredging operations has been rather slow.

The way port trusts are organised, they are unable to keep pace with the emerging challenges. In the resulting vacuum, state governments are now actively developing their ports through PPP. Their efforts need to be encouraged as this is leading to the much needed capacity enhancement on a competitive basis.

Airports

The airport sector presents a mixed picture. The opening up of air services to competition has galvanised this sector like never before. The decline in airfares leading to a rapid rise in passenger traffic is clearly indicative of a success story. The construction and operation of four metro airports at Delhi, Mumbai, Bengaluru, and Hyderabad through PPP is also a quantum jump, though doubts continue to persist about some elements of these deals. The remaining airports pose a serious challenge.

The Airports Authority of India (AAI) was never a shining example of efficiency, nor was it given the opportunity to grow as such. Its airports generally present a dismal picture. From that extreme, it is now swinging to the other by building high-cost terminals even at low-traffic airports. Efficiency in capital and operational expenditure seems to be a casualty in its newly acquired expenditure culture. Ultimately, this would add to airport user charges and offset part of the benefits arising out of lower airfares. Moreover, the efficient upkeep of high-cost terminals would seem beyond the present capacity of AAI. PPP may perhaps be the best solution for managing these terminals.

AAI has also shown a singular lack of vision in building new airports. As a result, it seems to have ceded this function to the private sector. Though one would expect market forces to drive the creation of new airports, planning and development of new airports, based on a national vision, cannot be abdicated by the government. There is also an urgent need to restructure the management of AAI to meet the emerging challenges. In particular, air traffic control (ATC) services need to be hived off into an independent entity for attaining international standards, as the efficiency of ATC can make or mar the overall performance and utilisation of airport infrastructure. Clearly, some reinvention of AAI seems inevitable.

Railways

The turnaround story of the railways sector is well known. What is lacking is a firm assurance that the reforms are irreversible. Tariffs and business policies continue to depend on the wisdom of the incumbent minister, and unless these are adequately institutionalised, the risk of a downslide is real. In that sense, the railways are in an urgent need of institutional reforms.

The growth potential of Indian Railways is simply enormous. Its asset value is virtually sky high. The railways have initiated policies that would allow redevelopment of railway stations, construction of new tracks, development of logistic parks, etc., through PPP. This initiative has the potential to mobilise large volumes of private investment. The opening up of container train services to competition is another step in the right direction. The railways offer great hope but, as they say, the proof of the pudding lies in its eating.

Power

The biggest challenge undoubtedly lies in the power sector. The state utilities are making huge losses on account of very high T&D losses—in the region of about 40 per cent, among the highest in the world. A major contributing factor is the rampant theft of electricity, which is a cancer-like ailment eating into the vitals of the economy. The number of people and the quantum of money involved have created strong vested interests that would not be easy to dislodge. The problem cannot be resolved except by campaign-style efforts, with political backing, across the country.

Competition is virtually absent in the electricity sector because state utilities continue to be monopoly suppliers in their respective areas. Though competition in supply through open access to the distribution networks is common to the developed world and also mandated by the Electricity Act, 2003, the incumbents have erected several barriers that have prevented the introduction of open access and competition. Not only would this perpetuate the present inefficiency and losses, it would also continue to act as a barrier to the much-needed private investment in the power sector. Any challenge to the stranglehold of incumbents would clearly require a firm commitment of the political leadership.

In sum, reduction in T&D losses and introduction of competition are the key challenges in the power sector. Though policy statements recognise and emphasise their importance, no concrete plans are so far visible in this direction. The current situation in the power sector should not only be regarded as critical for the health of this sector, but also for the growth prospects of the economy as a whole.

CONCLUSION

There can be little room for doubt that investment in infrastructure needs to be increased from a level of $218 billion in the Tenth Plan to about $515 billion in the Eleventh Plan. However, the 'business as usual' scenario would deliver only $351 billion, implying that the remaining $164 billion would depend on the ability of the government to take measures that can make this happen. If it were China, a government diktat backed by opening of the coffers of cash-rich state-owned banks would have done the trick, as indeed it has. Not so in India, more so in the era of coalition politics.

The challenges to be addressed are embedded in governance and raise questions of political economy. Can the government get its ministries and departments to cede control and relent on the 'contract raj' in favour of competitive private investment? Will projects be structured transparently to reduce costs and user charges? Can public sector enterprises be reformed to function on commercial principles? Will incumbent policymakers forego their discretionary powers and enable adoption of standardised MCAs and bid processes? Can the politician–engineer–contractor nexus be overcome to contain the menace of over-engineering and cost overruns? Can our archaic port trusts be restructured? Can a campaign be initiated against rampant power thefts? Can the stranglehold of state-owned monopolies in the power sector be overcome for introducing competition and enabling private investment? Such are the challenges that must be overcome to give the people of India the infrastructure services they deserve in order to take this nation to its rightful place as an economic power-house of this century.

POSTSCRIPT

The challenges of governance identified in this essay remain to be addressed. 'Command and control' form of governance continues to persist in most infrastructure sectors and so does the 'contract raj'. Public sector enterprises suffer from inefficiencies and corruption while private participation is often encumbered with rent-seeking. Moreover, public sector entities have been erecting multiple barriers to prevent entry of competing private entities on a level playing field. As a result, government's ambitious targets for attracting private investment to bridge the infrastructure deficit have not materialised, except in the case of mobile telephony.

One of the major roadblocks for private participation is the incumbents' unwillingness to roll out projects despite a robust appetite among domestic and foreign investors to participate in infrastructure projects. When projects are indeed rolled out, they are routinely gold-plated and users get short-changed through high tariffs compounded by lower-than-expected quality of service. There is a tendency to justify these sub-optimal outcomes by comparing private sector performance with the low benchmarks set by the erstwhile public sector provider whose inefficiency was the cause for private participation in the first place. Though there has been a significant improvement over the past five years in the policy framework for different infrastructure sectors, the pace of implementation continues to be wanting.

Neither the public sector nor the private sector has been able to deliver efficient and affordable infrastructure services, mainly on account of failures of governance. The process of reform continues to be weak and far too slow to overcome the challenges outlined in this essay. In sum, the growth prospects appear compromised and the promise of an improved quality of life would take much longer to fulfil.

II
Infrastructure Reform:
Missed Opportunities

2 Rescue Reforms*
Players cannot also be umpires

The charges of match-fixing in cricket attracted so much attention because people expected cricketers to play the game. But when it comes to governance, expectations of fair play have sunk so low that foul play is opposed mildly, if at all. Indeed, in different facets of government, players are also umpires, and so they keep batting even when they should have left the crease.

That explains why reforms in India have moved so slowly even in critical areas. A decade of reform in the power sector has brought little tangible gain; toll roads are still a distant dream in most parts of the country; private participation in airports has not taken off; ports have improved only marginally; and railways have deteriorated. Telecom alone has moved ahead in the recent past. Are there any lessons in all this? Clearly, an all-pervasive factor obstructing reforms is the inherent conflict of interest that plagues the entire process.

No man can be the judge of his own cause. This is an underlying principle that guides public affairs in a democratic polity where checks and balances play a critical role.

The Constitution prohibits legislators, other than ministers, from holding any office of profit in the government. The independence

* Originally published in *The Times of India*, 24 July 2002.

of the judiciary is jealously guarded. Other institutions such as the Comptroller and Auditor General, Election Commission, and Public Service Commissions have been created for functioning independently. The incumbents are forbidden from accepting post-retirement employment from the government lest the lure of favours cloud their judgement.

In the numerous tribunals and regulatory commissions, a member cannot have any subsisting personal interest in the subject matter of his jurisdiction. Similarly, company laws require a director to abstain if he has a personal interest in the issue under consideration.

In the last US presidential election (2000), Governor Jeb Bush of Florida refrained from intervening in matters affecting his candidate brother, George W. Bush, citing conflict of interest as the rationale. The president of the Nasdaq Stock Exchange must divest himself of his broking business before taking office (it took several scams before the Securities and Exchange Board of India [SEBI] ruled that brokers cannot be directors on a stock exchange). The Attorney General of the US is staying away from Enron-related investigations, as he had received political donations from the company. When it was revealed that the Labour government in the UK had accepted donations from the organisers of the Grand Prix and permitted the advertising of cigarettes, the donations had to be refunded.

Public life in developed democracies is characterised by examples where evidence of any conflict of interest is instantly recognised and adequately addressed. The raging controversy in the US regarding the acceptance of lucrative consulting assignments by the auditors of Enron and the growing pressure to ban auditors from accepting other jobs that can create conflicts of interest is a case in point.

By contrast, public life in India has no dearth of persisting conflicts that are conveniently brushed aside until a crisis or scam forces some action. Governance often gets flawed when economic policies affecting entrenched interests are at stake. Routinely, government functionaries who benefit from the powers and privileges of the existing system are entrusted with the task of reform that would strike at the very roots of their fiefdoms.

It is no surprise that when the electricity laws were amended in 1991 and 1998, private investment was enabled only through contracts with state-owned entities, thus perpetuating the stranglehold of government functionaries. Similarly, expansion in the highways sector is based on large-scale contracting by government functionaries who have 'discovered' umpteen reasons why privatisation is not feasible.

A good illustration of this phenomenon is the telecom sector where private investment languished for years, as long as the Department of Telecom called the shots. Things moved with speed and success only after the reform strategy was determined by an empowered task force outside the department and implemented by an independent regulator. Similarly, disinvestment in state-owned enterprises moved at a snail's pace as long as the ministries concerned controlled the show. The creation of the Department of Disinvestment changed all that.

It is unrealistic to expect ministers and officials to forgo their powers, particularly when they relate to contracts and fiefdoms. It is vain to anticipate progress when fundamental principles of human behaviour are violated. The suggestion for setting up an economic law commission is a move in the right direction, as it will arrest the tendency of the ministries to make partisan laws. Similarly, reform strategies for infrastructure should be devised by the Ministry of Finance, as has been the case in several developed countries.

For reforms to succeed, decision-making will have to be vested in institutions that are free of any conflict of interest. The failure to recognise this basic tenet of governance will only deliver flawed outcomes that would delay development and confine India to the Hindu rate of growth.

POSTSCRIPT

Conditioned by an era when virtually every economic activity was dominated by the public sector, the Indian psyche does not as yet recognise the conflicts of interest inherent in the functioning of incumbent ministries in a liberalised economy. The role of ministries as owners of public enterprises often comes into conflict with their role as policymakers responsible for creating an enabling environment that would promote competing private investment on a level playing field.

There are numerous examples of failures arising out of conflicts of interest, such as in the case of national highways where the projects offered for private participation have been less than 20 per cent of the agreed targets, year after year, while in ports sector, the corresponding achievement was less than 15 per cent of the targets. The story has repeated itself in power, airports, railways, and other sectors where the incumbents have often erected barriers to competition and private investment, mainly to protect their own fiefdoms. All this was happening when foreign and domestic investors were queuing up to invest in Indian infrastructure, but in vain. As a result, the infrastructure deficit has continued to rise, imposing a heavy price on the economy and the people. The challenge is essentially one of governance.

3 Yes, But Do Let's Pay for It*

The national highways (58,000 km) and state highways (1,35,000 km) have suffered from prolonged neglect. This has been dramatically reversed by the ongoing National Highway Development Project (NHDP). It envisages four-laning of the golden quadrilateral connecting Delhi, Mumbai, Chennai, and Kolkata, to be followed by four-laning of the east–west and north–south corridor and port connectivity. The quadrilateral is about 5,850 km long; the corridor's length is about 7,300 km; and port connectivity would involve about 1,000 km; over 14,000 km in all. Four-laning of the quadrilateral is expected to be near complete by December 2003 and work on the corridor and port connectivity has also begun.

The physical achievements of NHDP are indeed impressive when compared to the work done during the past several decades. Construction contracts aggregating, about Rs 20,000 crore have been farmed out and work is in full swing. This has had a very positive impact on the road sector; it has given a boost to transport infrastructure as a whole. Where does the highway sector go from here? Is the present approach replicable and sustainable for meeting the needs of this sector?

• Besides the NHDP comprising about 14,000 km, the remaining 44,000 km-long network of national highways (NH) would also need

* Originally published in *Financial Express*, 30 December 2002.

to be upgraded. About 10,000 km outside NHDP would need to be four-laned and about 20,000 km of single-lane highways would have to be two-laned. About 5,000 km of four-laned highways would also need to be six-laned, besides construction of a few expressways. Expansion of the existing NH network would also be necessary for creating an improved grid across the country. This may require addition of about 20,000 km to the NH network during the next decade.

• State highways constitute the next important part of the road network. Of the 1,35,000 km-long state highways, less than 1 per cent are four-laned; about 22 per cent have two lanes; and the remaining 77 per cent are single-lane. Their upkeep is generally poor. The resources required for upgrading and maintaining the state highways are equally daunting and seem nowhere in sight.

• As per current operations, the cost of four-laning 1 km of an NH is about Rs 4 crore. The cost of NHDP alone will, therefore, be about Rs 56,000 crore. The total requirement for the national and state network would thus be several times greater. The cess on motor fuels yields only about Rs 3,500 crore per annum for national and state highways while a corresponding amount is available from plan allocations of the Central and state governments. There is little clarity on how this vast resource gap is to be bridged if holistic development of the highway sector is to be undertaken.

• It is evident that budgetary resources, including the cess on motor fuels, would be grossly inadequate for meeting the resource requirements of highways. Raising public debt is not a credible option because of the high fiscal deficits staring at the Central and state governments. Moreover, raising debt for a non-revenue earning asset can at best be a short-term exercise.

• All infrastructure services such as power, telecom, railways, airports, ports, irrigation, and water supply rely on levy of user charges. In several states, even rural roads are funded out of levies paid by farmers. User-paid development of highways, therefore, seems to be the only pragmatic and feasible way of forging ahead. Several developed and developing countries have relied heavily on toll-based roads to meet their growing needs of transport infrastructure. India too needs to imbibe these lessons.

• Given the resource constraints, there seems no option but to commercialise highway projects and raise private capital and market borrowings to be sustained by user charges. If highways can be developed through a self-sustaining approach, the programme can grow manifold without too much reliance on scarce budgetary resources. If better services are provided at a reasonable and affordable user charge, there will be general acceptability for this approach.

• Starved of funds in the mid-1990s, the Central Government had settled for public–private partnerships (PPPs) through the BOT (build–operate–transfer) approach. A fairly elaborate framework was evolved and approved by the Central Government way back in 1997. This included a tolling policy for imposing user charges on all four-lane national highways, and a stretch of 100 km was successfully tolled in 1998.

• With great fanfare, the NHDP was launched in 1999. It gave highway development the priority that it had long deserved. As reforms were gathering momentum, the Central Government imposed a cess on motor fuels to augment resource availability for this sector.

• The approach to development of national highways seems to have changed when cess revenues became available. Somehow, the entire focus shifted from BOT toll roads to construction contracts. A fully evolved BOT project, the Jaipur–Kishangarh section of NH-8 was turned unviable when prospective BOT operators were asked to construct six lanes as against four lanes in the rest of the golden quadrilateral. That caused this single BOT project to languish, giving rise to an impression that private investment was not forthcoming. Award of construction contracts then proceeded full speed.

• To show some progress in private participation, a few highway projects were awarded on annuity basis. The scheme was based on deferred payments by the government in place of toll collection by the concessionaire (private entity). It implied assured bi-annual payments by the government to the contractor. In essence, these were construction and maintenance contracts based on deferred payments by the government over a period of 15 years. This approach did not commercialise the highway projects, nor was it self-sustaining.

• Annuity approach for road construction is not a preferred option anywhere else in the world; except in the UK where about 10 such projects have been undertaken, mostly as shadow toll projects. It does not bring any additionality of resources. In fact, it is based on high-cost debt and equity that is passed on to the government through annuity payments.

• Annuity scheme was what construction companies preferred because they would take no traffic risks and get assured bi-annual payments from the government. So where private participation did take place on a limited scale, it seemed to suit the preferences of construction companies, resource constraints and international experience notwithstanding.

• Seeing the extravaganza enabled by cess funds, there was no stopping the construction contracts. Huge borrowings have since been contracted for multiplying the funding for this programme, though such commercial borrowings for road construction were hitherto unknown. These borrowings include loans from the World Bank and the Asian Development Bank. A great opportunity to build self-sustaining highways is thus being missed.

• In support of the ongoing approach, it is argued that government would levy user charges after construction is completed. This would imply a series of tolling contracts across the country. It is indeed perplexing why construction should be farmed out to one set of contractors, maintenance to another, and tolling to yet another. A typical BOT toll road arrangement, as it prevails in rest of the world, allows a single concessionaire to do all this in a far more efficient and cost-effective manner; but that presupposes parting of control by incumbent players.

• Some of the states have also adopted the BOT approach for attracting private investment in state highways. The objective seems ostensibly right. But a closer look in case after case reveals that the design of BOT concessions is not in line with the established principles and international best practices. Efficiency and economy in investments, or even consumer welfare, may not be adequately served by such projects.

• In sum, the much needed impetus has been provided to the highway sector. It has assumed its rightful place and the industry is flourishing. Response of the user community is also positive and better highways would certainly accelerate economic growth besides providing cheaper and safer transportation. The challenge, however, is to maintain the tempo and to accelerate it.

• The only way to support a larger programme of road development is to rely on user charges. In order to keep these charges at affordable levels, upgradation of highways and related capital costs should be phased out over time so that self-sustaining projects are undertaken with minimal support from budgetary resources.

• By commercialising road development and making it financially sustainable, it should be possible to expand this programme multifold. As in China and several other developing countries in East Asia and Latin America, toll-based road development is the key to better infrastructure and economic growth. That would be a win-win situation for all stakeholders and users.

POSTSCRIPT

The author has been closely associated with the highways programme since 1997 when he was Joint Secretary (Infrastructure) in the Ministry of Finance. He helped evolve the entire policy and regulatory framework for PPP in the highways sector. He wrote the model concession agreement in 1998, which was later published in 2000. This model was used for the first PPP project on a 95-km section of National Highway 8 between Jaipur and Ajmer. Several similar projects have since been undertaken and a revised version of his model concession agreement has been adopted by the government for application to all highway projects.

In 2005, the government adopted PPP as its main strategy for building and financing national highway projects across India. It approved an enlarged NHDP that envisaged an investment of Rs 2,20,000 crore over a length of about 45,000 km, of which over 80 per cent would be undertaken through

PPP. *The idea of leveraging limited budgetary resources espoused in this essay and adopted in the Jaipur–Kishangarh project culminated in the Viability Gap Funding (VGF) scheme that has helped expand the scope and coverage of the PPP approach.*

Up to June 2011, projects for a length of 15,028 km have been awarded, with a likely investment of about Rs 1,28,751 crore. But for the global financial crisis and the resistance of the NHAI to PPP projects, the progress could have been significantly greater. The entire policy and regulatory framework for private investment in highways has been simplified, streamlined, and standardised. As a result, there is enormous appetite among foreign and domestic investors for investing in highway projects.

Though the aforementioned could be regarded as significant achievements, they fall woefully short of what was within easy reach. The achievement during the past four years has been less than 20 per cent of the target for awarding PPP projects, primarily because NHAI has been slow in offering projects for bidding. Moreover, since NHAI is mandated by law to act on business principles, its routinely over-engineered projects result in higher costs that cannot often be serviced by the existing toll rates. This would ultimately lead to a shrinkage in its programmes, forced by the hard budget constraints. Allegations about inadequate competition or cartelisation also seem to surface from time to time. For one reason or the other, the incumbent NHAI has been slow in awarding PPP projects, thus delaying the much needed investment in the highways sector.

4   Salvage Reforms*

No man can be the judge of his own cause, so goes an age-old dictum. This is also a basic tenet of jurisprudence in a democratic polity. In cricket too, a player cannot be an umpire if the game is to be worthwhile. Yet, in pursuit of economic reforms in India, this very principle has been compromised time and again.

The command and control structure of the economy that India adopted post-independence was a corollary of the socialistic philosophy of that era. It gave vast powers to government functionaries in the guise of public interest. They ran the nation's economy through public sector undertakings (PSUs) and the licence-permit raj. Over time, perpetuation of government control virtually became an end in itself while the laudable objectives of socialism took a backseat.

The crisis of 1991 spelt the end of business as usual and economic liberalisation became imperative. The captains in the government and in the PSUs, however, were unwilling to part with the considerable fiefdoms that they had acquired. Being in positions of control, they redefined reforms all the time with an eye on their turf. In the process, policies often got subverted and their implementation was compromised.

* Originally published in *Seminar, India 2002: A Symposium on the Year that Was*, Annual Issue, No. 521, January 2003.

That explains why reforms in India moved so very slowly in several critical areas. Ten years of 'liberalisation' in the power sector have brought little tangible gain; a network of toll roads is still a far cry; private participation in airports has not taken off at all; ports have improved marginally; the railways have only deteriorated; and divestment of state-owned enterprises moved at a snail's pace except during the past two years. Only the telecom sector has surged ahead in the recent past. An all-pervasive 'conflict of interest' seems to have plagued governance in these areas. Are there any lessons to learn?

Going back in history, the administrative system that evolved in India during the colonial era embodied the principle that no one should sit in judgement over his own cause. This proposition was also enshrined in common law as adopted in India. It also became an inviolate norm in judicial functioning, so much so that if a litigant expressed any misgivings about the impartiality of a judge, the latter was expected to transfer the matter to another court. It was recognised that in public affairs, a subjective or partisan approach had no place.

The founding fathers of the Constitution of India carried this principle to its logical conclusion. The Constitution thus prohibits legislators, other than ministers, from holding any office of profit in the government with a view to maintaining separation between the legislature and the executive. Independence of the judiciary is jealously guarded.

The Constitution has also created other authorities such as the Comptroller and Auditor General, Election Commission, and public service commissions to perform their roles independently and objectively, without fear or favour. The incumbents are forbidden from accepting post-retirement employment from the government lest the lure of favours cloud their judgement while dealing with the latter. Such provisions are necessary as a democratic polity relies heavily on checks and balances. Constitutional democracies in other parts of the world have acted likewise.

In the numerous tribunals and regulatory commissions functioning in India under different laws, a serving member cannot have any subsisting personal interest in the subject matter of his jurisdiction.

Similarly, laws governing the conduct of companies require a director to abstain from board deliberations if he has a personal interest in the agenda under consideration.

During the last presidential election in the US, Governor Bush of Florida refrained from intervening in matters affecting his candidate brother, George W. Bush, on grounds of potential conflict of interest. The President of Nasdaq Stock Exchange in the US must disinvest his broking business before taking office (it was only after several scams that the Securities and Exchange Board of India (SEBI) directed brokers not to act as directors on a stock exchange). The Attorney General of USA stayed away from Enron-related investigations, as he was the recipient of political donations from the company.

During an earlier term of the Labour government in the UK (1997), it was revealed that the Labour Party had accepted large donations from organisers of the motor racing Formula 1 Grand Prix events (which were heavily dependent on tobacco advertising), and the government had later agreed to continue the exemption of motor racing from the ban on public advertising of cigarettes. Following much controversy and embarrassment, the party refunded the donations (but the exemption stayed).

More recently, in January 2002, the Labour government was under pressure as a result of its links with Enron. The company had funded a number of Labour Party events, and admitted it did so to facilitate access to ministers. Subsequently, the government took a number of decisions, such as releasing the moratorium on building gas-fired power stations, for which Enron had been lobbying.

Public life in the US, the UK, and other developed democracies is galore with examples where the evidence of any conflict of interest is instantly recognised and adequately addressed. The constant vigil due to public awareness does not allow tolerance of any lapses once they are detected. The raging controversy in the US regarding acceptance of lucrative consulting assignments by the auditors of Enron and the intense pressure of public opinion in favour of banning auditors from accepting other jobs that may cause conflict of interest is a case in point.

Conflict of interest and judging one's own cause are two sides of the same coin. Be it a court judgement, board decision, or policy formulation, conflict of interest leads to outcomes that tend to be fundamentally flawed. Western democracies keep resolving such conflicts as and when they surface. The level of awareness in India being comparatively low, conflicts of interest tend to persist in several areas of public affairs. As a result, delinquent individuals and institutions get away with mayhem.

A survey of economic reforms suggests how persistent interventions of incumbent stakeholders have compromised the outcome. There is no dearth of instances where conflicts of interest are conveniently brushed aside until a crisis or scam forces some action. Routinely, government functionaries who benefit from the powers and privileges of the existing system are entrusted with the task of change and reform that would strike at the very roots of their own authority and patronage. It is only to be expected that they would devise policies aimed at protecting their fiefdoms.

Take the case of power reforms in India. The law enacted soon after independence had created a nationalised industry consisting of the vertically integrated state electricity boards (SEBs). These monolithic SEBs were virtually bankrupt by the 1980s and their mounting losses ruled out the possibility of large investments necessary for creation of additional capacity. Reforms became an imperative for improving operations and enabling private participation. Besides the Central Government, Orissa was the first state to initiate power reforms, and seven other states have since followed that path.

Power reforms in India have broadly comprised of (a) setting up of independent regulatory commissions for determination of tariffs; (b) enabling private investment; (c) unbundling of SEBs and corporatisation of the generation, transmission, and distribution segments; and (d) privatisation of state-owned entities. These are briefly described subsequently.

Regulatory commissions were considered necessary for depoliticising and rationalising tariffs. This was also seen as a device for increasing tariffs, which meant more funds in the hands of incumbent players. It, therefore, received their support.

In 1993, private investment, domestic as well as foreign, was opened up in generation, followed by a similar move in the transmission segment four years later. But such investments could only be made through long-term agreements with state-owned SEBs. Thus, government functionaries retained control through monopolistic agreements. Producers were not free to sell their produce directly to consumers, bulk or retail. This was a welcome measure for incumbent players; and the chosen private producers also favoured long-term agreements with state-owned entities in order to mitigate their risks and seek higher prices.

Despite willingness on the part of government functionaries, private investments in generation and transmission could not fructify on the basis of contracts with SEBs simply because they were perceived as bankrupt entities. Financial institutions were unwilling to finance projects based on monopolistic contracts where payment defaults by SEBs would cause the projects to go bust because they were not allowed to sell to anyone else. On the other hand, some of the cases where private investments fructified led to disastrous consequences, such as in Dabhol.

Unbundling and corporatisation of SEBs meant introduction of commercial discipline and threat of subsequent privatisation. This was stoutly opposed by employee unions and associations. However, when the respective governments agreed to protect their service conditions through appropriate legislative guarantees, they fell in line. Eight states have so far unbundled their SEBs.

Privatisation of state-owned distribution companies was first undertaken in Orissa about four years ago. But it was based on creation of private monopolies. Control over the power sector was thus apportioned between chosen private entities and incumbent government functionaries through a chain of interconnected monopolies—public and private. Absence of competition and choice inevitably led to rising tariffs and poor quality of service. The recent privatisation of distribution companies in Delhi is also based on a similar model and the dominant private players happen to be the same in both the states. It is unlikely that the outcome in Delhi would be materially different from Orissa.

The aforementioned illustrates how reform strategies were influenced by incumbent players to protect their turf. In the process, consumer interest and economic growth took a beating. Tariffs have risen significantly while the quality of service remains poor. Even after a decade of reforms, investments are confined to the public sector and the industry remains virtually nationalised.

The world over, successful power reforms—in developed as well as developing countries—were predicated upon introduction of competition and open access, leading to efficiency and price gains for the consumer. In India, a producer of power can sell his produce to a state-owned entity alone; he cannot access the market or a consumer, howsoever large. That is precisely what incumbent players seem to be perpetuating in India and the outcome is there for everyone to see. The power sector in India seems where it was in 1991, perhaps worse.

The story of reform in the highways sector is no different. Starved of funds in the mid-1990s, the incumbent players settled for public–private partnerships through the BOT (build–operate–transfer) approach. A fairly elaborate framework was evolved and approved by the Central Government way back in 1997. This included a tolling policy for imposing user charges on four-lane national highways, and a stretch of 100 km was successfully tolled in 1998.

With great fanfare, the National Highway Development Programme was launched in 1999. It consisted of the golden quadrilateral connecting the metros of Delhi, Mumbai, Chennai, and Kolkata, and the east–west, north–south corridor, all adding up to about 13,000 km. It gave highway development the priority that it had long deserved. As reforms were gathering momentum, the Central Government imposed a cess on motor fuels to augment resource availability for the sector.

Things changed when cess revenues became available to incumbent players. They took over reins of the entire programme and private participation was quietly buried. A fully evolved BOT project, the Jaipur–Kishangarh section of National Highway 8 was served a lethal blow and made financially unviable by requiring construction of six lanes as against four lanes in the rest of the golden quadrilateral. That caused this single BOT project to languish, enabling incumbent players to declare that private investment was not forthcoming. That was justification enough for awarding construction contracts at breakneck speed.

To show some progress in private participation, a few highway projects were awarded on annuity basis. The scheme was based on deferred budgetary payments by the government in place of toll collection by the concessionaire. Annuity scheme was what construction companies preferred because they took no traffic risks and got assured bi-annual payments from the government. So where private participation did take place on a limited scale, it was designed to suit the preferences of construction companies, public interest and international experience on toll roads notwithstanding.

Seeing the extravaganza enabled by cess funds, there was no stopping the construction contracts. Huge borrowings were contracted for multiplying the funding for this programme even though such commercial borrowings for road construction were hitherto unknown. The World Bank and the Asian Development Bank also stepped in with loans of a couple of billion dollars, never mind the accretion to fiscal deficit and setback to the reform agenda.

No government can go on building roads out of debt funds. As soon as the borrowing option gets exhausted, the programme will suffer a setback. Instead, privatised toll roads could have expanded faster without much burden on the exchequer. A great opportunity to build self-sustaining highways was thus missed.

Incumbent players explain that government would undertake direct tolling after construction is completed. This implies yet another series of tolling contracts across the country. It would be perplexing to any independent observer why construction should be contracted out to one set of contractors, maintenance to another, and tolling to yet another. A simple BOT toll road arrangement as it prevails in the rest of the world allows a single concessionaire (private entity) to do all this in a far more efficient and cost-effective manner; but that presupposes parting of control by incumbent players.

Some of the states have since ventured into the BOT approach for attracting private investment in state highways. Ostensibly, the objective seems right. But a closer look in case after case reveals that the design of BOT contracts is largely intended to suit the preferences of incumbent government functionaries and construction companies. In a manner of speaking, this is akin to distribution of spoils. Efficiency and economy in investments, or even consumer welfare, seem fairly low in their order of priorities.

Reforms in the telecom sector were initiated in the early 1990s, and following open competitive bidding, licences were granted for basic and cellular telephony in 1995–96. In the absence of an independent regulator, interconnection and other agreements could not be finalised as the incumbent Department of Telecom (DoT) virtually set conditions that lenders and private investors were unable to accept. In the meanwhile, other developments overtook the process and the licences began to be perceived as unviable. Though an independent statutory regulator (the Telecom Regulatory Authority of India) was constituted in 1997, it could not resolve matters as the requisite policy changes were not forthcoming from DoT. Evidently, the expectation that DoT would help promote competition against itself was flawed.

In order to resolve the continuing stalemate and respond to the demands of private investors, the government set up a Group of Ministers in November 1998, under the chairmanship of Jaswant Singh, then Deputy Chairman of the Planning Commission and Minister for External Affairs. The setting up of this group outside DoT enabled formulation of an independent policy that balanced the conflicting viewpoints of prospective investors and the incumbent operator, the DoT. The National Telecom Policy (NTP) 1999, as formulated by the Group, laid the foundation of telecom reforms and galvanised the sector, leading to a growth of 19.6 per cent in 2002, next only to China.

The spectacular growth of teledensity, massive inflows of private capital, phenomenal infusion of technology, intense competition, efficiency improvements, and lower consumer tariffs are here to stay. Economic growth has thus been facilitated. The lesson is writ large; reform strategies must be formulated and implemented outside the control of incumbent players. Absence of a level playing field does not augur well for growth and progress.

In the implementation of NTP 1999, several issues have since cropped up. It is DoT that determines the policy on matters not covered by NTP 1999, and it tends to help itself to the detriment of its private sector competitors. When the incumbent operator also doubles up as the policymaker, partisan policies are inevitable. The rising levels of discomfort among private players and the increasing litigation are symptoms of this malady. It is time for another independent group to formulate NTP-II if the momentum of growth is to be sustained. Better still, an independent arrangement should be institutionalised.

Indian Railways continue to run on a monolithic inward-looking model. Several attempts to introduce reforms and restructuring were stillborn. Being a closed organisation that does not entertain much external scrutiny, it determines its own policies and strategies largely on the basis of internal perceptions and compulsions. Few external checks and balances are available by way of self-correcting mechanisms. The vast potential of railways thus lies substantially untapped. On the contrary, a steady deterioration in many of its fundamentals is obvious to any observer.

Given the mould in which railways seem to operate, there is little hope of substantive reforms. It is futile to expect that incumbent players will be harbingers of change. Railways may thus continue to deteriorate unless a multidisciplinary Railway Commission consisting of eminent persons is set up for devising a reform strategy that would rejuvenate this sector.

For the past several years, there has been talk of privatising the major airports. Here again, incumbent players have been devising the reform strategy over the years. If lessons of other sectors were any indication, successful privatisation would remain elusive as long as incumbent players continue to determine the strategy. If and when privatisation occurs, conflict of interest may well deliver flawed outcomes.

Reforms in ports, water supply, and urban infrastructure are undergoing similar centrifugal pulls. Progress is, therefore, visible only in fits and starts.

Telecom reforms can be truly regarded as a success story. Though much ground remains to be covered, what has happened so far is truly of monumental proportions when compared to any other sector. The consumer and the economy share a win-win situation. If such history could be created in the telecom sector, others can surely learn a few lessons.

Another success story that proves the benefits of liberalisation and competition is the policy of open skies. When the monopoly of Indian Airlines ceased and competition was introduced, domestic air travel improved by leaps and bounds.

Creation of a Ministry of Disinvestment has ensured divestment of several government-owned companies. There has been a sea change in the progress of disinvestment after the ministry started functioning. This has proved how important it is to empower an independent entity to carry forward the process of reform and change, unshackled by the forces of incumbent players.

Writ large in these illustrations is the lesson that no person should be the judge of his own cause. It is unrealistic to expect ministers and officials to pursue reforms that would truncate their powers, particularly when contracts and fiefdoms are at stake. It is vain to expect that governance can succeed when fundamental principles of human behaviour are overlooked.

The telecom revolution in India would be unthinkable if DoT was in the driver's seat.

The traveller's plight could not have improved if Indian Airlines had determined the open sky policy. Would anyone have expected the Ministry of Petroleum to carry out disinvestment of its PSUs if it was in control of the process of disinvestment?

If the lessons are clear and beyond doubt, should anyone expect the incumbent players in power sector to part with their monopolistic stranglehold and let the sector open up? Would you expect incumbent players to give away national highways to private sector concessionaires? Is it realistic to expect incumbent players to privatise railways or airport operations? Would local authorities voluntarily give up their control over water supply or urban infrastructure?

Incumbent players acting in tandem with entrenched interests cannot only subvert reforms but also hijack governance. For reforms to proceed in the best interests of the nation, the evolution of a process that vests decision-making in individuals or bodies free of any conflict of interest is a pre-requisite. Failure to recognise this basic tenet of governance will only compromise development and economic growth.

In developed countries, their respective finance ministries have guided the reform strategy, particularly in critical areas such as infrastructure services. In the Indian context, the Ministry of Finance does not seem sufficiently empowered to carry out this task. Incumbent players can thus formulate self-serving policies. In addition, partisan law-making is also common, suggesting the need for an independent Economic Laws Commission.

If the methodologies and processes continue to be inadequate, and players act as umpires, can there be hope of successful reforms? The challenge facing the government is not reforms per se; it lies in empowering an independent forum to formulate reform strategies. Indeed, the horse will have to come before the cart.

POSTSCRIPT

Incumbent ministries continue to be players as well as umpires. This enables them to regulate and restrict the role of competing private entities that can contest their hegemony. As a result, barriers to private participation have virtually remained intact and only a small proportion of bankable projects has been rolled out in different sectors despite the continued rise in infrastructure deficit and the enormous interest among domestic and foreign investors to participate in the Indian infrastructure.

The power sector has been affected the most. State-owned monopolies and the entrenched interests associated with them have managed to keep competitive private investment at bay. As a result, peak shortages have risen from 11.3 per cent in 1997–98 to 16.6 per cent in 2008–09, causing a loss of millions of jobs, besides an adverse impact on the quality of life of the common man. The commercial losses of distribution utilities have increased from Rs 21,382 crore in 2002–03 to about Rs 58,200 crore in 2009–10. This rapid rise in losses is primarily on account of excessive profiteering by traders. In 2009–10 alone, about 6,590 crore units were sold by traders to the distribution utilities at an average bulk price of Rs 5 per unit, implying profiteering of about Rs 20,000 crore. This would have been easily averted if the market was opened to competition, as in the case of telecom. In the entire developed world, the power sector has been liberalised and opened up, but not so in India, thanks to incumbent government players and vested interests.

In the case of airports, the state governments in Andhra Pradesh and Karnataka took the initiative to set up new airports as the incumbent Airports Authority of India (AAI) was unable to augment its airports to keep pace with the rapid growth in traffic. The two airports at Delhi and Mumbai were taken up for redevelopment and modernisation largely because of a push from the Ministry of Finance and the Prime Minister's Office (PMO). The ball was set rolling in 2002 and the projects were finally awarded in 2006. The incumbents have since struck back and PPP has been shown the door while large construction contracts have become the preferred mode for AAI.

In the case of highways and port sectors too, private investment is only a fraction of what was eminently feasible, only because the incumbent ministries are unwilling to yield turf and allow competition against their own entities or to give up the award of lucrative construction contracts. For the past several years, the National Highways Authority of India (NHAI) has been awarding less than 20 per cent of its own targets for PPP projects, simply because of its pre-occupation with and preference for construction contracts. Though the progress of contract awards has improved since 2010–11, it remains far short of the target. The story has been similar in the case of port projects. But for the private ports coming up in the state sector, India would have faced a crippling congestion at its ports.

In the case of railways, private participation is still a pipe dream because the Indian Railways continue to function in an archaic form of government monopoly while the economy bears its burden. Several railway ministers have routinely announced more and more PPP initiatives in their successive annual budget speeches with little concern about the lack of progress in the past.

The only sector that has delivered a spectacular success is telecom. It has demonstrated beyond an iota of doubt what competition can deliver. It has also reinforced the faith and confidence in what India can achieve. Yet, the incumbent policymakers in other sectors find it convenient to pretend that the case of telephony is entirely different and its lessons do not apply to other sectors.

Conflicts of interest are all-pervasive in most infrastructure ministries that preside over large public enterprises and are unwilling to cede territory to competing private players. As a result, inefficient, resource-starved, and corruption-ridden public enterprises are unable to meet the growing demand for infrastructure, while at the same time, barriers to private participation have choked off a potential source of expansion. The economy and the common man continue to pay a heavy price.

5 Up in the Air*
Projects grounded by bad governance

Why should the government of Karnataka want to close down a fairly efficient facility and substitute it with a new airport 30 km away? Why can't both airports function simultaneously to the best advantage of the users? New York and Washington have three airports each while London has two.

Closing down a flourishing public sector facility in favour of a private monopoly does not stand to reason. It is becoming customary to pick up a large infrastructure project and make it a symbol of reform and development. Any criticism is dubbed as anti-reform and the flaws in policy are thus perpetuated. The epitaphs of many infrastructure initiatives bear testimony to this cavalier approach to good governance.

The airport project in Bangalore reflects a similar trend. Proponents of the new airport argue that it would not be viable unless the present one is closed. They maintain that without making a sacrifice, Bangalore cannot have this showpiece. If indeed a new airport finds favour with the government, let it be used for international flights to start with. Domestic flights could continue at the existing airport to the extent its capacity permits.

* Originally published in *The Times of India*, 3 November 2003.

Limited usage of the new airport will also help reduce its capital and operational costs. If it still remains unviable in the initial years, let the state government provide a capital or operational subsidy to be recovered through a cess on users of the existing airport. Assume that in order to be financially viable, the airport project would require a net revenue of Rs 100 per trip from all air travellers. This could well be raised through a development cess to be levied on users of the existing airport who should normally be willing to bear a reasonable cost for creation of a new airport rather than bear this cost and travel an extra 30 km too.

The use of state power to coerce them to a distant airport would militate against public interest. Let there be an open debate involving the users. Their opinion should matter. Policymakers seem to have turned a Nelson's eye to the junking of huge public investments in the existing airport. No one seems to have quantified the loss of a public asset and its recurring income. Nor have the costs of additional travel to the new airport been quantified. One wonders if there have been similar cases elsewhere in the world.

On a conceptual plane, the creation of monopolies must be regarded as an unacceptable form of government interference in the markets. It is conceded that airports are natural monopolies and governments cannot be expected to create multiple airports, as the required investments will outweigh the likely user benefits. However, in cases where two airports do come into existence, the mandatory closure of one in favour of the other should normally be viewed as detrimental to consumer welfare.

It seems Hyderabad is planning to set up a new airport. One can only hope that the proposed airport is not predicated upon the closure of the existing one. Infrastructure projects in India are flawed because the underlying policy is guided by prospective investors. Governments often lack the in-house capacity to formulate infrastructure policies and projects. This gap can easily be bridged by deploying independent experts. Private participation should be invited only after the policy framework is finalised.

Choosing a private entity and then working out the project frame-work is fraught with several dangers. Remember how the Cogentrix power project in Karnataka was based on a tariff that was virtually the highest in Asia. Thankfully, the project failed to materialise for a host of reasons, including the sobering influence of the Union finance ministry. The airport proposal is no friendlier to the consumer than the Cogentrix project was. It is, perhaps, worse. The prospective investors simply want to secure a monopoly with assured returns.

The failed privatisation of electricity distribution in favour of private monopolies in Orissa is another example to learn from. The more recent monopoly privatisation of electricity distribution in Delhi has also attracted adverse attention, including a recent indictment from the Comptroller and Auditor General (CAG). Consumer response has been mixed too. In power generation, the flight of private investors, who were required to sell to bankrupt state monopolies only, is yet to be reversed. Road projects, such as the Mumbai–Pune expressway and the Noida toll bridge, are unable to service their unsustainably large capital costs.

The National Highway Development Project, though otherwise laudable, is based on debt-based government funding that will soon reach its limits. A policy for sustainable development of highways is yet to be put in place. Quite clearly, India has not been able to get its act together on much of its infrastructure governance. A closer scrutiny reveals several flawed projects in other states and sectors. Telecom seems the only exception.

If the Bangalore airport is actually closed, forcing users to the new one, opposition is bound to intensify, as we saw in the case of Enron. The project needs to be people-friendly. After all, airports are for the people and not vice-versa.

POSTSCRIPT

When the existing airports at Hyderabad and Bangalore were closed in 2008 to create monopolies in favour of the respective concessionaires of the new airports, there was widespread criticism and several challenges in the courts of law. In particular, the 'silicon valley' in Bangalore was up in arms. However, this outcry proved to be of no avail. While the airport operators have acquired a flourishing business, the users of both airports are not only travelling an extra 30–40 km each way, they must also pay airport charges that are two to three times higher than what they paid earlier.

In 2006, the airports at Delhi and Mumbai were also awarded to private entities under long-term concession agreements, which neither cap the capital costs nor provide for any oversight by the government in controlling capital costs. As a result, the costs projected by the respective concessionaires are much higher than the costs anticipated at the time of award. This implies a significant increase in user charges since the tariff structure is based on a 'cost plus' methodology, which means that higher capital costs will be converted into correspondingly higher user tariffs. Further, there has been legitimate criticism in the media relating to the treatment of some revenue streams which have since been excluded from sharing with the Airports Authority of India. In effect, such redefining of revenues implies post-bid capital subsidies. Despite these significant subsidies, the passenger charges have already been increased sharply, and viewed from the user perspective, the benefits of private participation have been compromised.

6 Lessons from Infrastructure Reform in India*

A decade of economic reforms in India has resulted in many a tangible achievement. The growth rate has accelerated; liberalisation and de-licensing have increased competition, improved efficiencies, and reduced costs; shortages have virtually disappeared; investments and savings have shown good progress; exports have boomed; and forex reserves crossed the $100 billion mark. Against these impressive achievements, however, the progress in the development of infrastructure has been below expectation. Reforms in the power sector have so far brought little improvement; a network of good roads across the country is still a far cry; ports have improved marginally; private participation in airports has not taken off; and the railways have deteriorated. Only the telecom sector has forged ahead in the recent past. The failure has not been of infrastructure reforms per se. This poor showing is largely an outcome of flawed governance that has kept the Indian economy from taking a tiger-like leap. Unless the governance associated with the reform process is purged of its obvious frailties, the history of past failures could repeat itself.

* This paper was presented at the Annual Bank Conference on Development Economics (ABCDE) held at Bengaluru on 21–23 May 2003. It was a part of the proceedings which were published subsequently by National Council of Applied Economic Research (NCAER) in 2003.

The inadequacy of public resources and efficiency improvements associated with the private sector have been widely acknowledged as the rationale for private investment in infrastructure development. Central and state governments have made several policy pronouncements towards this end; yet the progress has been marginal and virtually all infrastructure services continue to remain in the public sector. Well-publicised efforts to attract private participation were initiated from time to time, but only to be flogged and declared unsuccessful, thereby justifying a further expansion of the public sector. This seems to have happened with remarkable similarity in virtually all the infrastructure sectors.

It should be obvious that a sustainable development of infrastructure through public resources is a pipedream, and private participation is inevitable. Yet, the government seems to have thrown in the towel and settled for public investment in the short and medium terms, though continuing to emphasise the role of private participation. Owing to failures in the past, political energy in favour of privatisation seems exhausted. In an environment of repeated failures, incumbents are being aided by sceptics in promoting the view that privatisation has not worked. Distinction has not been drawn between the privatisation of existing utilities, on the one hand, and the induction of competing private operations, on the other. There has been neither an analysis of the underlying causes of these failures nor any evaluation whether such failures were the outcome of misconceived and self-serving policies crafted by incumbent players to preserve the status quo.

A decade has been lost to trial and error, though it has led to a great deal of learning. There is greater recognition than before that infrastructure services—whether public or private—have to be paid for. Solutions and credible approaches are now better known and understood. It is time to pursue an aggressive programme of infrastructure development with a greater role for private participation. Drawing from past experience, the reform process needs to be initiated all over again.

This essay briefly examines the lapses in governance that induced failures in the past; it also attempts to identify remedial measures that would make a success of infrastructure reforms. The potential is enormous and the likely social and economic gains could be phenomenal. An open and informed debate would help prevent the oft-repeated hijacking of governance and bring the quantum gains necessary for transforming the Indian economy.

POWER SECTOR

The Electricity (Supply) Act, 1948, enacted soon after independence, mandated a nationalised industry consisting of vertically integrated state electricity boards (SEBs). In their initial years, the SEBs played a vital role in extending the network to the hinterland, but by the mid-1980s they were virtually bankrupt owing to irrational tariffs, increasing pilferage, and declining efficiencies. As a result, investment in generation shifted from state-level entities to the Central Government's public sector enterprises (PSEs) such as the National Thermal Power Corporation (NTPC) and National Hydroelectric Power Corporation (NHPC). While central PSEs played an increasingly dominant role in creating generating capacity, the underlying unviability of the distribution segment increased the moral hazards of the states.

Competing demands on public resources ruled out large outlays necessary for capacity expansion in the early 1990s, particularly because fiscal deficits were posing binding constraints. Reforms thus became imperative for enabling private investment and for improving operations. Besides the Central Government's initiatives to enable private investment in generation, Orissa was the first state to initiate power reforms in 1995, and seven other states have since followed. The enactment of the Electricity Regulatory Commissions Act, 1998, by the Central Government and State Reforms Acts by the state governments were steps in that direction.

The 'reforming' states adopted the so-called Orissa model of power reforms—described in international literature as the 'single buyer' model. It consists of an interconnected chain of monopolies where all power producers must sell to a state-owned transmission company, which in turn sells to a monopoly distribution company. 'Single buyer' implies the absence of a market where competing producers can set up capacity and sell to multiple buyers. As a consequence, private investment must rely on long-term power purchase agreements (PPAs) with payment security, generally in the form of sovereign guarantee. Such PPAs are typically based on negotiated 'cost plus' tariffs that tend to be comparatively high. The arrangement fails to incentivise efficiency improvements and cost reduction; and reliance on monopolies is incompatible with economic liberalisation. In addition, the uncertainty created by year-to-year determinations of tariffs and operational norms only compounded the problems. Predictably, these reforms failed to deliver.

In the absence of independent experts or an open debate, the agenda for power reforms was largely evolved by the incumbents who kept their turf intact. As a result, power reforms in India broadly comprised of: (a) enabling private investment in generation through long-term PPAs with state-owned entities; (b) setting up independent regulatory commissions for fixing tariffs; (c) unbundling and corporatising SEBs based on the 'single buyer' model; and (d) privatising distribution in a monopolistic mode. The bedrock of reforms—competition and open access—was simply kept out until the Electricity Act, 2003, came into force. The report card on reforms is briefly stated in the following.

Private Investment

In 1992, the Central Government opened up the generation segment to private investment—domestic as well as foreign—but only through long-term PPAs with SEBs. Government functionaries thus retained full control through these monopolistic agreements, because producers did not have the freedom to sell to any other entity. On their part, private producers favoured PPAs with state-owned entities in order to secure assured returns through 'cost plus' tariffs.

A close scrutiny of the PPAs would reveal that each of these agreements was drafted by the respective sponsor, and formed the basis for negotiated deals sans competition. The PPAs were usually very complex and opaque, thus difficult to comprehend, particularly in the absence of relevant expertise within the government. Yet, with overt and covert pressures working in favour of the sponsors, most SEBs ended up signing PPAs that were unsustainable. The Dabhol power project is an obvious example, but a public scrutiny of several other PPAs could send their signatories running for cover.

These PPAs stipulated several provisions that lacked economic rationale. For example, people were led to believe that assured returns to independent power producers (IPPs) were to be in the region of 16 per cent. The fine print, however, guaranteed these returns post-tax and with exchange risk cover. Moreover, these returns could be secured at fairly low levels of performance. If the IPPs performed at NTPC's efficiency levels, they could romp home with returns of 30 per cent or more. In addition, the 'cost plus' approach encouraged IPPs to settle for expensive state-of-the-art equipment, with some gold-plating added. Yet, the gains of efficient equipment were denied to the consumer because the operational norms were determined on the basis of historical performance of state-run stations, thus enabling IPPs to pocket savings equivalent to about 10 per cent of fuel and other costs that were nevertheless recovered from the consumer. Several other provisions were equally permissive.

In order to simplify the process and make it transparent, the Ministry of Finance issued guidelines on how to negotiate PPAs and also followed up with a model PPA. But there were few takers. The states were generally willing to go by the PPAs that were drafted by the IPPs, with marginal modifications. Even if motives are not to be attributed, professional inadequacy and naive responses of incumbent officials were recipes for hugely flawed outcomes.

The aforementioned arrangement explains the mad rush of foreign and Indian investors in the mid-1990s to set up power stations in India. More than 250 project sponsors were moving heaven and earth to make a quick buck. PPAs with bankrupt SEBs, however, were not financeable because payment risks were not manageable. This compelled investors and lenders to seek sovereign guarantees against payment default by the SEBs and the state governments. Thankfully, the Union finance ministry restricted its guarantees to eight 'fast track' projects, and following the controversial PPA for the Dabhol project, it also decided to reopen and renegotiate the remaining PPAs before extending its guarantee. The PPAs thus renegotiated resulted in unbelievably huge savings for the SEBs.

In the absence of sovereign guarantees, few PPAs were able to reach financial closure. On the other hand, the absence of sustainable reform of the SEBs hastened the demise of several PPAs. Clearly, the unwillingness of the finance ministry to provide sovereign guarantees averted a financial disaster that these high-cost PPAs would have brought about. The sagacity of the finance ministers of that era must, therefore, be acknowledged. But for the finance ministry's efforts in the face of prevailing currents, India would surely have acquired a dozen or more Dabhols.

The story of private investment in transmission is no different. Though opened to private participation in 1997 through amendments in law, private investment in transmission has not fructified so far. The control by public sector incumbents of the transmission segment continues to be total and little private investment is to be expected for years to come; and in the stray cases that it fructifies, the terms are likely to be dictated by the incumbents.

Independent Regulation

Another area of reform was the introduction of independent regulation with the objective of depoliticising and rationalising tariffs. This move received full support from the incumbents in the hope that higher tariffs would place more funds for investment in their hands. However, the regulatory commissions brought to light the high levels of inefficiency and pilferage in the system. They declined to increase tariffs for meeting the full 'cost' of supply based on inefficiencies and pilferage that accounted for almost half the cost in several states. Yet, the annual tariff revisions added substantially to the consumer's burden, but without improving the quality of supply. From the SEBs' perspective, however, these revisions were inadequate as far as restoring their viability was concerned. The consequent stalemate has virtually stunted the growth of this sector.

The evolution of a regulatory framework was certainly a step forward. It has made tariff-setting and loss recognition a comparatively transparent exercise. However, the current regulatory framework suffers from serious flaws. The process of selecting regulators is opaque and largely controlled by the political masters of the day. But once appointed, these regulators are not accountable to anyone even though they wield vast powers of licensing, regulation, and policy formulation. They have so far demonstrated little success in improving the performance of state-owned utilities; their commitment to the introduction of competition seems conspicuous by its absence; their capacity and expertise seem limited; and the absence of effective checks and balances opens avenues for an abuse of power and regulatory capture.

Unbundling of SEBs

Yet another significant reform initiative was the unbundling and corporatisation of SEBs in eight states. These were regarded as necessary steps towards commercial viability and privatisation, particularly in the context of growing losses of SEBs. Assistance from multilateral development banks provided the requisite incentives and employees were pacified by guarantees protecting their conditions of employment. However, restructuring SEBs was based on the 'single buyer' model that helped retain incumbents' control through an interconnected chain of monopolies. As a result, the corporatised entities have been working virtually in the same manner as their predecessor SEBs, with marginal improvements in their quality of service.

In common perception, unbundling has come to be associated with rising tariffs, and not with improvement in the quality of supply. For this reason, power reforms have received little public support. It should be clearly understood that though unbundling is a necessary step for restructuring the electricity industry, it is not sufficient for achieving the goals of power reforms. States will need to liberalise the sector and introduce competition in the generation and supply of electricity with a view to improving efficiencies and cutting costs, besides eliminating shortages.

Privatisation of Distribution

Privatising state-owned distribution companies was said to be the ultimate reform measure. This was first carried out in Orissa about five years ago, but only through creating private monopolies that had inevitably led to rising tariffs without much improvement in the quality of service. After seven years of reforms, including five years of privatised operations, transmission and distribution (T&D) losses continue to be over 45 per cent and bankruptcy in the state's power sector is all-pervasive.

The recent privatisation of distribution companies in Delhi is equally flawed. T&D losses at the beginning of the reform process were pegged at 51 per cent. The private companies are to bring them down to about 34 per cent over a period of five years, with reduction in the first and second years to be only 0.5 per cent and 1.5 per cent, respectively. During the first two years, these losses are to be absorbed through a government grant of about Rs 4,000 crore ($900 million). Thereafter, tariffs will have to rise, though Delhi consumers are already paying the highest tariffs in India. Moreover, these monopoly entities are unlikely to bring in a significant improvement in the quality of supply that would have otherwise occurred in an industry structure based on competition and choice.

The current strategy relies merely on privatising the existing utilities. It should, however, be recognised that given the size and complexities of the distribution network in India, its privatisation will, at any rate, take several years. So far, only Orissa and Delhi have been able to privatise their distribution companies, albeit without introducing any competition in the supply of electricity. For power reforms to succeed, focus will have to shift to introducing competition in generation and supply, which will accelerate private investment and galvanise the power sector.

Lack of Competition

Unbundling and corporatising SEBs was based on electricity reform laws passed in eight states—Orissa, Haryana, Andhra Pradesh, Karnataka, Uttar Pradesh, Rajasthan, Delhi, and Madhya Pradesh. These states adopted several provisions of the UK Electricity Act of 1989. However, the most fundamental element of the UK law relating to introducing open access and competition did not figure in any of these state laws.

Of the aforesaid eight states, seven were assisted by multilateral development banks. Apparently, the desire to expand their lending portfolios, coupled with the need to carry along incumbents, persuaded the banks to support a reform programme wanting in competition. Though the co-existence of reforms with a monopolistic structure was evidently a contradiction in terms, and lessons relating to the introduction of competition were available from the UK and other countries of Western Europe, the US, and Latin America, conditionality relating to open access and competition was conspicuous by its absence. Strangely, open access and competition did not figure in the lexicon of power reforms in India until the draft Electricity Bill of 2000 was made public.

Viewed in perspective, it is interesting to note that when mono-polistic control over the electricity industry was to be acquired, the government took only one year in replicating the UK Electricity Act of 1947 by enacting the Electricity (Supply) Act, 1948. On the other hand, when the UK Electricity Act of 1989 restructured the British electricity industry and introduced competition, it was completely overlooked by incumbent policymakers in India. In the late 1990s, when eight states enacted their electricity reform laws, they borrowed heavily from the UK model, but excluded the element of open access and competition that constituted the rationale for restructuring.

The Outcome

During the past decade of power reforms, tariffs have risen signifi-cantly but the quality of service remains poor. Investments have been largely confined to the public sector and the industry remains virtually nationalised. A quick look at the national five year plans and the state plans, including those of the eight reforming states, suggests that public investment and state control would continue to dominate. Private investment has been relegated to insignificance, ostensibly on the grounds that it has not materialised despite efforts by the government. As a result, the power sector in India seems where it was in 1991, or perhaps worse. Even now, a producer of power can sell his produce to a state-owned entity alone; he cannot access the market or bulk consumers. Such regimentation does not exist in any other sector in India. But that is how incumbents have so far managed to perpetuate their control.

The SEBs continue to be financially unviable; their T&D losses have been hovering in the region of 40–50 per cent; virtually half the households in rural India have no access to electricity; and millions of farmers are in long queues to secure electric connection for their agricultural pump sets. By any standards, the entire sector continues to be sick despite a decade of so-called reforms.

The Electricity Act

The recent passing of the Electricity Act, 2003, by Parliament represents a quantum jump because it places open access and competition at the centre stage of power reforms. The drafting of such a Bill (it was drafted by this author) was possible only because its evolution remained largely outside the control of incumbents, though they actively participated as stakeholders. Based on a resolution adopted at the Chief Ministers' Conference, presided over by the Prime Minister in February 2000, the Bill was subjected to a national debate and went through a wide consultative process unprecedented in the legislative history of India. That process enabled the Bill to reflect international best practices in the larger interests of the economy. Given the track record of power reforms at the Centre and in the states, it was unlikely that such a Bill could have evolved if incumbents controlled the process.

Vested interests, however, got their opportunity when the Bill was being finalised by the Ministry of Power prior to its introduction in Parliament. They managed to influence several provisions of the Bill, and introduced barriers aimed at delaying the introduction of open access and market forces. Nevertheless, the debate in Parliament reinforced the original architecture of the Bill and removed several of the induced barriers. In sum, the Electricity Act should be able to drive the restructuring of the electricity industry and bring quantum improvements within a few years. Incumbents, however, may obstruct the process and add to the turbulence of transition. The evolution of the new industry structure would, therefore, pose enormous challenges in terms of management of change.

The evolution of the Electricity Bill constitutes an excellent case study of how the incumbents influenced the law in their favour, on the one hand, and how an open and informed debate helped contain the pressures, on the other. It indicates how an open process based on wide consultations with diverse interest groups led to rational and sustainable provisions of law; how a closed process within the power ministry allowed incumbents to distort several provisions; and again when these provisions were openly debated by the Standing Committee of Parliament, much of the earlier consensus was restored. A consultative process based on open debate, on the one hand, and reliance on independent experts, on the other, were the two factors primarily responsible for the success of this initiative. It is an example that illustrates how the governance of reforms is critical to their outcome.

HIGHWAYS

Roads in India have suffered from prolonged neglect. This was sought to be reversed by the ongoing National Highway Development Project (NHDP), which envisages making a four-lane golden quadrilateral connecting Delhi, Mumbai, Chennai, and Kolkata, and the east–west and north–south corridors running through the length and breadth of India. The NHDP has accorded the priority that roads have long deserved. It has set in motion a large programme of highway development in India.

Besides the NHDP project of about 14,000 km, the remaining 44,000 km of National Highways (NH) will also need to be upgraded. In addition, some of the four-lane highways would have to be made six-lane, and the expansion of the existing network will also be necessary. Expressways with controlled access would also need to be planned and initiated on select routes with high traffic intensity. Upgrading the state highways network (1,30,000 km) deserves attention.

The NHDP alone would require about Rs 60,000 crore ($13 billion), while the requirement for the entire network would be a few times greater. On the resources side, the cess on motor fuels yields about Rs 3,000 crore ($0.7 billion) per annum, in addition to a similar outlay in the budgets of the Central and state governments. These limited resources cannot fund a programme of the aforementioned proportions. On the other hand, reliance on public debt is not a viable option owing to fiscal constraints. As a result, there is little option but to commercialise highway projects for raising private capital and debt, to be sustained by user charges. There is convincing evidence to suggest that users across the country are willing to pay a reasonable charge if it is accompanied by commensurate improvement in services. Yet, the incumbents have so far chosen to rely on public debt for financing the NHDP.

Debt-based Financing of NHDP

Following the launch of the NHDP in 1999, the Central Government imposed a cess on motor fuels to augment resource availability for this sector. This was a significant step forward in earmarking resources for road development. However, the resources thus generated were not leveraged for financing a much larger programme of road development. On the contrary, soon after the cess revenues became available, the entire focus of the incumbents shifted from public–private partnerships (PPPs) to the usual construction contracts.

This programme was then multiplied through large borrowings from external and domestic sources. As a result, the total public borrowings for the NHDP alone may well exceed Rs 40,000 crore ($8.5 billion), including multilateral development bank loans. These borrowings have, in fact, retarded the reform process by relegating private participation to insignificance and by relying on public expenditure alone.

The explanation given in support of construction contracts is that the government would undertake to levy tolls directly in due course after construction is completed. This implies yet another series of contracts for toll collection across the country. It would indeed be perplexing to an independent observer why construction should be farmed out to one set of contractors, maintenance to another, and levying tolls to yet another. A simple build–operate–transfer (BOT) concession approach would allow a single concessionaire to undertake this entire activity in a far more efficient and cost-effective manner; but that presupposes incumbent players parting control.

Continued allocations of debt-based outlays for road construction cannot be regarded as a sustainable approach in a resource-starved economy. The government has, therefore, inevitably shifted to the BOT approach for securing private capital to fund road development. In his Budget speech for 2003–04, the Union finance minister allocated Rs 2,000 crore ($450 million) for road projects, relying on PPPs. This is certainly a welcome step, but the opportunity to attract private capital for the more viable golden quadrilateral has been lost. Moreover, the implementation of a successful BOT programme by the incumbents remains to be seen. The ability of the government to get the road projects and associated contracts out of the control of incumbents is a governance issue that has several facets. If the government is unable to address this issue, its current efforts would only have a short-term impact. And besides exhausting the debt-based funding that is currently the mainstay of NHDP, the maintenance of the assets created will also pose serious difficulties.

Private Participation

Starved of budgetary resources in the 1990s, the Central Government had opted for PPPs through the BOT concession approach. After extensive consultations, it approved a fairly elaborate framework for BOT road projects in 1997. This included a toll policy for imposing user charges on all four-lane national highways; and based on this policy, a stretch of about 100 km was brought under the toll system in 1998.

Prior to the evolution of the model framework, some BOT concessions for bypasses around urban centres were awarded by the government. Like PPAs in the power sector, these concession agreements were drafted by the respective private sponsors and were, therefore, imbalanced in many ways. The adverse implications of some of these deals will gradually come to light when the users feel exploited. But thankfully, with the adoption of a model framework by the government, sponsor-led BOT concession agreements have been largely eliminated in the highway sector.

The evolution of the BOT framework was led by the Ministry of Finance, and it consisted mainly of a bankable concession agreement developed through a process of extensive consultations with stake-holders, including prospective investors, lenders, legal experts, and highway personnel. Based on an independent scrutiny by the financial institutions, the model concession agreement (drafted by this author) was found bankable and the government approved it. Private partici-pation, therefore, had a fair chance of success, and such success would have threatened the incumbents' turf, both in terms of territory as well as lucrative contracts. It was, therefore, no coincidence that this approach was side-lined.

Based on the aforesaid framework, the bidding process for the Jaipur–Kishangarh highway (NH-8) was initiated in 1998, well before the NHDP was launched. However, when incumbents got an opportunity, they introduced several modifications that obstructed the project's progress. In particular, the project scope was expanded from four-lane highways to six-lane (with toll rates of a four-lane facility), even though for all other highway projects in the NHDP, it was four-lane, except in urban stretches. These modifications put the project in a spin, and the bids were kept pending for almost three years. Yet, the project has happened and it is currently under construction.[1]

The Jaipur–Kishangarh project constitutes a very illustrative case study. Its capital cost is about Rs 720 crore ($160 million), which makes it the single largest project in the Golden Quadrilateral that formed part of NHDP; and its cost to the government is perhaps the lowest. The burden on the exchequer, in the form of grant element, is about Rs 211 crore ($47 million), which translates into Rs 2.3 crore ($0.5 million) per km. It is to be noted that had the project scope conformed to a four-lane one, as in the rest of the NHDP, no grant element would have been required and the project could well have been self-sustaining. If replicated, this approach could have made a world of difference to the highway development programme. This episode has demonstrated the basic strength of a fair, balanced, and transparent framework; it has established beyond doubt that private participation in BOT road projects is feasible in Indian conditions, contrary to the myth that private investment in roads is not a feasible option in India.

Private investment in highways is sometimes difficult to attract because of the perceived volatility of traffic risks. This is not true of the highway programme in India, where traffic risks are generally negligible because the ongoing programme is based on augmenting the existing highways where traffic streams are well determined. This is significantly different from BOT road projects in other countries where a new tollway has to compete with an existing freeway, causing greater traffic uncertainty.

Some states, too, have adopted the BOT approach to attract private investment in state highways. The objective seems ostensibly right. But a closer scrutiny reveals that the underlying agreements

[1] The Jaipur–Kishangarh Highway was inaugurated by Prime Minister Dr Manmohan Singh on 23 May 2005.

in most cases are loaded heavily in favour of the respective project sponsors. Some of these projects are typically based on a 'cost plus' approach that has virtually incentivised high costs. Others allow unjustifiably high returns without commensurate benefits to the users. The evolution of a credible BOT framework in the states is yet to happen.

Annuity Approach

In order to meet the growing criticism relating to the relegation of private participation, a few highway projects were awarded by the National Highways Authority of India (NHAI) on an annuity basis. The scheme was based on bi-annual payments by the NHAI as a substitute for toll collection by the concessionaire (private entity). In essence, these were construction and maintenance contracts based on deferred payments spread over a period of 15 years. They enabled the incumbents to poach on future budgetary outlays for expanding their current programme.

The annuity approach for road construction is not a preferred option elsewhere, except in the UK, where about 10 such projects have been undertaken for entirely different reasons. In Indian conditions, this approach implies high-cost debt and equity that is to be borne by the government through annuity payments. The scheme eminently suits the preference of construction companies, which are to receive assured returns from the government without bearing any commercial risk.

Disintermediation of Multilateral Development Bank Loans

As a separate matter, it was decided in 1997 that the role of the Central Government in routing multilateral development bank loans to the NHAI should be disintermediated in line with the practice followed for lending operations in other infrastructure sectors. Direct lending by banks to the NHAI would require the latter to repay the loans from its toll revenues, instead of relying on budgetary support from the government. Such disintermediation also helps in reducing the fiscal deficit correspondingly. The first disintermediated loan to the NHAI was approved by the Asian Development Bank in 1998 for augmenting the Surat–Manor stretch of NH-8.

However, this too received resistance from incumbents. The NHAI lobbied for a return to the budgetary route, with the multilateral development banks extending a helping hand. The lending programme of the banks soon reverted to the budgetary route, thus overlooking the benefits of commercialisation and fiscal consolidation, in favour of the exigencies of the lending programme and the preferences of incumbents.

Need to Revisit Private Participation

In sum, the much-needed impetus to the highway sector has certainly been provided by the NHDP, widely regarded as a welcome initiative. The challenge, however, is to evolve a sustainable approach for a much larger programme of highway development. As in several developing countries in East Asia and Latin America, toll-based road development is the key to a successful highway programme. That, however, would be possible only if public resources are supplemented by private participation for ushering in multifold investments and efficiency gains. The requisite framework is available, and it has also been tested. It only needs to be activated by independent policy formulation outside the control of incumbents.

TELECOM

Reforms in telecom were introduced in the early 1990s, and licences for basic and cellular telephony were issued in 1995–96. For want of an independent regulator, interconnection and other agreements could not be finalised because the incumbent department of telecom (DoT) had set conditions that the investors and their lenders were unable to accept. Meanwhile, the steep upfront payments offered by the licensees during the bid process began to be perceived as unviable.

Though an independent statutory regulator, the Telecom Regulatory Authority of India (TRAI), was constituted in 1997, it could not resolve matters because the requisite policy changes were held up in DoT. Clearly, the expectation that DoT would enable competition against itself was flawed.

Independent Policy Formulation

In order to resolve the continuing stalemate and respond to the demands of private investors, the Prime Minister set up a group of ministers and experts to formulate an independent policy that balanced the conflicting viewpoints of prospective investors and DoT. The National Telecom Policy (NTP) 1999, as formulated by the group, laid the foundation of telecom reforms and galvanised the sector, leading to a growth of 19.6 per cent in 2002, next only to China. There were several factors that contributed to this, but the single most important factor associated with the governance of these reforms was the setting up of an independent policy group outside the incumbent's control.

The phenomenal growth of mobile telephony, massive inflows of private investment, rapid strides in the evolution of technology, relentless competition, efficiency improvements, and remarkably low consumer tariffs are here to stay. Economic growth has thus been facilitated. The lesson is writ large; reform strategies must be formulated and implemented outside the control of incumbent players and free from conflicts of interests while the absence of a level playing field must be regarded as a barrier to growth and progress.

Challenges Ahead

During the implementation of NTP 1999, several issues have cropped up. It is DoT that interprets policy on matters not covered by NTP 1999; it usually helps itself to the detriment of its private sector competitors. When the incumbent operator also doubles up as policymaker, partisan policies are inevitable. The problems arising out of the dual role of DoT were compounded by the summary removal, in January 2000, of the chairperson and members of TRAI, who were perceived to be 'too independent'. The amendment of the law for this purpose did not set a happy precedent. The independence of TRAI, as reconstituted in 2000, is now taken with a pinch of salt, particularly after the recent disputes between cellular and WLL licensees. It is time for another independent group to formulate NTP-II for sustaining the momentum of growth. Better still, an independent arrangement should be institutionalised for this purpose.

RAILWAYS

The Indian Railways continue to run on a monolithic inward-looking model. Several attempts to introduce reforms and restructuring have been stillborn. Being a closed organisation that does not entertain much external scrutiny, the Railway Board determines its own policies and strategies largely based on internal perceptions and compulsions. Few external checks and balances are available by way of self-correcting mechanisms. The vast potential of the railways thus lies substantially untapped. On the contrary, a steady deterioration in many of its fundamentals continues unabated.

Given the mould in which the railways seem to operate, there is little hope for substantive reforms. It is futile to expect that incumbent players will be the harbingers of change. The railways may thus continue to deteriorate unless an independent forum such as a multi-disciplinary railway commission consisting of eminent persons is set up for devising and implementing a reform strategy that could rejuvenate this sector.

AIRPORTS

Here is yet another story of incumbent players keeping private participation at bay. There is always a semblance of some activity aimed at private participation, but no private investment seems visible on the horizon, except in the case of Bengaluru, where a sponsor-led initiative may see a new airport, albeit after a forced closure of the existing airport. Several cities in the world have two or more airports. The decision to close a flourishing public sector airport and substitute it with a private monopoly operating on a 'cost plus' basis is open to question, especially since the new airport will be located at a distance of about 35 km from the city, thus adding to the time and cost of commuters. In sum, private participation in airports on a credible basis is some distance away, and the Bengaluru approach is obviously flawed.

OTHER INFRASTRUCTURE SECTORS

For the past several years, there has been talk of reforming the ports sector. However, progress is visible only in fits and starts. If lessons from other sectors were any indication, successful privatisation would remain elusive as long as incumbent players continued to determine strategy. Reforms in water supply and urban infrastructure are undergoing similar centrifugal pulls. If and when privatisation occurs, inherent conflicts of interests may well deliver flawed outcomes.

SUCCESS STORIES

Telecom reforms can truly be regarded as a success story. Though much ground remains to be covered, what has happened so far is monumental compared to any other sector. The consumer and the economy share a win-win situation. If such history can be created in the telecom sector, other sectors can surely imbibe a few lessons.

Another success story that testifies to the benefits of liberalisation and competition is the policy of open skies. After the monopoly of Indian Airlines ceased and competition was introduced, domestic air travel has improved by leaps and bounds.

ISSUES IN INFRASTRUCTURE REFORM

It is unrealistic to expect ministers and officials to pursue reforms that would truncate their powers and patronage. Should anyone expect incumbent players in the power sector to part with their monopolistic control over a vast fiefdom? Would incumbents in the highway sector voluntarily cease to farm out contracts and shift to BOT concessions? Is it realistic to expect incumbents to privatise the railways or airport operations? Would local authorities voluntarily give up their control over water supply or urban infrastructure? The telecom revolution in India would have been unthinkable if DoT was in the driver's seat. The traveller's plight could not have been different if Indian Airlines were to write the open skies policy. It is vain to expect governance to succeed when fundamental principles of human behaviour are overlooked.

Incumbents acting in tandem with entrenched interests would not only try and subvert reforms but also manipulate their governance. For incumbents to part with control, they have to be exceptionally enlightened, or external pressures must compel them to act. To enable reforms to proceed in the best interests of the economy, the evolution of a process that vests decision-making in individuals or bodies free of any conflict of interests is a pre-requisite. Failure to recognise this basic tenet of governance will continue to compromise development and economic growth.

Conflict of Interests

No man can be the judge of his own cause, so goes an age-old dictum. This is also a basic tenet of jurisprudence in a democratic polity. This proposition is enshrined in common law too. It is also an inviolate norm in judicial functioning, so much so that if a litigant expresses any misgivings about the impartiality of a judge, the latter is expected to transfer the matter to another court. It is well recognised that in public affairs, a subjective or partisan approach has no place. A player cannot be an umpire if the game is to be worth its while. Yet, in pursuit of infrastructure reforms, this basic principle has been compromised time and again.

The crisis of 1991 had spelt the end of business as usual. Economic liberalisation became imperative and it was recognised that growth could be accelerated only if the woefully poor infrastructure services were upgraded by virtue of massive investments and efficiency improvements. The government, therefore, announced several policy initiatives aimed at opening these sectors to private investment. The prevailing thinking in the government, however, was on a different track. The command and control structure of the Indian economy had in the past entrusted vast powers to government functionaries in the guise of public interest. They ran the nation's economy through public sector undertakings (PSUs) and the licence-permit raj. Infrastructure reforms were thus perceived by the incumbents as a threat to their enormous fiefdoms that had come into being during the past five decades. Being in positions of control, they chose to redefine reforms at each stage in order to protect their turf. Conflicts of interests and sitting in judgement over one's own cause are two sides of the same coin. Be it a court order, a board decision, or policy formulation, the presence of a conflict of interests can lead to an outcome that may be fundamentally flawed. With greater public awareness and open debate, Western democracies keep resolving such conflicts as and when they surface. The level of such awareness being comparatively low in India, coupled with the absence of open debate and consultations, incumbents do not have much difficulty in influencing the reform agenda to suit their interests, even if it means the end of a reform initiative. These conflicts of interests, thriving in an opaque environment, seem to be the biggest stumbling block in the pursuit of infrastructure reforms in India.

Absence of Competition

A natural outcome of incumbent control is the absence of competition, coupled with a 'cost plus' approach that would generate assured returns. Efficiency improvements and cost reductions are obvious casualties. It is truly amazing how infrastructure reforms in India, other than in telecom, have remained unencumbered by competition, thanks to the clout of incumbents.

Competition should have been regarded as the key to infrastructure reforms. A restrictive market structure not only obstructs the inflow of private investment, it also makes it inefficient. It is competition, and not privatisation, that acts as the engine for efficiency and price gains. Economic growth and consumer welfare will remain hostage to incumbent control unless a clear policy on competition is put in place.

Flawed Regulatory Framework

Regulatory commissions have come to occupy a dominant role in several critical sectors of the economy. But often, regulators are not perceived as effective, honest, and credible. Their selection process inspires little confidence because it is virtually controlled by the political executive of the day. Predictably, the choice has generally fallen on favoured bureaucrats on the verge of retirement. As stated earlier, some time back the government amended the law to sack all the five telecom regulators and nominate a fresh lot. This was widely seen as a debatable exercise of power.

Juxtaposed against subjective selection is the lack of accountability. These commissions bear no consequences of their acts of commission and omission. They are answerable neither to the government nor to Parliament or the state legislatures. They enjoy complete 'independence' and cannot be removed during their specified term. Yet, they wield enormous powers over consumers, investors, and the economy without being subjected to any legislative oversight, which is contrary to established practice in developed democracies.

In the power sector, for example, the regulator will make regulations having the force of law; he will have powers of search and seizure; he will adjudicate and impose heavy penalties; he will issue licences and have powers to suspend or revoke them; he may issue directions that will be binding on all; he will levy his own fees; and he will pass his own budget. He is arguably very powerful, and with accountability to none, at that. To top it all, his appointment will be determined by the political executive.

The emerging regulatory environment negates the fundamental principle of effective checks and balances, upon which a modern democratic state rests. In particular, the absence of effective checks and balances will increase the possibility of regulatory capture by vested interests, simply because a lot of money is at stake. Fraud and abuse in regulatory affairs will be a real issue. The regulators will increasingly lose credibility and fail to provide the much-needed independent regulation. This could well lead to the emergence of 'rogue regulators', a term already in vogue in regulatory literature.

Lack of Professional Approach

Government functionaries in India are accustomed to the public sector mode of functioning, where risks and obligations are loosely defined and rarely carried to their logical conclusion. The private sector, on the other hand, functions through well-defined contracts where rights and obligations are precisely defined. The move from the public sector to the private sector mode of operations is, therefore, complex and requires a great deal of professional expertise.

Be it PPAs, concession agreements, or privatising public services through other means, government functionaries have had to manage these complex affairs without much experience or capacity building. In the process, they are often guided by private sponsors, thereby failing to ensure adequate value for public money. They are sometimes able to hire advisers, but the interaction is often superficial compared to the complexity involved. At any rate, governments at the Centre and in the states have failed to build the capacity or expertise necessary for dealing with the new challenges. As a result, the responses of government functionaries are often unprofessional and impose a heavy toll on growth and development.

Role of Multilateral Development Banks

The traditional role of multilateral development banks in providing loan assistance to sovereign governments needs to be redefined for meeting the emerging challenges of infrastructure reforms, particularly for economies in transition like India. The compulsions of maintaining or expanding their respective loan portfolios often lead to a continued financing of public investment in infrastructure sectors. On the other hand, multilateral development banks seem deficient in expertise relating to privatisation, and their efforts in this direction have not been particularly successful.

Multilateral development banks continue to provide significant loan assistance in India in support of public investments in power, highways, railways, ports, urban infrastructure, etc. But in reforming the telecom sector, where successful privatisation has already occurred, the role of multilateral development banks has been negligible, both in terms of financing and in providing expertise.

The failure of power reforms in several multilateral development bank-assisted states, coupled with the absence of substantive reforms in other infrastructure sectors, brings into focus the inadequacy of the role of such banks in this critical area of growth. Their failure to bring in open access in the power sector, followed by its introduction entirely through an indigenous debate within India, should serve as a case study for a critical evaluation of their role in infrastructure reforms.

A close scrutiny of their operations would reveal that though their declared objective is aggressive privatisation, their lending programmes tend to thwart it. For assisting the developing countries in formulating and implementing infrastructure reforms, multilateral development banks would need to rethink their role and strategy. Besides assisting in credible privatisation, they should help fund adjustment costs and also enable leveraging larger volumes of private investment through loan assistance to the governments. Merely the investment financing of public entities may be counter-productive in the long run, particularly when these entities can access adequate borrowings from domestic and external markets.

Role of Indian Financial Institutions

Indian financial institutions (IFIs) have provided loans for infrastructure projects largely on the strength of government guarantees. In doing so, they have developed little expertise in appraising projects and taking commercial risks. The market for domestic debt in support of infrastructure projects, therefore, remains underdeveloped.

With a view to building capacity and expertise, the Central Government, in association with private sector entities, promoted the Infrastructure Development Finance Company (IDFC) six years ago. This initiative has made little impact so far because the institution is small and its expertise is limited. Moreover, its role as an adviser is suspect, because that often comes in the way of its interests as a lender. This tends to compromise its position.

Even comparatively small neighbours such as Bangladesh and Sri Lanka have created independent outfits for project and policy development. In the absence of such segregation, the IDFC has not been able to play an effective role as an adviser in infrastructure policies and projects.

International Success Stories

Infrastructure reforms in developed countries have been usually led by their respective finance ministries or by independent statutory bodies. A good example is the role played by the UK treasury. Among other measures, it initiated a private finance initiative (PFI), which mobilised over £20 billion in private investments during the past decade. This initiative operated through a treasury task force and was later converted into a corporate entity. As stated earlier, Bangladesh and Sri Lanka seem to have recently adopted a somewhat similar course by setting up independent entities for policy and project development.

LESSONS FROM INFRASTRUCTURE REFORMS

From a decade of experience in infrastructure reforms across different sectors, it should be evident that the underlying causes of failure lie in governance. In conceptual terms, the emerging lessons can be briefly identified as follows.

Eliminating Conflicts of Interests

It should be clear that incumbent players cannot be trusted with formulating reform strategies that may strike at the roots of their powers or privileges. While their participation in the reform process is essential, they should not have the final say in determining the strategy or its implementation. The overall control over the reform process must vest in an independent entity sufficiently empowered to enforce its decisions.

In developed countries, the head of state or government seems to have empowered the finance ministry or set up independent statutory authorities to steer the reform strategy, particularly in critical areas such as infrastructure services. In the Indian context, the finance ministry does not seem sufficiently empowered to carry out this task. Incumbent players can thus formulate self-serving policies. In addition, partisan law-making is common, suggesting the need for an independent Economic Laws Commission.

Typically, the finance ministries/departments at the Centre and in the states are best suited for steering the reform process. However, this presupposes sufficient capacity-building for dealing with the complexities of infrastructure reform. Specialised outfits such as PFI of the UK could also be considered, but their roles and powers would need to be clearly defined.

Key Role of Competition

De-licensing and liberalising several segments of the economy have enhanced competition, thereby eliminating shortages, improving efficiencies, and reducing costs. Competitiveness as a whole is dependent on open and fair competition in each and every segment. The gains of competition in telecom and air travel are recent and powerful examples.

In infrastructure sectors, the network is often referred to as 'carrier'. It has attributes of a natural monopoly that attracts close regulation. On the other hand, content portions such as voice in telephony, electric current in the power sector, and gas in the piped gas supply sector are amenable to competition. Adopting an approach similar to telecom for the generation and supply of electricity should usher in phenomenal gains; and gas should follow. In the absence of competition, reforms of these sectors would continue to be superficial.

Independent Regulation

The provision of a level playing field that would enable investment to flourish in a competitive environment is a pre-requisite for the orderly growth of infrastructure, particularly because it is capital-intensive. The need to protect consumer interests is equally critical. The regulatory framework would need to rely on effective checks and balances for eliminating fraud and misuse by vested interests. It is, therefore, necessary to build consensus on regulatory best practices across different sectors with the objective of enacting an overarching law that will provide effective and credible regulation.

Open Consultative Approach

The laws and policies to be evolved as part of reforms should go through an open consultative process where different stakeholder interests get adequate opportunities to put across their concerns. The balancing of conflicting interests is critical to the success of reforms as well as for their acceptance by the stakeholders.

Open consultations are very useful in pre-empting any stake-holder interests from unduly steering the process to their respective advantage. Notable examples are the formulation of the NTP 1999; the evolution of the Electricity Bill; the role played by the Standing Committee of Parliament on Energy in enlarging the debate on the Electricity Bill; and the formulation of a concession framework for privatising highways. These episodes, as briefly described in this essay, sufficiently establish the critical role of open consultation and transparent policymaking.

Professionalising the Reform Process

Moving from public ownership to private participation in infrastructure is a complex phenomenon. It requires a change in the prevailing mindset and practices. It also implies a shift to the complex world of contracts that should not only facilitate private participation but also ensure good value for public money.

It would be necessary for the government to build capacity to deal with the emerging challenges. Typical government organisations and their usual responses fall well below the minimum requisite expertise necessary for dealing with these complex issues. Besides recognising the need for government functionaries to acquire some degree of specialisation, the government should engage independent experts of proven calibre in view of the high stakes involved. Without adequate professional and expert input, infrastructure reforms will continue to limp, thereby imposing a heavy cost on the economy.

CONCLUSION

The potential for reform in India is vast. There has been some progress too, but it is much less than expected and far below the potential. It needs to be recognised that there can be little hope of sustainable reform if players can continue to act as umpires. The challenge facing the government is not reforms per se; the real challenge lies in evolving a governance philosophy that ensures an open and objective consideration of reform strategies with the participation of experts and stakeholders. If governance is in order, it should be possible to address the aforementioned concerns in a professional and transparent manner. Economic growth and consumer welfare will then reinforce each other.

Formulating policies and strategies through an empowered process independent of the control of incumbents; introducing competition for efficiency improvements and cost reduction; effective and accountable regulation; capacity-building and involvement of experts;

and open consultation with experts and stakeholders should form the cornerstone of infrastructure reforms in times to come. A method for institutionalising these concepts would need to be established.

POSTSCRIPT

This essay concluded that the real challenge lies in governance—in eliminating conflicts of interest, promoting competition, ensuring independent regulation, and professionalising the reform process. India has a long way to go in each of these aspects of governance. Sustainable reform is unlikely if players continue to act as umpires because they are sure to obstruct an objective evolution of reform strategies. For the same reason, a level playing field will continue to be denied and the benefits of fair competition will remain elusive; neither will regulatory commissions emerge as independent and accountable institutions.

The essay emphasises the need for an empowered process that is independent of the control of incumbents; a process based on consultations with experts and stakeholders. The setting up of the Committee on Infrastructure (2004) under the chairmanship of the Prime Minister could be regarded as a significant step in that direction. It provided a platform for evolution of policies, processes, and documents that conform to international best practices. It also tried to address the governance issues with some degree of success. The work done so far has placed several infrastructure sectors in a 'take off' stage that could lead to transformation of their services, besides spurring growth and employment. The next big challenge is implementation, where the success so far has been limited, yet again owing to incumbent resistance. An equally daunting challenge is to contain, if not eliminate, the menace of rent-seeking.

7 Crisis of Credibility*

Warning signals suggest the possible exploitation of consumers at the hands of regulatory commissions that now play a dominant role in several critical sectors of the economy. Often the regulators are not effective, and are not seen as honest and credible. They have vast authority with little accountability; their selection process inspires little confidence; and redressal from their actions is elusive.

As a result, they are a law unto themselves. Here are some samples. Compared to three members constituting the electricity regulatory commissions in all the states, the Government of Delhi appointed only one member in 1999, with no legal or financial expertise. His tariff orders in favour of private distribution companies have been challenged in several court cases. Recently, a senior staff member questioned the regulator's integrity because the latter's son was on the payroll of a private licensee whose tariffs and licence conditions he determined.

Consumers could well suspect that this scenario could push up their tariffs. Imagine the confidence that a high court judge would inspire if his son were in the employment of a litigant before him. The same regulator has also drawn a daily allowance of $500 per diem while travelling abroad. Moreover, these expenses were disbursed by the Delhi Power Supply Company that he regulates. A furore that followed the Comptroller and Auditor General (CAG's) report

* Originally published in *The Times of India*, 22 January 2004.

on similar allowances drawn by the Telecom Regulatory Authority of India (TRAI) members some years ago was obviously no lesson. In addition, he also drew an excess payment of Rs 91,000, which was returned after one full year, following an audit objection. In a developed democracy, such conduct could attract summary dismissal.

As for the telecom regulator (TRAI), the editorial of a leading economic daily recently titled its actions as crony capitalism. The editorial stated, 'So now, all we have are vague promises from a regulator with little credibility or independence that real reforms will follow after six months.'

An editor of another economic daily described some decisions in telecom as largesse. Not to be outdone, an insurance regulator recently donated enough funds (several crores of rupees) to an institution that later provided a comfortable lifetime sinecure for him. The expectation of independent regulation seems vain because the extant laws offer no such hope.

The first flaw lies in the choice of regulators through selection committees that are controlled by the political executive of the day. Predictably the choice has generally fallen on favoured bureaucrats on the verge of retirement.

As politicians become wiser, the next round could go to their cronies. This is already beginning to happen. We could well see the emergence of rogue regulators, a term already in vogue in Western regulatory literature. Sometime ago, the government amended the law to sack all the five telecom regulators and nominate a fresh lot. This was indeed a debatable exercise of power. Imagine the fabric of the IAS and other services if recruitments were entrusted to committees nominated by the political executive.

Statesmen like Nehru and Sardar Patel may well have ensured fair selections through this route, but they opted for the Union Public Service Commission to conduct this task without fear or favour and enshrined its independent status in the Constitution. While considering the Electricity Bill, the Standing Committee of Parliament on Energy did recommend selection of regulators through the public service commissions, but to no avail.

Subjective selection of the regulators is compounded by their complete lack of accountability, as these commissions bear no consequences for their acts of commission and omission. They are answerable neither to the government nor to Parliament or the state legislatures. They enjoy complete independence and cannot be removed during their term of five years.

Yet, they enjoy enormous powers over consumers, investors, and the economy. Another worrisome trend is the empowerment of regulators to levy their own fees and spend the receipts at will. No legislative oversight has been mandated, contrary to established practice in developed democracies. Each commission can set up its own fund; even the Supreme Court does not have such a privilege.

In the power sector, for example, the regulator will make regulations having the force of law; he will have powers of search and seizure; he will adjudicate and impose heavy penalties; he will issue licences and have powers to suspend or revoke them; he may issue directions that will be binding on all; he will levy his own fees; and he will pass his own budget. He is arguably very powerful and not accountable to anyone. To top it all, his birth will be an accident of political favour. That standards of political behaviour are not exactly on the ascendancy would only compound matters.

The emerging regulatory environment negates the fundamental principle of effective checks and balances upon which a modern democratic state rests. In particular, the absence of effective checks will increase the possibility of regulatory capture by vested interests, simply because a lot of money is at stake. Fraud and abuse in regulatory affairs will be a real issue.

We can safely predict that these regulators will increasingly lose credibility and fail to provide the much-needed independent regulation that affects every citizen. What we really need is a states-man who will build consensus for an overarching law that will straighten economic regulation before it extracts a heavy price from the common man.

POSTSCRIPT

The reservations expressed in this essay about the electricity regulatory commissions have not been belied. The regulators have virtually failed the economy and the common man. Viewed as sinecures to be doled out to favoured retiring bureaucrats for services rendered, they carry little conviction with the people at large. In several cases, the incumbent chief secretaries of states as well as a Union power secretary have shifted seamlessly to the regulatory commissions, thus compromising the credibility of the selection process. In most cases, these commissions have not been able to deliver even a small fraction of what was expected of them.

For example, the mandatory provisions of the Electricity Act regarding introduction of competition and open access in the supply of electricity to bulk consumers are being followed in their breach. Seven years after enactment of the Electricity Act, 2003, not a single consumer across the territory of India has been able to buy electricity regularly from a competing supplier or producer, as he remains hostage to the distribution monopoly of his area. Absence of competition has resulted in low investment, continued shortages, and excessive rent-seeking. The manner in which the incumbents and vested interests, aided by the regulatory commissions, have prevented the introduction of competition and held the entire economy hostage is testimony to the failures of governance.

The interconnected chain of monopolies in the supply of electricity has enabled unprecedented profiteering in trading of electricity. Average bulk prices of traded electricity during 2008–09 and 2009–10 have been nearly three times the production costs. These excessive and unearned profits have imposed an unjustified burden of about Rs 40,000 crore on the exchequer and the common man. The regulatory commissions have thus failed in discharging their primary role, which is to protect the ordinary consumer from the monopoly supplier.

Yet another example of failure is the ports sector where the regulator seems to have suffered from regulatory capture in allowing excessive and unprecedented returns to private operators at the expense of users and the port trusts. The only example of success is the telecom sector where competition in the market did the trick.

Partisan selection processes as well as the lack of accountability have been the root causes of regulatory failure in India. Though the Common Minimum Programme announced by the government in 2004 promised regulatory reforms, the government could not muster enough political will to carry them through as it involved restraining the ministries that had developed a cosy relationship with the regulatory system. Nevertheless, the Eleventh Five Year Plan document and the Approach Paper on Regulation have recognised the need for an overarching legislation to set the house in order. When and how these reforms would see the light of the day is anybody's guess.

8 To Market, To Market*
Dismantle government control over infrastructure

Imagine how the Indian economy would have looked if the licence raj had not been abolished in the early 1990s. 'India Shining' was clearly a product of the economic liberalisation that unbound the spirit of enterprise from the stranglehold of a control and command structure. The rest, as they say, is history.

While the markets were booming, the resulting economic expansion increased the demand for infrastructure services that were hitherto in the public sector domain. Conforming to the mantra of liberalisation, the infrastructure ministries announced their respective policies for inviting private participation to bridge the yawning investment gaps. In practice, however, the ground rules were so laid out that the prospective investors were short of a level playing field and the requisite regulatory framework.

Over the years, private investment remained elusive for want of an enabling environment and its shortfall served as a justification for expanding the role of incumbent government entities. The political masters and bureaucrats saw this as an opportunity to reinvent control and command through contracts. The loss of economic power

* Originally published in *The Times of India*, 4 November 2004.

following the demise of licence raj was thus made good through the commanding heights of 'contract raj'.

Take the example of the power sector. The world over, introduction of competition constituted the rationale for successful power reforms. Not so in India. Private investment in generation was introduced, but only via contracts for sale of power to the state electricity boards (SEBs)—solely by invitation, Dabhol style. No producer was allowed to sell directly to consumers, howsoever large. Since these monopolies were perceived as bankrupt, the virtual absence of private investment was predictable. In the shortages that so prevailed, the role of public investment expanded. As for its sustainability, there seemed little concern. Even today, electricity continues to be the sole industry where a producer can sell only to an SEB or a state-mandated monopoly.

Highways were no different. Public–private partnerships (PPPs) were eminently feasible and the golden quadrilateral, for example, could have been completed at less than one-fourth the cost to the exchequer, with far greater speed and efficiency. The example of the Jaipur–Kishangarh section of the Delhi–Mumbai highway should serve as an eye opener. It is the largest highway project in India; its capital cost exceeds Rs 700 crore; it is being built through a PPP; and is nearing completion despite apathy of the incumbent government entities that took five years to award the concession. This model is eminently replicable, if only the policy formulation is wrested out of the incumbent's control.

Government entities in the highways sector seem preoccupied with construction contracts that are typically followed by maintenance contracts and contracts for tolling. It should be obvious that combining construction, maintenance, and toll collection into a BOT (build–operate–transfer) concession is an internationally accepted norm that enables private investment in highways. Yet, PPPs have been a no-no owing to the attendant loss of contracts and controls.

The story was no different in telecom where the incumbents created a stalemate that kept private investment at bay until 1999 when multi-pronged pressures persuaded the government to set up an independent task force under Jaswant Singh. It wrote the National Telecom Policy (NTP), 1999, that transformed the sector beyond all expectations. The key was creation of a framework that enabled competing service providers to market their services directly to the consumers and not by sale to the government under a contract.

Even now, the Department of Telecom continues to seek control whenever the occasion arises, such as by restricting the broadband service providers from accessing the network of government-owned entities. Consumers will be able to secure low-cost broadband services if competing service providers are allowed to use Bharat Sanchar Nigam Ltd (BSNL) wires on the analogy of similar access in telephony. It is time for another NTP to contain the incumbent's hegemony that is withholding an impending explosion of broadband services.

The examples are many and all-pervasive. They reflect the command and control psyche of the respective ministries and departments. The dishonest see the contract raj as an opportunity to gratify their avarice, while the self-appointed guardians of public interest regard it as a device for containing what they regard as exploitation by the private sector. The net result is a modified version of the licence raj in infrastructure services.

If all infrastructure sectors were truly opened up to competitive private investment, the Indian economy would be in striking distance of 8 per cent annual growth. Remember how India achieved an average growth rate of 7.5 per cent from 1994 to 1997 following the demise of the licence raj. In the subsequent years, this robust growth petered out to an average of 5.3 per cent owing to various constraints, including infrastructure. All these years, the enormous potential in infrastructure has been waiting to be tapped. But for that to happen, the contract raj would have to go. Abolition of the licence raj did enormous service to the common man. Demolition of the contract raj will lead to the same results. Telecom is a live example. The recent initiatives announced by Prime Minister Manmohan Singh suggest light at the end of the tunnel. In 1991, he gave India the much-applauded economic liberalisation. It is sheer providence that he will now lead the second-generation reforms. His emphasis on reforms in infrastructure services bodes well for the nation.

POSTSCRIPT

The Committee on Infrastructure, chaired by the Prime Minister, has steered the reform initiatives which have helped create the requisite policy framework for private participation in a competitive environment. However, the incumbent ministries have been slow to respond and investment in infrastructure continues to be lower than expected. The extent of private participation varies significantly among different sectors. While private investment in telecom accounts for more than 80 per cent of the total investment, the railways continue to languish below 5 per cent. A quick survey across sectors would seem to suggest that wherever private investment and competition have been introduced, the improvement in quality of services has been significant.

The public sector simply does not have the resources or the capacity to meet the infrastructure challenge. Yet, it is not willing to let go of its command and control, thus restricting the much needed private investment. As a result, the infrastructure deficit continues to rise. The key really lies in implementation of the policy framework for liberalisation of the infrastructure sector through competitive private participation, and that is where the entrenched interests would need to be dealt with.

9 Challenge is to Tackle Governance Issues*

The infrastructure deficit in India is widely recognised as a constraint on growth. Congestion on highways, ports, airports, and railways has increased, as have power shortages.

They impose additional costs and constraints, which in turn compromise the competitiveness of the agriculture, manufacturing, and services sectors in the domestic as well as global markets. This widening deficit is characterised by the fact that the demand has grown much beyond the anticipated levels and the creation of infrastructure has persistently fallen short of the targets set by the government.

Efficient infrastructure is also a critical input for broad-based and inclusive growth aimed at improving the quality of life, generating employment, and reducing poverty across regions. China and other East Asian economies have been investing over 10 per cent of their gross domestic product (GDP) in infrastructure as compared to about 5 per cent in India.

The Eleventh Five Year Plan (2007–12), therefore, aims at ramping up the investment levels to about 9 per cent of GDP by 2012. In absolute terms, the investment of about Rs 8,71,450 crore ($218 billion) during the Tenth Five Year Plan would have to rise by 2.4

* Originally published in *The Economic Times*, 6 January 2008.

times to Rs 20,60,193 crore ($515 billion, at an exchange rate of Rs 40 per dollar)) during the Eleventh Plan.

This would amount to an annual average of 7.65 per cent of GDP. Without an effort of this order, GDP growth rate of 9 per cent could be compromised. Investment in irrigation, rural roads, and in the water supply and sanitation sectors will have to be made from budgetary resources.

Given the allocations required for social sectors and rural infrastructure, the resources available for funding large infrastructure projects would be increasingly inadequate. Not only would public sector undertakings be required to enhance internal generation and raise market borrowings, greater reliance would have to be placed on public–private partnerships (PPPs) in infrastructure projects.

As compared to 20 per cent during the Tenth Plan, the share of private sector would have to increase to 30 per cent during the Eleventh Plan, implying a jump from Rs 1,72,188 crore to Rs 6,19,591 crore in absolute terms.

'Business as usual' projection of total investment in infrastructure during the Eleventh Plan is about Rs 14,05,059 crore or $351 billion. To raise this level to the projected Rs 20,60,193 crore would constitute an enormous challenge for the government. The prospects of achieving this level would largely depend on the steps that it is able to take for creating an enabling environment.

The ability to raise resources for large infrastructure projects would depend critically on a regime that would enable recovery of economic user charges where risk allocation is clearly defined.

Investment in large infrastructure projects would, therefore, need to be structured on sound commercial principles and legal structures that rely on competition and credible regulatory practices, thus enabling financially viable projects that deliver efficient and affordable services to users. Since 70 per cent of the projected investment would have to be raised from internal savings, market borrowings, and private investment, commercialisation of infrastructure is inevitable.

The key challenge would lie in addressing governance-related issues. These would include introduction of competition, elimination of the dominance of incumbent government entities, reform of regulatory institutions, and standardisation of documents, procedures, and processes.

On the one hand, there is huge demand for infrastructure. On the other hand, there is enormous appetite among investors and lenders to finance infrastructure. If only the barriers can be removed, then the infrastructure story would come into full bloom.

POSTSCRIPT

This piece reiterates the theme of several essays in this volume viz. the critical role of governance and the removal of barriers to competition and investment. It brings out the scale of the challenge, especially the need for ramping up private investment rapidly. It also refers to the investment target for the Eleventh Five Year Plan (2007–12) which was more than double the actual investment during the preceding Plan period. The Mid-Term Review of the Eleventh Plan suggests that the overall investment target may still be achieved but growth across sectors would be uneven. The performance of the telecom sector will clearly exceed the targets while there would be significant shortfalls in some of the other sectors, especially railways and ports. This vindicates the role of governance in introducing competition and removing barriers. There is irrefutable evidence to establish that wherever reforms have been structured and implemented well, the outcomes have been impressive. Equally true is the proposition that sectors which are lagging behind are typically encumbered with serious governance issues.

The story that keeps emerging time and again is that financing of infrastructure is not a problem, as there is enormous appetite among investors. The problems arise primarily from barriers to private investment, which have been erected by incumbent government entities. If only the government can get its act together, investment in infrastructure is set to grow at an unprecedented pace.

10   Lessons from the CWG Scams[*]

Can the engineer–contractor–politician nexus be demolished?

It is scam season in full bloom: award of telecom licences, contracts relating to Commonwealth Games (CWG), Adarsh housing complex in Mumbai, land allotments in Karnataka, etc. There have been scams in the past too, though not on the same scale. All of them seem to attract media glare, put the government on the defensive for a while, and lead to investigations and court cases that linger on till public memory fades away.

In the past, little effort was made to identify the systemic failures that allowed a scam to happen. As a result, effective safeguards have not been introduced for eliminating the possibilities of recurrence. So scams keep repeating themselves in different forms but with predictable frequency. While men and morals may continue to falter in giving precedence to personal greed over public interest, good governance is all about checks and balances that channelise behaviour in the right direction.

Take the example of the recently held CWG. According to several press reports, not only were the projects of Delhi Government hugely delayed, their costs were doubled from about Rs 2,000 crore to

[*] Edited and published in *Hindustan Times*, January 2011.

Rs 4,000 crore. Yet, little has been said about the system failures that caused this imbroglio.

In contrast, redevelopment of the Delhi Airport, with an investment of over Rs 10,000 crore, was completed well before the Games. The construction of the Games Village was also finished in time. Some deficiencies in construction work remained, but these were amenable to correction through enforcement of the stringent penalty clauses in the construction contract. The reported controversies relating to the Games Village were mainly about furnishing and other jobs that were assigned to different agencies. The point here is that a huge construction project involving an expenditure of over Rs 1,500 crore got completed in time and without cost overruns while several smaller projects undertaken by the CPWD, DDA, PWD, etc., were barely completed just before the Games opened, and at much higher costs.

Nothing seems to have been written about the basic reason for this stark difference in outcomes. However, the distinction is quite simple and straightforward. All projects other than the Delhi Airport and the Games Village were undertaken through an outdated mode of contracting that has potential for delays, cost overruns, and corruption. On the other hand, the Delhi Airport and the Games Village were built through a more rational and modern mode of contracting where the entire risk and responsibility was assigned to the contractor who was also required to bear the burden of any time and cost overruns.

In a conventional PWD-style contract, bids are invited for the unit rates payable in respect of each item of work. The government engineer measures each unit of work and makes a running payment for the work done. In this process, the costs of additional quantities and new items are also paid by the government. Moreover, delays on this account are borne by the government and the contractor is compensated for inflation during the construction period. In effect, this is like an open contract which offers enormous opportunities for time and cost overruns as well as for corruption. The engineer and the contractor have little incentive to complete the work in time and within the estimated costs. The result of this approach was evident in all the Games related projects handled, for instance, by the PWD.

On the other hand, the Delhi Airport was constructed through the public–private partnership (PPP) mode which allocates all the construction risks to the concessionaire. Experience suggests that PPP projects usually get completed ahead of schedule. Since the concessionaire also gets to collect the user charges from the new facility, he pushes even harder for early completion. These are very powerful incentives for completion without time and cost overruns. In the case of the Games Village, the contractor was given a turnkey contract which also required him to bear the burden of time and cost overruns. As a result, this project also got completed in time and at no extra cost to the government—unlike the PWD projects related to the Games.

The message is simple and straightforward. Allocate the construction risks to the contractor and let him have an incentive for timely completion. It would change the entire scenario. All that needs to be done is substitution of the item rate contracts by turnkey contracts. If this were done, the construction of highways, flyovers, bridges, buildings, dams, etc., would not suffer from time and cost overruns. The potential for corruption would be minimised too. Sounds logical, so why is it not done?

The problem with turnkey contracts is that the government engineer loses his day-to-day control over the project. Nor can the engineer and the contractor collude to increase the project costs at government expense. Moreover, it would directly affect the contractor–engineer–politician nexus that is known for its relentless pursuit of rent extraction. As a result, while the developed countries as well as the private sector across the world have moved towards the turnkey approach, all the engineering departments in India seem opposed to this reform.

In plain terms, this is an issue related to good governance. Hopefully, the shame and embarrassment that India faced before the entire world during the run up to the CWG will lead to some systemic reforms. The money thus saved can help build many more projects that would accelerate growth.

POSTSCRIPT

The cost and time overruns as well as the charges of corruption relating to the CWG projects have since been examined by the Comptroller and Auditor General as well as by an independent high-level committee. Their respective reports clearly suggest that the procurement methods currently in vogue are eminently prone to corruption and delays. They need to be reformed and modernised.

While the developed countries and several developing countries have enacted their respective procurement laws, India continues to rely on administrative rules and procedures that lack statutory backing and do not serve as effective deterrents against malpractices and corruption. Though 15 to 20 per cent of the GDP is spent on public procurement, the governance associated with it is starkly inadequate. The groundswell of public opinion relating to the perceived corruption in CWG projects and other cases of public procurement illustrates the gravity of the problem. Yet these cases only reflect the symptoms. The disease lies in governance—in the lack of a credible legal framework for regulating public procurement, compounded by the lack of accountability. These failures of governance are manifested in the popular belief that malpractices and corruption can go scot-free.

III
Power Reforms

11 Whither Electricity Reforms?*

The electricity reform strategy currently being pursued in the seven states of Orissa, Haryana, Andhra Pradesh, Uttar Pradesh, Karnataka, Rajasthan, and Delhi is not in the right direction. It is neither perceived as people-friendly nor is it likely to attract the much-needed investments in the power sector. The reform process seems to be working as a sedative that suppresses symptomatic pain without addressing the disease. Worse is the situation in the remaining states where reforms are yet to be initiated. In most parts, the debate on reforms is inadequate and without much clarity on the issues involved, leave apart their possible resolution.

The structure of the electricity industry in independent India was laid down by the Electricity (Supply) Act, 1948, that created the state electricity boards (SEBs). In their initial years, the SEBs performed yeomen service in carrying electric power far and wide, but over the years they have become unsustainable, thanks to their mismanagement and politicisation coupled with the economic and technological developments of the past decade. It is high time that the electricity industry is denationalised and restructured on commercial principles.

Though the legal framework was amended in 1991 and 1998 to facilitate private investment in generation and transmission,

* Originally published in *Economic and Political Weekly*, Vol. 36, No. 17, 28 April–4 May 2001, pp. 1389–91.

respectively, it enabled private entities to sell or transmit power only through long-term contracts with state-owned entities. Such contract-driven privatisation through state-owned monopolies can have little chance of enduring success. Similarly, the setting up of regulatory commissions under the 1998 Act, though a welcome move, can only have a limited impact on the state-owned monopolies. It should surprise no one that these piecemeal changes in the name of reform have not been able to arrest the deterioration of this industry.

To overcome the outdated structure stipulated in the central laws, the seven 'reforming' states have enacted their own laws and adopted the so-called Orissa model for unbundling their monolithic SEBs into generating, transmission, and distribution companies, to be regulated by an independent regulatory commission in each state. The argument in favour of unbundling was the pressing need for creation of viable commercial entities that would lend themselves to efficiency improvements and privatisation, as in the West.

The similarity of the Orissa model with the restructuring under-taken in other countries virtually ends with the unbundling of SEBs. Unlike the West, where competition in generation and supply is the engine for efficiency gains and tariff reduction, the Orissa model relies on an interconnected chain of monopolies where competition is conspicuous by its absence. In effect, it has only tin-kered with the structure without incorporating any sound economics of regulation.

SINGLE BUYER MODEL

Orissa represents a 'single buyer model' where all generating companies (Gencos) are required to sell their produce to a state-owned transmission company (Transco). This implies that even if Gencos are willing to offer spot sales, or enter into short-term contracts, there cannot be a credible market in the absence of multiple buyers. Gencos cannot, therefore, bear the market risk and must rely on long-term power purchase agreements (PPAs) with the Transco. As a result, new capacity can only be contracted through the state-owned Transco that continues, like its predecessor the SEB, to negotiate PPAs on a 'cost plus' basis, leading to comparatively high tariffs.

In the Orissa model, the absence of competition does not stop at generation. Since Gencos must sell their produce to the Transco, distribution companies (Discoms) can buy from the Transco alone, and the consumer must, in turn, source all his requirements from the Discom of his area. The industry structure thus continues to be in the command-and-control mode, unencumbered by competition and consumer choice. In this chain of monopolies, public as well as private, all prices are determined on a 'cost plus' basis either through negotiations or by the regulator, and this constitutes a perfect recipe for delivering high-cost power to the consumer.

At the distribution end of the Orissa model, the prevailing tariff structure coupled with the high transmission and distribution (T&D) losses does not permit adequate cost recovery by Discoms, which persistently default on their payment obligations to the state-owned Transco. The use of Transco as a free banker for Discoms, carrying their unpaid bills aggregating about Rs 900 crore, negates the very rationale of commercialisation and privatisation. Privatised Discoms in Orissa are virtually being allowed to accumulate unsustainable losses year after year without any clear road map as to when, if at all, these losses will be wiped out, and by whom.

The losses/receivables of Discoms in Orissa are currently being accumulated on the balance sheet of the Transco whose outstanding payments to the state-owned Gencos continue to rise. With a negative net worth, the Transco may be able to contract new generation capacity, if at all, only on the strength of state guarantees and escrow arrangements that are widely regarded as unsustainable. In practice, therefore, Orissa as well as the other 'reforming' states may fail to attract much capacity addition and the prevailing power shortages would continue to persist.

The Transco in Orissa has already accumulated overdue payables of more than Rs 1,500 crore that continue to mount steadily, besides a debt burden of about Rs 3,000 crore. It seems to be caught in a debt trap that can only be addressed through steep tariff increases, which are unlikely to materialise. The state government may, therefore, have to rescue the Transco—a doubtful proposition in view of the precarious condition of state finances—or else this rising burden may stunt the performance and growth of the industry. Evidently, the Orissa model in its present form is not sustainable. This model was perhaps adopted as a first step towards restructuring, but the need to move forward is now imminent.

It appears that just as a reform package had to be evolved for dealing with the financial chaos that was the SEB, another package may be necessary for bailing out the Discoms and the Transco from their impending bankruptcy. The added complication, however, would be the legal and moral hazards posed by any state assistance to private Discoms for cleaning up their losses. Similar problems may arise if Discoms are allowed to charge higher tariffs from future consumers for offsetting their past losses.

BANE OF LONG-TERM PPAS

As a matter of principle, creation of monopolies must be regarded as an unacceptable form of interference by the government in the operation of free markets. It is pertinent to note that in several developed countries, induction of competition in telecom and power has resulted in significant tariff reductions during the past decade, but these lessons seem to have been completely missed in India insofar as power sector reforms are concerned. While competition in telecom is beginning to show dramatic results, there is yet no move towards introducing any worthwhile competition in the electricity industry.

It is important to recognise that in the emerging structure of the electricity industry across the world, long-term PPAs are no longer regarded as conducive to consumer interests. In India, too, there are a number of PPA-based projects where the capital costs and operating norms, as approved by the Central Electricity Authority (CEA) and the respective state governments, leave much room for improvement. These PPAs have typically allowed select private entities to procure power plants based on indicative capital costs approved by the CEA, even though similar approvals for public sector entities like the SEBs and the National Thermal Power Corporation mandate open competitive bidding. In a 'cost plus' regime where capital costs directly translate into tariffs, this issue deserves a more credible treatment. Compelling the consumer to buy power for 20 years or more from a source that has been determined through a sub-optimal process sans competition can hardly be regarded as a practice worthy of emulation.

In the UK, for instance, Gencos do not have the comfort of long-term PPAs to assure them of guaranteed sales and profits. Until recently, they were required to sell their produce through a 'pool' where half-hourly bidding determined the price and off-take. With a view to eliminating the possible manipulation of pool prices through the use of market power by some Gencos, the UK has recently amended its laws to facilitate licensees/consumers to buy directly from competing Gencos. In some of the other developed countries, existing PPAs have been terminated, with compensation, to allow for competitive sale of power in the market. Thus, the typical PPA seems to be facing extinction in the developed markets, and India can hardly hope to usher successful reforms by using the PPA as a vehicle for capacity addition.

In the reform strategy, the central objective should be the creation of a sound structure that promotes growth with efficiency. Towards this end, generation and supply should be separated from transmission with a view to subjecting the former to competition. The proposed separation between the carriage and content businesses is somewhat similar to telecom where several long-distance or cellular operators compete even where a single wire connects the consumer's telephone. Since generation typically constitutes over 75 per cent of the consumer tariff, competition among Gencos selling to multiple buyers would bring about significant price and efficiency gains, whereas overlooking this fundamental economic principle would be tantamount to ignoring consumer welfare in the reform design.

In the restructured industry, the Transco must not buy or sell power; it should only transmit on payment of regulated wheeling charges with a view to providing open access to its transmission network. At the distribution end, Discoms must provide similar open access to their wires for enabling bulk consumers to buy directly from Gencos. With these fundamental elements of restructuring in place, market forces can be relied upon to bring in rapid efficiency gains as well as new investments that have so far been elusive. It is important to recognise that an efficient and competitive industry is a pre-requisite for achieving the goal of universal access.

The industry structure proposed here is predicated on the provision of non-discriminatory open access to the 'transmission highways'. A Transco that buys and sells electricity would face a conflict of interest in transmitting the electricity owned by its competitors, and it is for this reason that companies operating transmission networks in the restructured markets abroad are prohibited from buying and selling power. This is critical for creating a free market where Gencos and suppliers can use a common network for selling directly to bulk consumers and Discoms. Besides providing a competitive environment, this arrangement would enable Gencos to assess market demand, enter into contracts with bulk consumers, and set up 'merchant power plants' without relying on government guarantees. The creation of such capacity would free some of the existing supplies of bulk consumers that would become available for the benefit of other consumers.

REFORM OF DISTRIBUTION CRITICAL

There is increasing recognition that reforms at the distribution end are critical for restoring the viability of this industry. This would require distribution to be depoliticised and privatised with a view to containing the large-scale collusive thefts and for upgrading the network. Though difficult to achieve, sustainable privatisation of distribution presupposes a well-designed and comprehensive regulatory framework that is transparent and predictable, unlike the present 'cost plus' year-to-year approach that does not sufficiently incentivise efficiency improvements and, on the contrary, fosters regulatory uncertainty.

Complete separation between the wire and content businesses at the distribution level may not be feasible without a substantial systems upgradation that is unlikely to be cost-effective at this stage. Yet, open access to the wires of a Discom must soon be introduced in respect of bulk consumers. Since these consumers possess the requisite bargaining strength and consume large quantities, they can buy directly from competing producers and bring about the desired competition in the entire industry. The introduction of third-party access to the distribution networks would thus usher the much-needed competition in generation and supply, besides providing a credible mechanism for adding generating capacity.

For ceding their bulk consumers to Gencos, the Discoms can be suitably compensated through the levy of a wheeling surcharge or electricity duty that would help in sustaining the subsidised farm tariffs. Cross-subsidies are here to stay, and competition cannot be postponed indefinitely until their elimination. The problem can, however, be tackled by simply isolating the cross-subsidies and collecting an equivalent surcharge or duty from bulk consumers. As long as they pay such a surcharge or duty, bulk consumers should have the freedom to buy from competing producers.

In the structure proposed here, continued regulation of tariffs payable by retail consumers, not being bulk consumers, would be necessary for guarding against volatility and speculative pricing. Adequate supplies would also have to be ensured by earmarking the existing sources of cheaper generation for their consumption. In effect, this would imply that the existing sources, exceeding 1,00,000 MW of generating capacity, would not enter the competitive market and would continue their supplies as per extant agreements. Only new capacity would be subjected to competitive markets, to begin with; and competition would thus be introduced at the margins. States would be free to subject the older power stations to a similar regime as the markets mature. Such an approach would ensure a smooth transition for the markets as well as the consumers.

It is nobody's case that subsidies should be eliminated; though there is an urgent need to target them towards well-defined recipients. Affirmative action by the government would continue to be necessary for providing universal access at affordable prices, particularly in rural areas and for the economically weaker sections. But decades of experience shows that governments alone, howsoever resourceful and well-meaning, cannot accomplish the task without the market. In fact, the poor would be better served by market-driven policies, topped with targeted subsidies.

While addressing the problems arising out of near-free supplies to the farm sector, it is important to recognise that cross-subsidies have pushed up industrial tariffs to almost double the household tariffs in India, whereas it is the other way round in several developed countries. If Indian industry has to face global competition, the quality and price of electricity would matter, and a sustainable approach to subsidies would be necessary. The surcharge proposed here would not only help in funding the subsidies, it would also ensure transparency in determining the extent of such subsidies as well as the government subventions necessary for this purpose.

PILFERAGE, THE REAL PROBLEM

Commercial accounting in the 'reforming' states is beginning to reveal the cesspool that the electricity industry seems to have become—how else does one describe a bizarre situation where more than 40 per cent of the produce does not get accounted or paid for? Pre-reform, the T&D losses were usually stated in the region of about 20 per cent, with poor systems maintenance and outlying rural areas being held as the main culprits. Pilferage by small and large consumers alike, apparently in collusion with the SEB employees, now seems to be emerging as the real problem. This is a shocking state of affairs as no civil society can afford to overlook such widespread prevalence of theft for which honest citizens are penalised, or worse, the burden is shifted to future generations by renaming these losses as 'regulatory assets' that would qualify for tariff increases in subsequent years. This failure of governance needs to be rectified through stringent and effective measures lest the judicial courts intervene, as in the case of pollution by the commercial vehicles plying in Delhi (1998), and take charge owing to government's abdication of its legitimate role.

In the debate on reform, there has been a sharp focus on the low tariffs that do not allow for cost recovery. This argument is being used for strengthening the case for tariff increases. There is, however, inadequate focus on pilferage and technical losses that account for over 40 per cent of the electricity generated. For example, Orissa continues to report T&D losses of about 43 per cent while in Delhi they reportedly exceed 50 per cent. The prevailing approach that relies on a 'cost plus' determination of tariffs on a year-to-year basis is not conducive to the reduction of these losses at a pace sufficient to restore the viability of the industry. A regulatory framework that incentivises loss reduction in a transparent and predictable manner is, therefore, essential. In addition, if competition were introduced in generation and supply of electricity, it is bound to push the tariffs downwards. As such, while some increases in tariff may be justified for ensuring cost recovery, these should be largely offset by reduction in T&D losses, on the one hand, and introduction of competition, on the other.

Whether India is able to realise the full potential of reforms depends crucially on the government and the regulators, whose role is vitally important. As California's power crisis of 2001 has shown, governments can make a big difference by getting it wrong, often under pressure from the industry's incumbents. In fact, that has been the sad story of India's power sector during the past decade. As for the regulators, they should be willing to trust market forces; they must make the rules of the game clear and refrain from arbitrary interference during the transition; they must detect and curb market abuses effectively; and should ultimately yield most of their powers to the market.

ELECTRICITY BILL

In sum, the industry structure being advocated here would help introduce competition, improve efficiency, add capacity, rationalise tariffs, and enhance consumer welfare. It would unleash latent energies, enterprise, and innovation that should galvanise the industry towards rapid growth and enable consumers to enjoy lower prices with improved services. On the contrary, continued adherence to the Orissa model in its present form would promote monopolies, raise tariffs, deny consumer choice, and constrain investments in the 're-forming' states. Reforms would not be perceived as people-friendly if tariffs rise without a perceptible improvement in the quality of supply. As for the remaining states, failure to initiate reforms expeditiously would lead to a virtual collapse of their power sector as well as the state finances.

During the past decade of economic liberalisation in India, electricity has perhaps been the only major industry that has failed to improve even though it is so vital to economic growth and human development. It has remained comparatively static in the midst of significant changes that are taking place elsewhere in the world. Several principles and practices that have universal relevance are yet to be applied to the power sector in India. If a GDP growth of 8–9 per cent is to be achieved, there is no way it can be done without a holistic restructuring of the power sector, and the proposed Electricity Bill should form the vehicle for this inevitable change.

POSTSCRIPT

At the request of the Ministry of Power, the author drafted the Electricity Bill, 2001, which gave a legislative form to the concepts and strategies outlined in this chapter. The Bill was enacted by Parliament as the Electricity Act, 2003, to replace the archaic laws of the past. Enactment of this new law was clearly a great leap forward, especially as it spelt out the framework for introducing competition in the generation and supply of electricity, based on proven experience in developed countries.

The Electricity Bill was drafted after extensive consultations, unprecedented for any law enacted so far in India. Over a period of 18 months, 41 seminars and conferences were held where various experts and stakeholders participated with a view to evolving consensus. In addition, 234 written interventions were received and addressed. The author drafted eight successive versions of the draft Bill to shape the emerging consensus. When this draft Bill, with some modifications carried out by the Ministry of Power, was introduced in the Parliament, it was referred to a Standing Committee of Parliament. It was once again subjected to an extensive process of consultation for over a year. The Bill was finally enacted in 2003. It retained virtually all the concepts and strategies described in the chapter.

Though India now has a modern and forward-looking law for the electricity sector, its implementation presents a dismal picture in the face of entrenched interests that continue to pose a governance challenge of enormous proportions. In particular, no consumer has been able to avail of the choice and competition mandated by the law, primarily because the entrenched interests have obstructed the creation of a market-based industry structure. Since power producers can only sell to monopoly utilities, which are generally bankrupt, private investment has shied away and shortages have persisted. Of late, opportunistic traders have entered the fray to engage in profiteering from the sale of bulk power to state-owned utilities. The average price of traded electricity has been about Rs 5 per unit (11 cents), which may perhaps be the highest in the world. This has led to a sharp increase in the commercial losses of state-owned utilities, which crossed Rs 58,000 crore in 2009–10. The entire power sector seems far more fragile than ever before. A reform law sans implementation has so far been counter-productive.

12 Power Failure in Orissa*

Whichever way you look at it, the Orissa model of electricity reform is not sustainable. But the lessons of Orissa are extremely important because reform is a must; people think that Orissa reformed and yet Orissa is a mess. So is reform the wrong way to go? Definitely not. The reason Orissa is a mess is that it did not do the reform right.

In recent press interviews, Montek Ahluwalia has virtually campaigned against the 'single buyer' model of electricity reforms. He was the chairperson of an Expert Group on the restructuring of state electricity boards (SEBs) (constituted by the Chief Ministers' Conference in March 2001) that included luminaries like K.V. Kamath, Rakesh Mohan, Jairam Ramesh, Deepak Parekh, and Harish Salve. The Group had noted that adoption of the 'single buyer' model in Orissa was fundamentally flawed and it should not be replicated in other states.

The present structure in Orissa consists of an interconnected chain of monopolies that eliminates any form of competition and the attendant efficiency gains. The sole buyer of all power from generating companies is the state-owned transmission company called Gridco; all distribution companies can only buy from Gridco and the consumers must buy from the distribution companies alone. As a result, there is complete lack of choice, and all tariffs are fixed on a 'cost plus' basis—a sure recipe for high tariffs and neglect of the consumer.

* Originally published in *Business Standard*, 27 August 2001.

The Orissa structure does not allow competing generating companies to have the benefit of 'open access' to the network for selling directly to bulk consumers, and this virtually implies a lack of market for electricity. In a paper published in December 2000, Laszlo Lovei, Lead Energy Specialist in the World Bank, says that 'This "Single-buyer" model has major disadvantages in developing countries; it invites corruption, weakens payment discipline, and imposes large contingent liabilities on the government.'

Gridco, the sole buyer, manages to draw electricity without making full payment to the public sector generating companies. The receivables of a privatised generating company, Orissa Power Generating Corporation (OPGC), have also exceeded Rs 200 crore; but it is unable to discontinue supplies for fear of coercive action under the Essential Service Maintenance Act (ESMA). Gridco thus owes more than Rs 1,500 crore to generating companies; it has been defaulting on its debt service obligations and is evidently bankrupt.

Gridco's lack of creditworthiness is no different compared to a typically bankrupt SEB in another state. Private investment is, therefore, unlikely to materialise except through government guarantees. Of late, the investment climate across the states has dampened further, with Enron wanting to pull out of the first major project involving foreign investment in the power sector.[1]

The prognosis at the distribution end is worse. The performance of all the four distribution companies that were privatised two years ago has been dismal—not because privatisation has failed per se, but because the policy and regulatory framework was inadequate and myopic. Reportedly, Charles Lenzi, Managing Director of the Central Electric Supply Company (owned by AES corporation of US), resigned recently on account of what he described as 'frustration with current regulatory and contractual structure of the distribution system in Orissa'.

---

[1] The Power Purchase Agreement for Enron's Dabhol power project was terminated by the Maharashtra State Electricity Board in June 2001.

CESCO is losing heavily and AES wants to exit by off-loading its equity. It is noteworthy that the equity stake of AES is about Rs 42 crore while the unsecured payables of CESCO to Gridco exceed Rs 420 crore. How the regulator allowed a private licensee to accumulate such liabilities and why it failed to cancel the licence in accordance with the law is an issue that would call for closer scrutiny.

All distribution companies in Orissa are bankrupt beyond redemption, and according to AES it cannot even pay the salaries of its employees. Transmission and distribution (T&D) losses continue to exceed 45 per cent and the efficiency gains expected from privatisation have so far been elusive. Nevertheless, consumers have to contend with tariff increases every year. The companies, of course, blame the regulatory environment while the regulator blames the companies—indeed a zero sum game for the hapless consumer.

Problems came to a head (in mid-2001) when Gridco recently tried to recover its receivables from CESCO by adjusting them against its payables to the AES-owned OPGC. Though legally untenable, one can sympathise with Gridco for trying to recover its overdues from a sister company of CESCO. However, the question that arises is whether Gridco will similarly recover its overdues from BSES that owns the remaining three distribution companies?

The recovery of overdues from privatised distribution companies is a sticky issue that has been brushed aside all along. It is not clear how the state-owned Gridco has extended unlimited credit to private entities without any worthwhile security. Such a situation can hardly be visualised in the private sector where the instinct of self-preservation would have prevailed against such irrational behaviour.

The four distribution companies owe over Rs 1,100 crore to Gridco and yet the latter continues to make unsecured supplies that are adding rapidly to its ballooning receivables. This has been compounded by the recent decision (in mid-2001) of the state government to pay the salaries of CESCO employees following the company's refusal to pay. On the day of reckoning, all these liabilities will be nothing but bad debts, and when the taxpayers' money is eventually used for a bail out, the outcome is bound to assume scam-like proportions. The writing is on the wall.

The entire power sector in Orissa is facing impending bankruptcy. Yet, the distribution companies are pressing the state government for release of long-term loans that are to be refinanced by the World Bank. The government may not find it prudent to turn a Nelson's eye for extending loans without any security whatsoever, and that would smash any residual hope of improving the network. The stalemate is virtually complete.

What really went wrong in Orissa? Clearly, the state followed the mantra of unbundling and independent regulation, but that is where the reform ended. It was a reform that neither created a market nor introduced competition. It also failed to incentivise the market players to deliver efficiency gains to the consumer. It simply created public and private monopolies that could avail of 'cost plus' tariffs and thwart any commercial discipline. The regulator set tariffs as well as efficiency norms on a year-to-year basis in a manner that lacked predictability, thus creating uncertainty where capital was bound to flee. On the other hand, the government's day-to-day control over the power sector continued through Gridco that plays a pivotal role in the 'single-buyer' model.

While devising the reform strategy in Orissa, international best practices and lessons were overlooked in order to 'accommodate' the interests and perceptions of the principal players. John Besant-Jones, lead economist at the World Bank, seems to be on the bull's eye when he says, 'The single-buyer model is an invention of the devil.'

The Orissa structure is terminally sick and a bypass is urgently required for stalling an irreversible event. The impending departure of AES (with the Enron episode in the backdrop) has dealt a body blow to power sector reforms as a whole, and their chaotic progress and lack of credibility have been compounded. If the Orissa experience is repeated in other states, then there is a serious danger that reforms will be discredited and pressures will be generated for a rollback. India can ill-afford to let power sector reforms fail.

POSTSCRIPT

Power reforms in Orissa are a classic example of half-baked recipes that emulate successful models of the West albeit with suicidal compromises aimed at accommodating the vested interests. Restructuring of the power sector in developed countries was aimed at introducing competition in the generation and supply of electricity—unbundling of utilities was only a means towards this end. In Orissa, the state-owned utility was unbundled sans the introduction of competition. What followed was the 'single buyer' model that required all producers to sell to the state-owned Gridco that formed part of an interconnected chain of monopolies. Several other states went the same way.

That a 'reform' based on monopolies would fail was entirely predictable, though it was somehow not evident to the mandarins of the World Bank that supported this initiative. After over a decade of privatisation, the T&D losses, mostly consisting of theft, have continued to exceed 30 per cent and the distribution companies are simply unsustainable.

The entire structure in Orissa would have surely collapsed but for the Electricity Act, 2003, which has been grossly misused to bail out the Orissa power companies, year after year, by exploiting consumers in other parts of India. All power producers in Orissa must continue to sell to the state-owned Gridco which, in turn, sells its surplus to monopoly utilities in deficit states at prices that yield a profit of over 300 per cent. In a manner of speaking, the rampant theft prevailing in Orissa is being paid for by consumers of other states whose tariffs have risen steadily while the tariffs in Orissa have not been revised for over a decade. This arrangement allows Orissa to subsidise its consumers by almost Rs 1,000 crore every year at the expense of consumers in other states. Unlike trading in any other goods or services, the prices charged by Gridco for the sale of bulk electricity outside Orissa are over three times what it charges for similar sales within Orissa.

The legality and constitutionality of this arrangement is entirely suspect as it creates inter-state barriers for trade and commerce and thus sounds the death knell of a common market that the Constitution of India guarantees. That the Central Regulatory Commission is a mute spectator despite its statutory responsibility to regulate inter-state trade suggests a regulatory capture.

13 Empower Consumers*
Plug loopholes in the Electricity Bill

The government is to be congratulated for getting the Electricity Bill passed in the Lok Sabha. However, the fine print offers cause for concern, especially if the goal of making power supply available to the common man at reasonable prices is to be achieved.

The Bill was introduced in the Lok Sabha in August 2001 and was referred to the standing committee on energy. The committee's 45 members, representing all the major political parties, presented their report in December 2002. Unfortunately, most of the committee's critical recommendations were not accepted by the government.

The committee proclaimed open access as the 'panacea for ushering in power sector reforms, especially for private sector participation'. It unambiguously stated, 'It is imperative that transmission and distribution are unshackled from restrictive use', and recommended that they should 'be subjected to non-discriminatory open access within a mandated time-frame'.

The rationale for telecom and power reforms has arisen from the introduction of competition and choice. Presently, the state-owned electricity boards are monopolies and all producers of power must sell to these boards alone. Introduction of open access will allow producers to sell directly to bulk consumers and distribution companies by

* Originally published in *The Times of India*, 16 April 2003.

wheeling power through the existing transmission lines on payment of regulated charges. This will increase supply, improve efficiency, and cut tariffs.

Yet, the Bill leaves the introduction of open access entirely to state regulatory commissions. They will declare within one year as to when and how they propose to introduce open access in their respective states. This amounts to excessive and unguided delegation. The commissions could well be persuaded by incumbent players to postpone open access for several years. For example, the Delhi state government believes that open access may take 10 years to arrive.

Freedom of trade and business is a fundamental right under the Constitution and allowing the commissions to deny open access for several years will abrogate this right, perpetuate private monopolies, and harm consumers. Delay in introducing open access means delaying competition and private investment. Shortages will continue and consumers will have to rely on the public sector, which does not have the resources for meeting the entire demand. This seems a sure recipe for power shortages and high tariffs.

The regulatory commissions are another area of concern. At present, nine laws provide for independent regulatory commissions—the Electricity Regulatory Commissions Act, 1998 (central Act), and eight state reform Acts. The Electricity Bill contains many significant departures from the existing laws and the standing committee's recommendations.

All commissions will now be placed under the administrative control and supervision of a retired judge, to be appointed by the Centre as chairperson of the appellate tribunal. The states have opposed this provision and the standing committee recommended its deletion. Yet, it remains in the Bill.

The committee recommended that these commissions be made answerable to the Parliament/state assemblies. This is eminently justified as the commissions perform licensing and regulatory functions that affect every walk of life. The recommendation has been rejected.

All the nine existing laws require the expenses of these commissions to be met out of the respective consolidated funds. This ensures transparency, accountability, and thrift. Even the Supreme Court and high courts meet their expenses from the consolidated funds. Despite strong representations from several states as well as the recommendation of the standing committee, the Bill proposes an independent fund for each commission. This may encourage profligacy, misuse of funds, and lack of accountability, leading to loss of public confidence in these commissions.

Under the nine existing laws, members of the commissions can be removed only by the president or the respective governors, upon enquiry by the Supreme Court or high court, as the case may be. The Bill provides for their removal by the Central Government/state government upon enquiry by a retired judge, acting as chairperson of the appellate tribunal. The standing committee's recommendation to retain the existing provisions has been rejected.

Contrary to the provisions contained in the nine existing laws, members of these commissions will become eligible for re-employment by the same government, thereby infringing on their impartiality. Here again, the recommendations of the standing committee have been overlooked. These measures will tend to make the regulatory commissions less independent and more pliable. Appointments to these commissions in the past are already a matter of public criticism. Such commissions may fail to guard public interest and end up serving vested interests.

With postponement of open access coupled with pliable regulatory commissions, the fate of power reforms may hang in the balance. Worse, the Bill proposes to supersede all state reform Acts, despite strong protests. In any case, rejection of the recommendations of an all-party standing committee does not stand to reason. It is still not too late to make amends.

POSTSCRIPT

The Electricity Act, 2003, requires the regulatory commissions to enable consumers to avail of open access to distribution networks for transmitting the electricity purchased by them from competing suppliers. The Act was amended in December 2003 to specify a time limit of five years for operationalising open access for all consumers of one megawatt and above. However, monopoly distribution companies have erected barriers that have withheld the introduction of open access and competition. Despite the mandatory provisions of law, state regulatory commissions continue to fix the tariffs for such bulk consumers even though the law requires them to buy at market prices. In a manner of speaking, the soul of Electricity Act, which is mainly about liberalisation of the industry structure for introduction of competition and choice, remains to be emancipated.

Though the Act was amended to remove the administrative control of the Appellate Tribunal over the regulatory commissions, accountability of regulators to Parliament/state legislative assemblies was not introduced, despite the emphatic recommendations of the Standing Committee of Parliament as well as the repeated interventions and assurances during the debates in Parliament. As a result, the performance of regulatory commissions in achieving the objectives of the Act remains dismal.

14   Open Access Bijli*
How to electrify our power sector

Imagine a toll road where the operator has a right to choose who can use the road. Sounds absurd? Everyone knows that there can be no discrimination among users as long as they pay the toll and abide by the traffic rules. This can be described as non-discriminatory open access to the toll road.

Much of the growth and tariff reduction in telecom is the outcome of competition enabled by open access to networks. A consumer can subscribe to a licensee of his choice, as access to other networks is no constraint. Non-discriminatory open access was clearly a pre-requisite of telecom reform.

In telecom jargon, open access is known as interconnection. A licensee carries his subscriber's call up to the point of interconnection from where the recipient's operator must carry it to the destination. There could also be intermediaries, such as long-distance carriers, operating between two networks.

Way back in 1994, several licences were granted to private entities, but the incumbent telecom department dragged its feet over interconnection and other issues. As a result, the licensees never took off until the National Telecom Policy (NTP), 1999, was formulated

* Originally published in *The Times of India*, 5 June 2003.

by an independent task force and implemented by the Telecom Regulatory Authority of India (TRAI).

More recently, in January 2003, the refusal of cellular operators to carry the calls of Reliance Infocom caused much anxiety and TRAI had to intervene to restore interconnection. This episode illustrated how a telecom company would be virtually ineffective if other operators could deny interconnection. Such is the importance of non-discriminatory open access.

For carrying the calls of another licensee, every operator is entitled to recover its costs in the form of an access charge. But a landline operator could extract an unreasonable charge since it has a virtual monopoly in its area. To prevent such exploitation, these charges are regulated by TRAI, which also ensures non-discriminatory open access across all networks.

The rationale for power reforms is similar. When competition was to be introduced in telecom, the incumbents tried to defend their monopoly by invoking national security, rural connectivity, and service to the poor. Predictably, power sector incumbents are also resisting introduction of open access.

Open access in power supply means that a distribution company will operate the network connecting your premises, but other licensees can also reach you through that network. Thus, a supplier need not lay a parallel network of wires for carrying electricity to your premises; he can use the existing network upon payment of an access charge, called the wheeling charge, to be determined by an independent regulator. Such non-discriminatory open access is a pre-requisite for competition and real reform.

Power tariffs in India have only moved upwards, largely because of the 'cost plus' tariffs of monopolies ridden with huge inefficiencies and transmission and distribution (T&D) losses. This must be reversed. The energy component accounts for over 80 per cent of consumer tariff, and if this segment is exposed to competition, consumers will benefit from tariff reductions and improvements in supply. Competition is the best guarantee for consumers.

The international experience on open access in the power sector has been very encouraging. During the last decade, electricity prices in the UK fell by over 30 per cent. Similar trends have been witnessed in European countries and the US. Several developing countries across the world have either introduced or are in the process of introducing competition in supply of electricity. The writing is on the wall.

Open access would encourage private investors to produce more power and sell directly to consumers. This can begin with bulk consumers and can be gradually extended to the household level. A surcharge on open access could fund existing cross-subsidies for the farm sector. Over time, these cross-subsidies could be substituted by transparent subsidies from the budget, with electricity duties being adjusted suitably.

Conceptually, open access in infrastructure services is character-ised by separation of 'carriage' from 'content'. Carriage refers to the fixed network like wires, sub-stations, and telephone exchanges; and content refers to the moving element such as voice in telephony and energy in power sector. Upon separation, carriage is typically subjected to non-discriminatory open access for enabling competition in the content segment.

Carriage usually has the attributes of a natural monopoly, as the costs of setting up multiple networks are greater than the likely gains of competition among multiple operators. As such, carriage networks tend to be monopolies or duopolies. It is, therefore, necessary to subject them to close regulation by an independent regulator who must fix the access charge and ensure non-discriminatory open access for enabling effective competition in the content segment.

Open access in the power sector would increase supply and reduce tariffs. That would mean a sea change. India's telecom sector grew 19.6 per cent in 2002, next only to China. The wonders of open access in telecom are here to stay, and it is only a matter of time before they overtake the power sector. Incumbents, however influential, cannot block the winds of change for long. But consumers need to assert their rights.

POSTSCRIPT

Seven years after the enactment of the Electricity Act, not a single consumer across the country has been able to get the benefit of competition among producers and suppliers of electricity. All distribution utilities continue to be monopolies and all producers of electricity must sell to these utilities alone. As a result, all consumers, howsoever large, must buy solely from their respective distribution companies that normally charge higher prices and provide poor quality of supply.

On the supply side, since power producers have no access to creditworthy bulk consumers, they must only sell to the near-bankrupt state-owned utilities. As a result, private investment has been slow and inadequate, resulting in a further increase in power shortages. This monopoly structure and the power shortages seem to be mutually reinforcing evils of the power sector. Competition and open access in telecom have done wonders in India and elsewhere. Competition and open access in the power sector have also proved their efficacy in the entire developed world. Yet, the incumbent monopolists would like us to believe that India is not yet ready for this reform in its power sector.

The prevailing shortages have also encouraged unscrupulous profiteering in trading of bulk electricity, with prices exceeding thrice the production cost, a phenomenon unknown to any other sector in India. With the exception of the infamous California crisis, there are perhaps no parallels of such profiteering anywhere else in the world. In California, the electricity traders exploited the shortage in the summer of 2000 and pushed up the prices through unscrupulous gaming. The law did not allow the distribution companies to pass on this increase to the consumers and as a result, they went bankrupt. Ultimately, the State of California had to provide a multi-billion dollar bail-out. A similar clock is ticking in India too.

15 Power Reforms to Empower People*

The Tribune is to be complimented for encouraging a debate on power reforms, so crucial for the growth of Punjab. Without doubt, the debate will help evolve a consensus and prevent vested interests from hijacking governance.

The article 'Reforming Punjab's Power Sector' (26 May) by M.G. Devasahayam requires special mention. It accuses the Expert Group on Power Reforms of writing a report to serve a 'private agenda in the garb of public interest'. It states that 'a donor agency trademark could be seen on every page of the report', and that it 'got approved from senior [World] Bank functionaries at Washington'. This implies that national interests were bartered to serve the agenda of foreign institutions. Such a charge is no ordinary matter.

It is a matter of public record that the donor agencies had no say in the evolution of the reform strategy in Punjab. The state government has not yet approached any of these agencies for assistance. Nor is any agency contemplating such assistance.

It was stated that the Expert Group report was synchronised with the passage of the Electricity Bill in Parliament. It is true that I authored the Electricity Bill, but that is history. Incumbent players had subsequently managed to distort some of the basic provisions

* Originally published in *The Tribune*, 10 June 2003.

of the Bill, and I opposed them openly. The 'Report of the Standing Committee of Parliament on Energy' has reflected my viewpoint on the Electricity Bill. Clearly, the Expert Group report does not suffer from the flaws in the Electricity Bill. To that extent, it is more in line with the best international practices.

My efforts (while serving in the Union Ministry of Finance) in saving the economy from several unsustainable private power projects are no secret. Of course, this was possible only because of the support and guidance that I received from the then finance ministers. It is also public knowledge that I have been a vocal critic of the World Bank–assisted Orissa model that was adopted in seven other states, including Haryana.

It was not my intention to burden the reader with my credentials. A healthy debate must be issue-based. But when motives are attributed, it becomes necessary to get 'suspicions' out of the way, to provide comfort to the readers that this debate is in the best interest of Punjab.

Coming to the basic issues, the objective of power reforms should be to provide reliable power at reasonable prices, and the consumer should be given a choice. If the Punjab State Electricity Board (PSEB) is able to provide improved services, consumers may choose to stay with it. If not, they should have the freedom to shift to whoever gives them better services. This makes robust common sense. It is also a fundamental right of the people.

On the other hand, some of the PSEB employees are opposed to open access and competition. Like all roads lead to Rome, the purpose of their arguments is to perpetuate the monopoly of the PSEB, never mind the interests of the people.

Unlike the Orissa model, Punjab's reform strategy aims at demolishing the monopolistic structure of the power sector because the creation of monopolies is an unacceptable form of government interference in the markets. It is neither conducive to consumer interests nor does it accelerate economic growth.

Though the telecom department and Indian Airlines are better organised than the PSEB, will anyone want the return of their monopoly?

A vast improvement in their services coupled with a reduction in the cost is there for everyone to see. Open access in the power sector is aimed in the same direction. That is also the way power reforms have succeeded in other countries.

There seems to be a phobia in some quarters against the privatisation of the PSEB. A careful reading of the 'Report of the Expert Group on Power Reforms' (2003) under the chairmanship of the author would clarify that it did not foresee privatisation in the near future. At any rate, the group did not rely on privatisation as the key to growth and welfare. Instead, it recognised competition as a critical element in the reform process.

Let public sector entities compete with private companies to provide better and cheaper services to the consumer. Reforms should not perpetuate public sector monopolies. On the contrary, they should expose these entities to the pressures of competition so that they serve their master—the consumer—better. The PSEB is meant to serve the people, and not vice versa.

Economic liberalisation has brought about much growth and welfare during the past decade. This was made possible by the demolition of the 'licence-quota-permit raj' that had enabled a handful of people to exploit the millions. The power sector, however, continues to represent the worst form of the licence raj. A producer of power can sell his produce only to a state-owned state electricity board (SEB). It cannot sell directly to anyone else. Why should a free society compel every producer to sell his produce to the state alone?

On the other hand, the SEBs are virtually bankrupt and thus unable to buy power from private producers. Moreover, when the SEBs manage to sign power purchase agreements (PPAs) with private entities, the role of corruption in raising power costs assumes significance.

Given the present structure of the PSEB, it should be little wonder that 3 lakh farmers in Punjab are waiting for an electricity connection, while the 8 lakh who have connections do not get electricity for more than eight hours a day. Why should an advanced state like Punjab, with its enterprising people, continue to suffer such a plight? This is not the making of the people. This has been imposed on them by incumbent functionaries who wish to perpetuate their stranglehold over this vast empire called the power sector.

There seem to be reservations in some quarters about World Bank assistance for financing power reforms. Is it the suggestion that Punjab should deny to itself a source of concessional finance? It should be obvious that Punjab needs to maximise investments as long as they support its own strategy of reforms.

Opponents of reform fear tariff increases as an outcome. That would indeed be the case if monopolies continue to rule the roost, be it in the form of the SEBs or their corporatised successors. For example, some employee associations of the PSEB have been demanding a sharp increase in tariffs. On the other hand, little is being done to reduce transmission and distribution (T&D) losses of 38 units for every 100 units sold. Competition could fundamentally change the present scenario. There would be efficiency improvements and cost reduction too.

The Expert Group has recommended that any tariff hikes should be commensurate with an improvement in services and that farmers and low-income households should continue to be subsidised, though with sharper targeting.

The message is simple and clear. Power reforms in Punjab are aimed at improving the lot of the people. The reforms will arm people with a choice and ensure better supply at cheaper rates. That indeed is the burden of the Expert Group's report, available on the Punjab Government's website for anyone to see.[1]

POSTSCRIPT

This essay was written when the author was advising the Government of Punjab on its strategy for power reforms. The author headed an Expert Group that wrote a report on power reforms in Punjab. He also drafted the Punjab Electricity Bill that was introduced in the Punjab Legislative Assembly by the then Chief Minister Amarinder Singh, with much hope and enthusiasm.

[1] See http://infrastructure.gov.in

Though the state government and the chief minister were convinced about this reform strategy and provided full support and commitment publicly, their resolve gradually withered away in the face of stiff opposition from the 90,000-strong employee force of the PSEB. The reform initiative eventually fell through and a historic opportunity of leading power reforms in India was lost.

From being a leader, Punjab eventually turned out to be a laggard, as it was among the last few states in India to unbundle its electricity board into generation, transmission, and distribution companies in April 2010, as a first step towards structural reforms. Not surprisingly, PSEB made commercial losses of Rs 4,238 crore and Rs 3,894 crore respectively in 2007–08 and 2008–09, while its peak power shortage was 15.4 per cent and 15.9 per cent, respectively. In 2009–10, these losses rose to about Rs 4,767 crore while peak shortage reached 24.3 per cent. With rising losses and persistent shortages, the people of Punjab continue to pay a heavy price that could have been avoided had the power sector been opened up to competition. A competitive industry structure would have inevitably led to lower costs, improved efficiencies, and elimination of shortages, but the incumbents seem to have forced a contrary outcome.

16 Does Power Privatisation Help?*

Economic liberalisation in most sectors—telecom, automobiles, televisions, airlines, you name it—has been about increasing choice for consumers. Competition has resulted in better quality and lower prices. The power sector has been an exception to this rule.

And the result is there for everyone to see. Power is the only sector where reforms are associated with repeated tariff hikes with marginal improvements in supply. Orissa, Punjab, Haryana, Uttar Pradesh, Rajasthan, Andhra Pradesh, Karnataka, and Delhi, each 'reform' state has seen successive tariff hikes over the years. In Delhi, the regulator hiked tariffs by over 15 per cent barely two years ago, and another hike is on the anvil. In Orissa, tariffs have gone up by more than 50 per cent over five years of 'reform'. And quality, as most consumers in Delhi are witnessing first hand nowadays, has clearly not improved.

Delhi's case is especially interesting. When the Delhi Vidyut Board (DVB) was being split and privatised, the government had kept aside Rs 3,450 crore for avoiding tariff shocks during the first five years of 'reform'. But in just the first 21 months of privatisation, this entire sum will be exhausted. So what happens after that? Obviously, tariffs may shoot up next year by over 50 per cent, unless the government provides backdoor subsidies to the distribution companies.

* Originally published in *Business Standard*, 11 June 2003.

BSES, Tata Power, and the Transco, between them, have stated before the regulator that there is a gap of Rs 4,400 crore, or Rs 3 per unit, between what they recover from customers and what it costs them to supply. This will have to be met either through a subsidy, which means higher taxes, or through a straight-forward tariff hike. At an average Rs 4 per unit, Delhi's power rates are the highest in the country, and customers are to be asked to pay another Rs 3, either directly or indirectly.

Look at it another way. After five years of reforms, the transmission and distribution (T&D) losses in Delhi are to be brought down from the current 51 per cent to 34 per cent, while the losses in the New Delhi Municipal Council (NDMC) area are currently 16 per cent and 10–11 per cent in Mumbai. So, even after five years of reforms, customers in Delhi will still be paying about 33 per cent more than they need to—after all, the 34 per cent T&D loss has to be paid for by someone.

So, if the slew of reforms is not going to result in lower tariffs, the question to ask is: what was wrong with the Dabhol plant? It was a first-class plant, very efficient; the only problem was that it produced very expensive power. Well, the current reforms are not doing anything different.

Reforms do benefit the consumer, but only if they are conducted properly. Let us take a situation in which you have 'open access', as has been promised in the new Electricity Bill. Once you have open access, consumers in south Delhi, say, can decide if they want to buy power from BSES that has the monopoly for the region right now, or from some other company, say Y. Naturally, competition between BSES and Y will lower prices, the same way competition between BSES and Tata Power has driven down tariffs for high-tension consumers in Mumbai. In the UK, where a similar model has been followed, retail prices for consumers have fallen 30 per cent over the decade.

Many critics have said that open access is a disaster and will prevent new investments as firms will no longer be certain about how long their profits will last. This is false propaganda. When firm Y uses BSES's power lines to carry power to your house, it will pay BSES a certain 'wheeling' charge for using its infrastructure. This charge, to be set by the regulator, will be enough to ensure BSES does not go bankrupt. And if it wishes to make profits, well, it will just have to become more competitive.

POSTSCRIPT

Privatisation of electricity distribution has been undertaken only in Orissa (1998) and Delhi (2002). In both cases, public monopolies were substituted by private monopolies, which is evidently a flawed approach. In the case of Orissa, the performance of private distribution companies continues to be dismal, both financially as well as operationally. In the case of Delhi, the results have been better as compared to Orissa, but at a huge cost to the consumer and the exchequer. The details are provided in other essays in this volume. Delhi is often lauded by some as a success story when compared to the erstwhile state-owned entity. Such comparisons with admittedly low benchmarks cannot be regarded as rational. The creation of private monopolies, along with their attendant ills, is a potently flawed approach that finds little support in international literature or best practice.

Privatisation, by itself, cannot be a goal, as it does not normally provide the anticipated gains in the absence of competition. It is competition which is the best guarantee for protecting consumer interests, and in the absence of competition, consumers would continue to be hostage to monopolies, with their attendant rents and inefficiencies. For this reason, the Electricity Act, 2003, mandates introduction of competition in generation and supply of electricity, but the law has so far been followed in its breach.

Nothing but sub-optimal outcomes should be expected from private monopolies, which must be regarded as an unacceptable form of government interference in the operation of markets.

17 Ray of Light*
Power tariffs may start declining

The demolition of the 'licence-permit raj' in the 1990s opened markets to competition. As a result of these reforms, quality improved and prices declined in telecom, airlines, automobiles, and consumer durables, to name a few sectors. The power sector seems to be the sole exception where 'reforms' got associated with repeated tariff hikes, mainly because incumbents manipulated the 'reforms' to keep their monopoly intact. And as long as monopolies rule the markets, consumers will continue to get short shrift.

The first reform initiative in the power sector was a policy of the early 1990s that enabled private investment in generation. It allowed negotiated deals where producers could sell only to state electricity boards (SEBs), thus protecting the SEBs' monopoly. Negotiated deals meant higher tariffs, the worst example being the Dabhol project. Predictably, the policy did not take off. But a decade was lost and the economic cost was enormous.

In eight states, beginning with Orissa in 1995, reforms were based on unbundling and corporatisation of SEBs. But all these states adopted the 'single buyer' model that implied an interconnected chain of monopolies. The outcome: repeated tariff hikes with only marginal improvements in supply. Evolution of the Electricity Act,

* Originally published in *The Times of India*, 19 June 2003.

2003, through an extensive process of consultation brought to centre stage the concept of 'open access' that enables competing suppliers to use the existing network of wires for reaching the consumers. Indeed, this was the rationale for reform in the telecom and power sectors across the world.

Introduction of open access and competition in the power sector, even if belated, should nevertheless be cause for celebration. Though incumbents have managed to raise some roadblocks, these cannot last for long, as the demand for better and cheaper services will overcome these barriers—sooner rather than later.

The real question is: will tariffs decline? In Mumbai, they will. The reason is simple. Power distribution in South Mumbai rests with BEST, a subsidiary of Mumbai Municipal Corporation, while the remaining areas are served by BSES, a private company. BEST also runs buses in the entire city, and the losses of its transportation business are subsidised by its power business. Its power tariffs are, therefore, higher than what they ought to be. The Mumbai Municipal Act, 1888, apparently allowed BEST to cross-subsidise buses by charging higher power tariffs. But in the process, residents of South Mumbai, who buy power from BEST, end up subsidising the bus services of the entire city. That is obviously unfair.

The Electricity Act, 2003, has superseded the Mumbai Municipal Act. Power tariffs will now be set by the Maharashtra Electricity Regulator/Commission that has no authority to subsidise bus fares through power tariffs. The electricity tariffs of BEST must, therefore, fall by about Rs 150 crore, against a total revenue of about Rs 1,500 crore from sale of electricity, which means a tariff cut of 10 per cent. That would be the first case of tariff reduction due to power reforms. Power minister Anant Geethe can claim some credit for that.

Tariffs of BSES are at par with BEST, even though the former does not subsidise buses. Reduction in BEST tariffs is bound to create a demand for tariff cuts in BSES areas as the two suppliers operate in similar conditions. The regulatory commission may either have to reduce BSES tariffs or explain to consumers why a private company's tariffs are higher than the public sector BEST. An interesting scenario may thus unfold. Moreover, Mumbai is an ideal ground for introduction of open access to the distribution networks. Incumbents often quote short supply and high transmission and distribution (T&D) losses as reasons for postponing open access. Mumbai suffers from neither. What was introduced in the UK in 1989 can surely be attempted in Mumbai in 2003. That will bring further decline in power tariffs—just as the UK tariffs have declined by over 30 per cent. Incidentally, BSES and Tata Power compete in Mumbai for supply to bulk consumers and that has led to virtually the lowest tariffs in India. Such competition will now spread elsewhere.

Delhi will see some action too, at least in the areas where the New Delhi Municipal Council (NDMC) supplies power to its constituents. Currently, T&D losses in NDMC areas are about 16 per cent compared with about 50 per cent in the privatised areas. However, consumers pay the same tariffs in both the areas. This is patently unfair to the constituents of NDMC who end up paying more than Rs 500 crore per annum against an actual expenditure of less than Rs 400 crore.

The Electricity Act requires Delhi's Regulatory Commission to fix tariffs in NDMC areas. That may see a decline of about 20 per cent in power tariffs. On the other hand, tariffs in privatised areas may soon go up by more than 10 per cent, despite a state subsidy of about Rs 2,000 crore this year. Such a steep difference in tariffs should sharpen the debate on the nature and impact of the monopolistic privatisation in Delhi.

When consumers see declining tariffs in Mumbai and parts of Delhi, the demand for enforcing open access and competition will grow. State governments will come under increasing pressure to show results to their voters. The turnaround could, however, be slow and difficult because of the influence that incumbents wield. Their resistance may also impose huge opportunity costs on the economy and the consumer. Yet, India's power reforms are surely on the right track. At last.

POSTSCRIPT

The enactment of the Electricity Act, 2003, was the cause of hope when the author wrote this essay. The Act mandated the introduction of open access and competition in the generation and supply of electricity. It was passed after more than a year of extensive consultations by the Parliament's Standing Committee on Energy, which reinforced the provisions relating to open access and competition. Introduction of the Electricity Bill 2001 in the Parliament was preceded by two years of consultations with diverse stakeholders and experts. Such extensive consultations at the drafting stage of a bill have been unknown to any other enactment in India. The author had the privilege of drafting the Electricity Bill and, therefore, carried the conviction and hope associated with it, especially as the policies of economic liberalisation of the 1990s had delivered rich dividends.

As events unfolded, the incumbents in the Ministry of Power, the respective state governments, and the state-owned utilities helped perpetuate the barriers that prevented the introduction of competition. As a result, the hope expressed in this essay was belied. Neither did the supply of electricity improve in terms of quality and quantity nor did the tariffs decline in the absence of competition. In sum, India continues to be a 'third world' economy so far as the power sector is concerned. Its peak shortage in 2009–10 was 13.3 per cent, while the losses of distribution utilities exceeded Rs 58,000 crore.

18 Unshackle Power Reforms*
Focus must shift to the consumer

The Electricity Act was passed by Parliament in May 2003, amidst great expectations. But little has changed since then. Incumbents continue to hold the leash that has shackled the power sector for several decades. Monopolies are still in command, and empowerment of the consumer through competition and choice continues to be a mirage.

Electricity is the sole industry in India where producers can only sell to state electricity boards (SEBs) that are bankrupt and cannot pay. As a result, private investors have stayed away while the public sector is unable to produce enough. If these barriers are removed, private investment is sure to chase the unsatisfied demand, thus eliminating shortages and the long queues for electric connections.

Incumbents have been opposing subsidies for everyone but themselves; they favour competition in every sphere but their own; and plead for transparency in everyone's actions other than their own. The attempt to perpetuate their control over the means of production and supply deserves to be checked because monopolies are an unacceptable form of government interference in the markets. Monopolies also violate the fundamental rights that the Constitution of India guarantees.

* Originally published in *The Times of India*, 6 April 2004.

The origins of our dysfunctional governance lie in the command and control economy that fostered shortages. Liberalisation has eliminated such shortages in many a sector. Consumers accustomed to a one-way upward movement of prices in the past are witnessing better services and declining prices owing to competition—be it automobiles, telephones, cola, or washing powder. Power sector is perhaps the only case where shortages and rising tariffs continue to persist.

Most 'experts' in the power sector are currently employed by the industry and their 'expert opinion' is often encumbered by conflict of interest. They have managed to disseminate doctored information aimed at preventing competition, or even a debate on how it could be introduced.

The benefits of competition have been demonstrated in Mumbai where bulk consumers can, for historical reasons, choose between Tata Power and Reliance Energy, thus securing quality power at virtually the lowest tariffs in India. If this limited competition is substituted by open competition, it will add significantly to consumer empowerment. Power reforms are not about substituting SEBs by smaller monopolies.

Way back in 1989, the Electricity Act of the UK mandated the introduction of competition in generation and supply of electricity. This was primarily achieved by requiring every distribution company to wheel (transmit) the electricity supplied by competing producers and suppliers to consumers located in its area. The network was thus subjected to non-discriminatory open access against payment of a regulated wheeling charge. Such open access was first provided to bulk consumers and then gradually extended to smaller consumers. During the 1990s, much of the developed world went the same way. Several developing countries in Eastern Europe, Latin America, and East Asia are now following suit. Efficiency improvements and tariff reductions have clearly demonstrated the efficacy of this approach.

Strangely, India remained oblivious to competition in the power sector until 2000. Even in the 'reforming' states that unbundled their SEBs on the UK pattern, there was no intent to introduce competition even though open access was the mainstay of the UK model. Predictably, the quality of supply improved marginally, but tariffs went up substantially. Power reforms were thus perceived as not being people-friendly; nor could they make the utilities viable.

The concept of open access was introduced in India through the first draft of the Electricity Bill that was presented in February 2000 at the Chief Ministers' Conference presided over by the Prime Minister. The conference resolved that the Bill be subjected to a national debate for evolving a consensus. Several conferences and revised drafts of the Bill followed, and open access thus gained momentum.

The Standing Committee of Parliament on the Electricity Bill stated in its report that open access was the 'key' to power reforms and a 'panacea' for the current problems. The debate in Parliament led to an amendment in the Act, mandating that open access for bulk consumers shall be introduced throughout India within five years. That is the law of the land. The Act has sounded the death knell of monopolies in power supply. Incumbents have nevertheless managed to erect barriers that would delay the progress of open access.

In particular, they want it postponed until the specified time limit of five years. But this limit is more suited to backward and hilly regions; metros and developed regions should have introduced open access within one year. Clearly, the interests of incumbents are in conflict with consumer interests, and incumbents would, therefore, have to be prevented from hijacking governance.

The heart of power reforms lies in the introduction of open access and competition. For this to happen, power reforms need to be unshackled. Investment will then take wings, quality will improve, and costs will be cut. Indeed, it is time for a quantum jump.

POSTSCRIPT

Notwithstanding the mandatory provisions of the Electricity Act, coupled with all the lip service paid to reform and liberalisation, the monopoly structure of electricity industry has remained intact. The incumbent players and entrenched interests have erected enough barriers to ensure that not a single consumer in any state is able to procure open access to distribution networks for a regular supply of electricity from a competing producer or supplier.

Failure to introduce open access and competition has led to the perpetuation of state-owned monopolies where the consumer is a hostage. As a result of the continued mal-performance of state utilities and their inability to attract investment, peak power shortage has increased from 11.3 per cent in 1997–98 to 13.3 per cent in 2009–10. On the other hand, over 40 per cent of the total households in India continue to await electricity connections. To make matters worse, the losses of state utilities increased from about Rs 11,800 crore to Rs 58,200 crore during the same period. The direct and indirect losses thus imposed on the economy and the people pose the single biggest challenge to India's growth prospects.

19 Power Play*
Electricity reforms scuttled at the outset

Electricity reforms seem to have lost their way. Former power minister Anant Gangaram Geethe, while urging the Rajya Sabha on 5 May 2003 to pass the Electricity Bill, said, 'I assure the House that amendments reflecting all the recommendations of the standing committee will be definitely brought forth in the next session.' Admittedly, the Act requires amendments. Its review, as part of the common minimum programme (CMP) is welcome, particularly for purging the distortions that it suffered in its long journey.

Geethe had called the Bill 'a revolutionary step' because it eliminated the monopoly of state electricity boards (SEBs) and enabled competing producers to access consumers. Earlier, producers of electricity could sell their produce to SEBs alone, and since the SEBs were bankrupt, private investors and financial institutions were unwilling to take the payment risk. As a result, little private investment materialised, despite decade-long efforts by successive governments. Enabling power producers to sell directly to consumers will surely attract investment and eliminate shortages. It will improve quality and reduce tariffs, too. In developed countries and in several developing countries, such competition has actually led to tariff reduction.

* Originally published in *The Times of India*, 9 October 2004.

As an industry, electricity can be broadly divided into two segments, namely, carriage and content. Carriage is used for transporting electricity from generating stations to the end consumer. Content is the electricity itself. The carriage segment encompassing the transportation network has attributes of a natural monopoly, as it is uneconomic to build multiple networks. It is, therefore, used as a common carrier providing equal opportunity to all producers who can then compete and bring home price and efficiency gains.

Providing non-discriminatory access to the transportation network is referred to as 'open access' under the Electricity Act that mandates its gradual introduction for consumers. In the UK, for example, all consumers of 1 MW and above got open access in 1990; consumers above 100 KW got it in 1994; and small consumers (about 24 million) got it in 1999. The developed world and several developing countries have introduced retail access on similar lines. The Electricity Act was evolved through a process of extensive consultation, unprecedented in the legislative history of India. The first draft was presented on 26 February 2000 before the Chief Ministers' Conference presided over by the Prime Minister. It was resolved to subject the Bill to a national debate with a view to arriving at a consensus. Over 40 conferences and workshops, more than 250 detailed written interventions, and eight successive drafts followed.

However, when the power ministry was considering the final draft (the 'consensus draft'), lobbying by interested parties led to several modifications. At the heart of the consensus draft was the introduction of open access and competition, aimed at providing consumer choice within a definite time frame. Provision was also made for substituting the cross-subsidy element with a surcharge. It was widely supported, though incumbents predictably opposed the move.

They later managed to introduce several barriers to competition and the Bill thus introduced in Parliament was flawed. The consensus draft had stipulated that as a first step, open access shall be provided to all bulk consumers (1 MW or more) within three years, but the power ministry quietly removed the time frame. However, the standing committee of Parliament gave a powerful endorsement for open access. It stated, 'Provision of open access is key to the power sector reforms' and 'panacea for ushering power sector reforms especially for private sector participation'. The committee stressed that there should be a 'definite time frame' for its introduction.

The power ministry failed to stipulate any time frame, leading to a furore in the Rajya Sabha, when the power minister had to concede, 'I completely agree with the members, I will bring forth amendments to provide for the time limit of three to five years.' However, the promised amendment came eight months later and with a time limit of five years. Moreover, five years were to be counted from January 2004 and not June 2003 when the Act came into force. In addition, several important recommendations of the standing committee did not figure in these amendments. Sixteen months after the Act came into effect, open access remains a pipe dream. Not a single consumer has got it so far.

It seems that the effort is to postpone competition by at least five years, if not more. At this rate, even Mumbai and Delhi may get open access only by January 2009 along with Bihar and Manipur. The regulatory framework stipulated in the Electricity Act is also flawed. The regulatory commissions have been given excessive powers, but with no accountability whatsoever. They will make regulations, grant licences, suspend or revoke them, undertake searches and seizures, adjudicate, impose penalties, and perform several other functions, but with no accountability to the legislature or to the people. On the other hand, the state governments will end up bearing the people's ire. In sum, let the review proceed in right earnest. It will only benefit India and its people.

POSTSCRIPT

In order to secure the support of the opposition parties who were demanding implementation of the recommendations of the Standing Committee of Parliament on Energy, the Minister for Power gave an assurance to the Parliament that he would bring an amendment to the Act in the forthcoming session. The Bill was passed only after this assurance was accepted. According to the assurance given, the time limit for introduction of open access and competition should have been fixed at three years but when the amendment to the Act was actually moved after some delay, the time limit was fixed at five years. This clearly reflected the stranglehold of incumbent players and vested interests over policy formulation and implementation. As events unfolded, open access and competition continue to remain a pipe dream even after eight years of enacting the Electricity Act, 2003.

The debate on open access had begun in 2000. The Electricity Act, 2003, as amended in 2004, had fixed January 2009 as the date by which all bulk consumers would be entitled to avail of open access and choice. While postponing the mandatory introduction of open access to January 2009, the Ministry of Power had argued that the process would have to be gradual and would, therefore, take time. This lack of commitment was more than shared by the state-owned monopoly utilities that erected enough barriers to ensure complete denial of competition and open access.

In the meanwhile, the distribution utilities started buying and selling electricity through traders at prices that are exorbitant by any standards. As a result, the prospects of bulk consumers being able to buy from competing suppliers have receded further since the market structure and trading prices have been severely distorted. There would be few examples where the subversion of the will and intent of the Parliament was so complete.

20 Candlelight Vigil*

People do not seem to realise that part of the electricity they consume costs over Rs 11 per unit simply because someone is making a quick buck. Unscrupulous traders are selling to distribution companies at about Rs 7 per unit. After adding distribution costs and transmission and distribution losses of 30 per cent, the delivered cost crosses Rs 11. Such profiteering in an essential commodity like electricity would have normally attracted strong reactions but it has not happened primarily because distribution companies blend this high-cost electricity with cheaper supplies from dedicated sources and the impact is thus diffused. This would, however, lead to ever higher consumer tariffs with each passing year.

According to the latest *Economic Survey* (2008–09), traders sold 2,192 crore units in 2008–09 at an average price of Rs 7.29 per unit as compared to Rs 3.14 in 2005–06, implying a rise of 132 per cent in just three years. In addition, over 2,150 crore units were 'traded' through Unscheduled Interchange (UI) at an average price of Rs 5.37 per unit. In the last eight months of 2008–9, two power exchanges sold about 270 crore units at an average price of Rs 7.49 per unit. The total payments for 'traded power' thus aggregated about Rs 30,000 crore in 2008–09, and this amount is sure to increase in 2009–10. Assuming an average generation cost of Rs 2 per unit, profiteering

---

* Originally published in *The Outlook*, 5 October 2009.

exceeded a whopping Rs 20,000 crore in 2008–09 alone. All of it would be passed on to the hapless common man, who also bears the brunt of power cuts.

This exploitation occurs because the consumer is hostage to an interconnected chain of monopolies. There is no power producer in India who has open access to any consumer, howsoever large. In other words, no consumer buys electricity from a competing producer or supplier. He can buy from none other than a state-owned distribution company. Even where privatisation of distribution has occurred, such as in Orissa and Delhi, public monopolies have been substituted by private ones. The scourge of monopolies has virtually decimated the power sector in India, and the peak shortage increased from 11.2 per cent to 16.6 per cent over a five-year period ending 2007–08.

State-owned monopolies have neither the creditworthiness to raise the required capital nor the ability to build the additional capacity necessary for meeting the rising demand. Nor can they inspire sufficient confidence to attract private investment, which accounts for only about 28 per cent of the total investment, including captive generation. As a result, about 40 per cent of the households remain without access to electricity even after six decades of independence, and those who do get electricity, suffer from poor quality of supply. The loss in terms of productivity, quality of life, employment, and incomes is enormous by any standards and diminishes India's hope to be at the forefront of emerging economic powers.

In contrast, a single private company has provided mobile phone connections to no less than 10 crore customers across India, and it is not a monopoly as it has four strong competitors. Every company can connect its subscribers to any other telephone through open access to the networks. This has created unprecedented opportunities, with about 65 per cent of the total investment coming from the private sector. As a result, teledensity increased from 7 per cent in March 2004 to 37 per cent by March 2009 when mobile connections exceeded 42.8 crore. Over a crore new connections are added every month while call charges in India are, perhaps, the lowest in the world. Thanks to competition and open access, the telecom revolution has reached the *aam aadmi*—not just as rhetoric, but in reality.

The debate on introducing competition in the power sector began in February 2000 when the draft Electricity Bill was presented at the Chief Ministers' Conference chaired by the Prime Minister. An extensive debate within and outside Parliament led to enactment of the Electricity Act, 2003, which provides the legal framework for competition and open access, in much the same way as the telecom sector has. Yet, no state has enabled open access to a single consumer during the past six years and the regulatory commissions have only been mute spectators. If there can be a good example of contempt of Parliament, this is it.

The electricity sold by power producers is only purchased by 20-odd state-owned utilities in what can best be described as a 'non-market'. Power-surplus states are 'exporting' to deficit states at exorbitant prices in violation of the constitutional provisions that prohibit barriers to inter-state trade. Electricity is, perhaps, the only commodity market where all buyers are state-owned; most are loss-making. In an environment of shortages, these state-owned entities are driven more by political impulses than economic considerations. What is being passed off in the name of 'trading' and 'markets' is no more than a camouflaged vehicle for rent-seeking of unprecedented proportions.

If all mobile users were to get their connections only from a state-owned monopoly, the telecom sector would have resembled the power sector. Remember how hard it was during the pre-1990s to get a telephone connection? A vibrant market got created only after competing players were allowed to access millions of potential consumers. Air travel went the same way; competition led to massive investment in expansion, besides reducing fares to less than half. As a result, the annual growth rate of air traffic exceeded 20 per cent for several years. In contrast, denial of open access to electricity consumers has meant the absence of a market, which in turn has led to scarcity of investment. If investors must remain confined to a handful of loss-making state-owned monopolies, they would rather venture elsewhere. If only open access to consumers was provided in pursuance of the Electricity Act, we would have seen a vibrant electricity market, leading to a lot more growth and welfare.

In 1990, the UK provided open access to all bulk consumers of 1 MW. This was gradually extended to smaller consumers and went right up to the household by 1999. Most of the developed world has followed this path over time. The electricity markets so created have benefited the consumers, suppliers, and producers, and the respective economies too. For example, a household in London can choose from among 12 competing suppliers of electricity. In India, even if you consume 5 MW, you can only buy from the area monopoly, your entitlement to choice under the Electricity Act notwithstanding.

The unmistakable objective of competition and regulation is to protect consumer interests. In the power sector, however, both seem to have deserted the common man. Competition is completely absent as no consumer of electricity is able to exercise any choice in the face of monopolies. As for regulation, the all-pervasive apathy of regulatory commissions to rampant profiteering in bulk supply suggests that they have been captured by entrenched interests. No less than the Central Electricity Regulatory Commission has recently, in September 2009, decreed that the price cap for bulk power will be Rs 8 per unit, thus legitimising sales up to that exorbitant ceiling in the name of 'ensuring reasonable prices'. A regulated wholesale price of 17 cents per unit would be a world record of sorts. In comparison, Enron was an angel at 7 cents.

Incumbents in the power sector argue that India is not yet mature for open access and the examples of telecom in India or the power sector in developed countries are irrelevant. They forget India is in the select club of nuclear powers, it is a software leader, and its growth in the telecom sector is second to none. It has enough entrepreneurs and capital for turning around the power sector if only the state-owned utilities would let go of their monopoly and licence raj. The power sector needs a shake-up. As a first step, the government needs to declare that come 2012 (by when it has promised electricity for all), government offices in the state capitals will observe a voluntary power cut of 2 minutes for an average outage of 100 minutes suffered by the common man. This would hopefully set the ball rolling. If not, it will at least demonstrate that the government identifies itself with the common man.

POSTSCRIPT

The impact of this 'trading' in electricity has since surfaced in the form of a steep increase in the commercial losses of state-owned distribution utilities. According to latest estimates, the losses of distribution companies in 2009–10 aggregated about Rs 58,200 crore as compared to Rs 28,356 crore in 2006–07. These losses already represent about 1 per cent of GDP and their steady rise would pose a serious challenge to fiscal stability year after year. In any case, the ability of distribution utilities to pay for this 'traded' power may be increasingly suspect. In such an environment, private investment is sure to be adversely affected and shortages coupled with high prices are here to stay.

It should be a matter of serious concern that this rank profiteering in 'traded' power is entirely at government expense since this high-cost power is being purchased by state-owned utilities alone. Yet, there seems to be no regulatory or governance response so far, while the losses of utilities continue to mount rapidly.

The systemic problem posed by the present practices is that while bulk power can be 'traded' at high prices, its impact cannot be passed on to the consumers in the form of correspondingly higher tariffs. One of the principal causes of the infamous California crisis of 2001 was that the traders jacked up the bulk prices to be paid by the distribution utilities, but the same could not be passed on by the latter to the consumers. As a result, the losses of distribution utilities mounted rapidly and led to the near-total collapse of the power sector, thus compelling the State of California to provide a large bail-out package.

There seems little doubt that if independent researchers analyse the present power situation in India, they may well conclude that regulation and governance of this sector seem to have withered away.

21   It's Wired to Trip[*]

The Central and State Electricity Regulatory Commissions were set up under the Electricity Act 2003 with the objective of protecting consumers, introducing competition, and facilitating the orderly growth of the power sector. They have singularly failed in achieving any of these objectives. Prices have shot through the roof, competition is conspicuous by its absence and the endemic power shortages have only increased. Losses of utilities have risen sharply to about Rs 60,000 crore per annum (over 1% of GDP), signalling a widespread sickness across the sector. The power sector in India seems more fragile than ever before.

The regulators seem to have been captured by entrenched interests which include a new breed of traders and merchant power producers who are being allowed to sell large volumes of electricity at prices unknown to the civilised world. Their bulk prices range in an average of Rs 5–6 per unit and the only buyers are the state-owned utilities. After accounting for transmission losses and other expenses, the cost of supply to consumers exceeds Rs 8 per unit. Yet they supply to bulk consumers at regulated tariffs of about Rs 4 per unit even though the law does not allow the regulators to fix tariffs for bulk consumers who are expected to buy at market prices, as is also the practice in the developed world. However, the regulators have been subsidising the

* Published in *Hindustan Times*, 15 November 2010.

bulk consumers at the taxpayers expense. Predictably, the losses of utilities have mounted rapidly.

Why is the power sector lagging behind when virtually all other sectors of the economy seem to be faring much better? The short answer is the monopoly in supply of electricity to consumers who must only buy from their area distribution company. Though the Electricity Act gives consumers the right to buy from competing suppliers while continuing to use the network of their distribution company—just as the voice from an Airtel or Vodaphone telephone can reach you through your BSNL land-line—the monopoly utilities and regulators have virtually conspired to keep competition at bay. In London, for example, a household can choose from among 12 competing suppliers of electricity, all of whom use the existing distribution network for their supply. Thanks to the regulators, this still appears a pipedream for India, despite the mandatory provisions of law and a lag of two decades compared to the UK.

The monopoly in distribution of electricity has been difficult to challenge. It benefits thousands of utility employees who lord it over their captive consumers—the same way your telephone linesman did when he represented a monopoly. The local politicians benefit too as they share this patronage. Then there is the large-scale pilferage of electricity, running into several thousand crores of rupees, which creates a huge vested interest. In addition, there are lucrative contracts to be awarded for the expansion and operation of this system. All this adds up to quite a heady mix for those in control. Understandably, they would not want to let go of their monopoly.

The State Electricity Regulatory Commissions (SERCs) were expected to clear all this mess by introducing competition, but none of them have risen to the occasion. They simply eat out of the hands of the utilities and the entrenched interests. They also seem to lack the will and the professional skills to walk the change. For they are usually retired bureaucrats upon whom these sinecures are bestowed for services rendered.

The Central Electricity Regulatory Commission (CERC) has outdone the SERCs. Its statutory duty is to protect the consumers of one state from exploitation by suppliers and traders of other states. Acting quite the opposite, the Commission has virtually legitimised the inter-state sale of electricity at prices often exceeding three times the production cost—all in the name of trading, which is evidently unlawful, and also anti-social if the interest of society is the yardstick.

The CERC has a duty to fix the trading margin for inter-state trade of electricity so that the consumers of importing states are not exploited. Though it fixed a margin of 4 paise per unit, it allowed traders to subvert this arrangement with impunity. Traders can evade this regulated margin by buying at unregulated prices within one state and then selling in another state through another inter-state trader who will only charge the regulated margin. Thus CERC pretends that it is enforcing an inter-state trading margin of 4 paise even though a preceding transaction in the same chain may have extracted a profit of Rs 3 per unit. This loophole has been created by none other than the CERC. The trading regulations earlier prohibited a sale from one trader to another, obviously aimed against manipulation of prices. But the CERC amended this rule to allow trader-to-trader sales, thus facilitating unchecked rent seeking. A regulator that has virtually enabled profiteering of over Rs 50,000 crore in the past three years can hardly carry conviction as an institution that has consumer interests at heart.

The regulatory commissions have failed so miserably because of two fundamental reasons: (a) a selection process that enables the appointment of favourites, howsoever incompetent and lacking in commitment, and (b) lack of accountability—the regulators are accountable neither to the government nor to the respective legislatures.

The unchecked loot that is going on in the electricity sector militates against any notion of economic regulation and good governance. Though India has created the most elaborate regulatory structure for electricity, it is nevertheless facing a regulatory capture. Whichever way you look at it, the matter is far too serious to be left to the regulators. It deserves attention at the highest levels in the government.

POSTSCRIPT

This essay was published in November 2010 and it is too early to write a postscript. It reinforces the concerns expressed in some of the previous essays and demonstrates how failures of the government and the regulators to take timely action lead to predictable pitfalls.

IV
Privatisation of Power
Distribution in Delhi

22 Blackouts Ahead*
Private monopolies are a dim idea

Private monopolies are a dim idea. Delhi's citizens tend to label Bihar as the epitome of chaos and misgovernance. A quick introspection will reveal that Delhi itself condones the vanishing of half its electricity supply day after day (value over Rs 3,000 crore annually) in the name of transmission and distribution (T&D) losses. The power scam in the capital is far in excess of Bihar's infamous fodder scam. And now, in an attempt to get out of this predicament, Delhi wants to hand over its electricity supply business to three private monopolies; never mind the failure of a similar experiment in Orissa. The tariffs will be determined every year on a cost plus basis by the state regulatory commission. This arrangement, if carried out, would be economically flawed and prejudicial to public interest, apart from being contrary to the law.

The structure adopted in Orissa is commonly known as the 'single buyer' model. It consists of a chain of interconnected monopolies where competition and consumer choice are conspicuous by their absence. According to Laszlo Lovei, lead energy specialist in the World Bank, this single buyer model has major disadvantages in developing countries. It invites corruption, weakens payment discipline, and imposes large contingent liabilities on the government. If the Orissa

* Originally published in *The Times of India*, 13 December 2001.

experience is any guide, tariffs would rise even when private companies default with impunity on the payments owed to the state-owned transmission company for power supplied; Rs 1,200 crore at the last count in Orissa. The complete breakdown of commercial discipline, at the taxpayer's expense, is inevitable.

In the restructuring of the telecom industry in India, no monopolies have been created for basic, cellular, or long-distance services. In developed countries, only the wires (carriage) businesses in telecom and power are regarded as natural monopolies; but such monopolies do not extend to the content (voice or electricity) business. Since the content typically exceeds 80 per cent of the tariff, competition in this segment delivers significant efficiency and price gains to consumers.

The Electricity Bill, as drafted by the National Council of Applied Economic Research (NCAER) after a national debate held under the auspices of the Ministry of Power, did not permit private distribution monopolies. Nor did the expert group, consisting of luminaries like Montek Ahluwalia (Chairman), K.V. Kamath, Rakesh Mohan, Jairam Ramesh, Deepak Parekh, and Harish Salve, validate the monopolistic model currently being pursued in Delhi. In fact, their recommendations were emphatically to the contrary. Complete separation between the wires and content businesses may take some time and investment. Yet, bulk consumers, who possess the requisite bargaining strength and consume large quantities of power, can be allowed forthwith to buy directly from competing producers, thus introducing much-needed competition. This would also provide a credible mechanism for adding generation capacity through private investment.

It is often argued that if bulk consumers do not buy from the state electricity board (SEB) or distribution company, its ability to cross-subsidise farm tariffs would be jeopardised. Ideally, the government should fund such subsidies directly, but until that can happen over time, bulk consumers who buy directly from producers can be required to pay a surcharge equivalent to the cross-subsidy element. In a liberalised environment, the totalitarian restriction that all power producers must sell only to a state-owned entity from whom alone the consumers can buy sounds like tyranny of the state. This becomes all the worse when the state-owned entities are bankrupt and thus incapable of procuring enough supplies for meeting the growing demand.Substitution of state monopolies by private monopolies will only compound the problem.

Monopolies must be viewed as an unacceptable form of government interference in the operation of free markets. Monopoly is to a market what a dictatorship is to a political system; monopoly is anathema to the philosophy of democracy and repugnant to the values of freedom and choice that form the bedrock of a democratic polity. The absence of choice, be it in governance or in the markets, inevitably leads to devastating consequences for the citizen.

The Monopolies and Restrictive Trade Practices Act, 1969, states that every monopolistic trade practice shall be deemed to be prejudicial to the public interest, unless such trade practice is authorised by any enactment. Section 20 of the Delhi Electricity Reforms Act, 2000, echoes the provisions of Section 3 of the Indian Electricity Act, 1910, which postulate the multiplicity of licensees in the same area of supply. The Delhi Act does not vest any authority in the government to create private monopolies. On the contrary, it enjoins upon the regulatory commission to promote competitiveness and ensure a fair deal to the consumers.

Above all, the constitutionality of any process that results in the creation of private monopolies is open to challenge. Article 14 guarantees equality before law and equal protection of the laws. If a power producer wishes to sell power that a bulk consumer wishes to buy, can the state restrict their freedom, if only for safeguarding the monopoly of the incumbent distribution company? Article 19 of the Constitution guarantees the freedom to carry on any occupation, trade, or business. In the heyday of socialism, however, Clause (6) of Article 19 was amended (in 1951) to enable the state to enact laws for legitimising state-owned monopolies. Exclusion of private monopolies from this amendment reinforces the interpretation that the state cannot, even by law, provide for private monopolies. The only situation where the Constitution would permit enactment of laws to sustain private monopolies is when they can be justified as reasonable restrictions on the aforesaid rights. The proposed monopolies, however, would fail to meet the stringent criteria laid down by the Supreme Court for this purpose.

It should be evident that any sell-off to private distribution companies on a monopolistic basis would be subversive of the extant laws and incompatible with the ongoing economic liberalisation. Yet, this is precisely what Delhi seems to be attempting. When the electricity industry was restructured and privatised in the UK in 1989, all bulk consumers drawing more than 1 MW were given the freedom to choose from among competing producers of electricity. This was gradually extended to smaller consumers. As a result, the prices of electricity have fallen by about 30 per cent over the last decade. If Delhi is not willing to attempt what was successfully done in the UK 12 years ago, it may well be pursuing a cure that is worse than the disease. The citizenry of Delhi needs to wake up to these challenges. The rest of the country must join in as well, for similar issues await it round the corner.

POSTSCRIPT

Electricity distribution in Delhi was handed over to private monopolies in July 2002. Contrary to the assurances given by the Delhi government at the time of privatisation and in violation of extant laws, open access and competition have not been introduced so far. As a result, not a single consumer has been able to buy electricity from a competing supplier even nine years after privatisation, notwithstanding the mandatory provisions of the Electricity Act. Sure enough, private monopolies can well be expected to prevent the introduction of any competition, especially when the governance of the sector is fundamentally flawed.

After privatisation, tariffs have risen by about 50 per cent, thereby belying the expectation that reduction in T&D losses would improve revenue collections and help avoid such tariff hikes. T&D losses were about 33 per cent in 2006–07, about 29 per cent in 2007–08, and about 19 per cent in 2009–10, compared to about 10.5 per cent in Mumbai and Ahmedabad, and 6 per cent in Surat. Outages are still common. Widespread complaints about over-billing have caused considerable public outcry.

The Comptroller and Auditor General (CAG), in its report on Government of NCT of Delhi (2004), stated that undue gains of several thousand crore rupees were doled out by the government to the private distribution companies during the bid process. Following the CAG report, the Public Accounts Committee (PAC) of Delhi Legislative Assembly recommended an investigation by the Central Bureau of Investigation (CBI) to nail the delinquent officials. However, in the absence of any accountability, no one has borne the consequences of so much wrong-doing while the hapless consumers have been denied the fruits of competition that would have led to greater efficiencies, elimination of outages, and reduction in tariffs.

23 Darkness Ahead*

The proposed power reforms in the Capital could result in 'Dabholising the Delhi Vidyut Board (DVB)', says Gajendra Haldea, a power sector expert, currently chief adviser and head of the Centre for Infrastructure and Regulation, NCAER. He explains why to Ruhi Batra:

RUHI BATRA (RB): Why are you opposing power reforms in Delhi?

GAJENDRA HALDEA (GH): I am not opposed to reforms. In fact, I congratulate the Delhi government for pursuing them. However, in my personal view, it is ill advised about the reform strategy. The plan is to set up an interconnected chain of monopolies where all generating companies (Gencos) must sell to the state-owned transmission company (Transco); the Transco will sell to three private distribution companies (Discoms); and all consumers, bulk or small, must buy from the area Discom alone. There will be no choice at any stage. This will create a bizarre situation where all producers of electricity must sell to a state-owned entity, and that too a bankrupt one.

Is it not absurd to have a mandatory state-owned middleman, the Transco, between private producers on the one hand and private licensees/consumers on the other? The international norm is that a Transco should only transmit power, not buy or sell power. That is

* This interview was originally published in *The Times of India*, 7 March 2002.

what Powergrid Corporation does at the national level. Why should the Transco wish to enter into long-term power purchase agreements (PPAs) for buying power, even after the Enron experience? This would clearly distort the industry structure and invite corruption.

At the distribution level, privatisation will lead nowhere if a private monopoly replaces a state monopoly. Competition may well lead to privatisation; the reverse is not true, as privatised monopolies will thwart competition. The consumer will thus remain hostage. Nowhere in the developed world are such monopolies being created. On the contrary, the objective is to encourage competition.

Privatisation is not an end; it is only a means for enhancing consumer welfare through efficiency and price gains. It is competition, not privatisation, that delivers these gains. For example, who cares whether or not Bharat Sanchar Nigam Ltd (BSNL) is privatised as long as there is a choice of service providers? Remember how BSNL slashed long-distance charges by 60 per cent, thanks to competition from Bharti Telecom?

The Indian Constitution enshrines freedom of trade and business as a fundamental right. By enacting appropriate laws, reasonable restrictions can be placed on this right, but only in public interest. The first amendment to the Constitution (1951) allowed state-owned monopolies as long as they were created by law. State electricity boards (SEBs) were thus protected. Private monopolies, however, are patently unconstitutional; they abrogate fundamental rights and are anathema to democratic philosophy. The last thing one wants to see as part of economic liberalisation is the creation of monopolies.

The Delhi Electricity Reforms Act specifies competition as one of its main objectives. Like the Electricity Act, 1910, it declares that the grant of a licence to a person 'shall not in any way hinder or restrict the grant of a licence to another person within the same area of supply for like purpose'. The law clearly postulates multiplicity of licensees. An example is Mumbai where bulk consumers get cheaper power because of competition between BSES and TEC.

It is not known who the real advisers of Delhi government are. Their ostensible advisers, however, have no experience or expertise in power reforms. Delhi seems unmindful of the recommendations of the expert group that included luminaries like Montek Singh Ahluwalia, Rakesh Mohan, Harish Salve, Jairam Ramesh, Deepak Parekh, and K.V. Kamath. All this will Dabholise the Delhi Vidyut Board (DVB).

RB: Why do you say so?

GH: The process of privatisation is suspect. The manner in which huge guaranteed returns have been assured after shortlisting of bidders vitiates the entire exercise. If you look at the fine print, the consumer will end up paying over 27 per cent by way of annual return on equity during the next five years. There is hardly any competition as only three bidders are in the fray for three circles—and no one can get more than two circles. Two of the bidders have a track record of defaulting on payments to state-owned entities by almost Rs 1,000 crore each.

Besides, if the Discoms reduce thefts beyond the agreed level, they can keep half the gains. Thus, for every stolen unit that is brought to book, the Discom can retain Rs 2.08 as its reward. Can a civilised society allow a policeman to retain 50 per cent of the value of stolen goods recovered? This could also tempt the policeman to declare an honest person a thief.

RB: Do you fear a repeat of the Orissa fiasco?

GH: Yes, of course. Orissa followed the 'single buyer' model that Delhi is now emulating. It did not enhance consumer welfare—only raised tariffs without much improvement in supply. It is not people friendly. Regulation was also flawed as it relied on cost-plus returns on a year-to-year basis. This caused lack of predictability, which is proposed to be addressed in Delhi by guaranteeing exceptionally high returns.

Power companies in Orissa are in deep trouble and face impending bankruptcy. AES (a US company) has already withdrawn from one Discom; the remaining three Discoms are surviving on huge defaults (about Rs 1,000 crore) to the state-owned Transco, which in turn has lost over Rs 1,500 crore.

The monopolists and incumbent players, however, refuse to admit the real lessons of Orissa and focus only on peripheral issues—because they wish to retain their stranglehold. Unfortunately, those charged with the responsibility for reform are the ones who will lose their fiefdoms if real reforms occur. No one should expect results in this scenario.

RB: What could be the alternative model for power reforms?

GH: First, we must understand the rationale for restructuring. It does not arise from the rampant thefts in DVB. Both in telecom and in power, the 1990s witnessed a separation between carriage (wires) and content (voice or electricity). Content typically accounts for over 80 per cent of the consumer tariff. So the telephone or electric wires connecting your home remain the same but competing long-distance operators vie for your custom, and in the same way Gencos compete too.

The strategy for reform must revolve around open access where wire companies carry electricity for a regulated charge while supply is exposed to competition. If producers are allowed to access consumers, they will take the market risk and invest in new capacity—like in any other industry—and also provide better service.

RB: Can competing suppliers at the household level be viable?

GH: This has already happened in several countries. For example, if you lived in London, Melbourne, or Auckland, you could choose from among competing suppliers. However, that would require upgradation of the network. During transition, consumers should continue to get electricity based on existing arrangements, to avoid any speculative pricing. Nonetheless, bulk consumers must be given a choice of buying from competing producers. This will open up the market, attract investment, and deliver price and efficiency gains to all consumers.

POSTSCRIPT

If we compare the outcome of the first eight years of private participation in telecom with what was achieved eight years after privatisation of electricity distribution in Delhi, the differences are stark. The telecom services did not suffer from any short supply and all services were available on demand and at competitive prices. In the case of electricity, however, outages are still common, especially during peak hours and in summer months, while tariffs have also risen. The single biggest reason for this divergence is the fact that telecom companies are required to compete in a free market while the power utilities enjoy a complete monopoly where consumers can only buy from the distribution company of their area, which is free to enforce outages, provide poor quality of supply, and recover higher charges. These are the obvious attributes of a private monopoly.

The way consumers as well as the public exchequer have been short-changed by the power distribution companies in Delhi has been the subject of scathing reports by the Comptroller and Auditor General as well as the Public Accounts Committee of the Delhi Legislative Assembly and the media. Consumers have often complained about outages, overbilling, and higher tariffs. Whatever the investment bankers, consultants, and interested parties may have said in favour of the Delhi model of privatisation, the government should have known better. If private monopolies continue to be perpetuated, we may see more rent-seeking and crony capitalism at the expense of the consumers and the economy.

24 Outdoing Enron[*]

Dabholisation of the Delhi Vidyut Board (DVB) is on its way. Riding on the tiger of public resentment, the DVB is sprinting to cut deals that would outdo Enron. The proposed structure is contrary to international practices and recommendations of the expert group that included Montek Singh Ahluwalia, Harish Salve, Rakesh Mohan, Jairam Ramesh, Deepak Parekh, K.V. Kamath, and this author. But if you object, the DVB top-brass could label you 'obstructive, obstreperous, and unruly'.

Private power producers got 16 per cent assured return on equity (RoE) plus taxes at normative generation of 68.5 per cent—derived from the performance of state-owned units. But handsome incentives for higher generation enabled returns to exceed 30 per cent.

History is being repeated. For performing as per their bids, distribution companies (discoms) will get 16 per cent RoE post-tax, which would be even higher (say, 27 per cent) when you add the benefits of a three-year moratorium on debt service that converts into a long-term interest-free loan of Rs 300 crore.

Further, if discoms achieve better loss reduction compared to their bids, they get windfall gains. So a discom that reduces transmission and distribution (T&D) losses by an additional 5 per cent gets an extra 20 per cent RoE, doubling it to 47 per cent. And any investment made

* Originally published in *Hindustan Times*, 19 March 2002.

for achieving loss reduction will also qualify for RoE, etc., implying double jeopardy for consumers who will pay twice.

These fabulous returns do not stop here. The consumer will also pay 6.83 per cent of the equity as an annual depreciation charge. In five years, he would have paid back over 34 per cent of the equity. In Mumbai, Kolkata, Ahmedabad, Surat, and Orissa, these payments reduce the capital base for computation of tariffs. But by changing the reference point from net capital to equity, discoms will get huge profits at consumers' expense.

Correcting the equity for depreciation repayments, the effective RoE will exceed 33 per cent in the fifth year, to which 5 per cent can be added on account of moratorium. And, if a discom improves on T&D losses by 5 per cent, the effective RoE could be a whopping 70 per cent.

Some of these substantial benefits have been offered after the bidders were shortlisted. This vitiates the entire bidding process. Bids have been invited for reduction in T&D losses that are assumed as 51 per cent. Since bidders for the three discoms are only three, the bids are likely to be conservative, more so as no one can buy more than two discoms. Incidentally, two of the bidders have defaulted elsewhere by about Rs 1,000 crore each.

With current losses of 51 per cent in DVB, the cream available is enormous, as discoms will retain half, that is, Rs 2.07 per unit for every stolen unit that they recover beyond the bid level—an invitation to excess billing indeed.

All this is being managed with the 'cooperation' of the Delhi Electricity Regulatory Commission (DERC) where no judicial or financial member has been appointed. Purposely? A sole chairman, electrical engineer by background, is flooded with legal and financial issues that he has little training to deal with. Moreover, he is acting under directions that are legally untenable.

DERC has been persuaded to fix bulk supply tariffs twice—once for sale by Gencos to Transco and again for sale by Transco to the discoms. Bulk tariffs should normally be fixed for Gencos, while transmission companies get a wheeling charge, as in the case of Powergrid.

Strangely, tariff for sale by Transco has been fixed at Rs 1.47 per unit even though its cost will be over Rs 2.50.

The loss (about Rs 1,400 crore in the first year) is to be borne by the government (read, taxpayer) so that privatised discoms can get assured returns. The law does not permit such an arrangement. But who cares? Didn't Mumbai overlook several laws for the Dabhol deal?

In Delhi, a monopolistic structure is being crafted to enable the favoured few to accomplish their grandiose business goals unencumbered by competition. Is it possible to stab consumer interests more fatally? All power producers will be required to sell to the bankrupt state-owned Transco—clearly an absurd proposition. If there are private producers and consumers, must the state insist on being the mandatory middleman? Would this not invite corruption?

Neither the Constitution nor the Electricity Art, 1910, allows private monopolies. The 1910 Act declares that the grant of a licence 'shall not in any way hinder or restrict the grant of a licence to another person within the same area of supply for a like purpose'. Thus, BSES and TEC compete for bulk consumers in Mumbai and their tariffs are nearly the lowest in India. Section 20 (9) of the Delhi Electricity Reforms Act echoes the aforementioned provisions, but it lies buried.

Competition may well lead to privatisation, but the reverse is not true since privatised monopolies will stifle competition. In no other sector has the government created private monopolies in the name of reform.

Telecom is a shining example of the benefits of competition. But trust the monopolists and incumbent players to confuse issues, for if competition is allowed, the house of cards that guarantees high returns will collapse instantly. What we need is a reform strategy that allows open access to the network on payment of a regulated charge while generation and supply face competition. If competing producers can access consumers, they will take the market risk and invest in new capacity and deliver price and efficiency gains too.

POSTSCRIPT

Regardless of the obvious pitfalls pointed out in the chapter, the Government of Delhi went ahead with its flawed privatisation of power distribution companies, which has exposed the taxpayer and the consumer to significant losses. Concerned about the enormous fallout of this ill-conceived initiative, the author took the unusual step of challenging the legality of this entire scheme through a writ petition filed in the Delhi High Court in April 2002. He received support from unexpected quarters such as P. Chidambaram, senior advocate of the Supreme Court (previously and subsequently the Union Minister of Finance) who argued the case, pro bono, in its initial stages.

With the Government of Delhi as well as some very powerful corporates as defendants, the battle in the high court was long-drawn and difficult. After five years of proceedings, the Delhi High Court in July 2007 declared that the directions of the Delhi government that mandated the structure of privatisation were unlawful. The matter currently rests in the Supreme Court where the Delhi government has gone in appeal.

Reports of the Comptroller and Auditor General (CAG),[1] the Public Accounts Committee (PAC)[2] of the Delhi Legislative Assembly, and several other fora have questioned the terms of privatisation, which remain controversial. Reports of the CAG and PAC have indicted the government as well as the officials concerned for providing unlawful gains of several thousand crores of rupees to the private distribution companies at the expense of the public exchequer and the consumer.

The monopoly in supply of electricity, created by the unlawful directions of the Delhi government, has enabled the private distribution companies to engage in various forms of rent-seeking, thus denying the significant gains that consumers would have secured through competition. The most damaging fallout of this episode has been that since 2002, no other state has talked of privatising power distribution, and in that sense, power sector reforms have suffered a setback.

[1] Report of the Comptroller and Auditor General (CAG) on Government of NCT of Delhi (2004).

[2] Report of the Public Accounts Committee (PAC) of the Delhi Legislative Assembly on privatisation of electricity distribution in Delhi (2006).

25 Match NDMC, Make a Killing*

The best business of the decade may well be the electricity distribution company of central and east Delhi (discom). If the soon-to-be-privatised discom equals the 16 per cent distribution losses of the New Delhi Municipal Council (NDMC) in five years, it can recover over 400 per cent in profits from the consumers. This could well happen considering that the distribution losses in Mumbai, Ahmedabad, and Surat are only 11 per cent, 14 per cent, and 15 per cent, respectively. Moreover, the monopoly status of discom will ensure that its profits remain unencumbered by competition; Delhi's power minister has declared that competition can be introduced only after a decade.

In this saga of privatisation in distress, the Delhi government issued directions to the Delhi Electricity Regulatory Commission (DERC), hiking the assured returns of discom, but only after a chosen few bidders were left in the bidding ring. The single-man Commission, manned by a retired electrical engineer, set the tariffs accordingly. It fixed the tariff payable by discom to the government-owned transco at Rs 1.32 per unit in the first year, while the average tariff to be charged by discom from its consumers would be Rs 4.08 per unit. Moreover, discom would charge Rs 6.52 per unit from Delhi government's Jal Board, the Municipal Corporation would pay Rs 6.95 for street lighting, and Delhi Metro would shell out Rs 4.80 per unit. For subsidising

* Originally published in *Business Standard*, 19 June 2002.

power purchase by the three distribution companies, the Delhi government shall provide loans of Rs 3,450 crore that would ultimately be borne by the taxpayer or the consumer.

The Delhi government has altered the tariff principles specified in the Sixth Schedule of the Electricity (Supply) Act, 1948 (ES Act). The tariffs of private discoms in the rest of the country, such as in Orissa, Mumbai, Kolkata, Ahmedabad, Surat, and Greater Noida, are determined as per the ES Act. Section 28(2) of the Delhi Electricity Reforms Act (DERA) requires that the ES Act be followed in Delhi too. However, Section 28(3) empowers the Commission to make departures after recording its reasons in writing, following a public hearing. Many argue that the government had no powers to usurp the statutory role of the Commission that was primarily set up as an independent tariff-setting authority.

The government directions are revealing. The ES Act allows a reasonable return equal to 5 per cent above the RBI (Reserve Bank of India) rate, which is ruling at 6.5 per cent. This return of 11.5 per cent is to be paid on the capital base, which is defined as original cost, less depreciation. The rationale for a declining capital base under the ES Act is that when consumers pay for depreciation in cash, the capital investment gets reduced to that extent. The Delhi government, however, has fixed a 16 per cent return, and that too on equity which remains constant, unlike the capital base that would reduce progressively. This manoeuvre alone will double discom's profits by the fifth year, as compared to the ES Act.

Discom will also get a moratorium of three years on a government loan of Rs 174 crore. The benefits, however, will not be passed on to the consumers who will nonetheless pay Rs 43.3 crore to discom on account of loan repayment, thus enabling it to increase returns by about 13 per cent. In fact, none of the actions of the Delhi government will reduce consumer tariff, which happen to be the highest in India after the Commission raised them by a hefty 22 per cent last year.

The best is yet to come. The Commission has determined the current distribution losses of discom at 57.2 per cent, and the government's negotiated pact requires discom to bring down these losses to

40 per cent in five years. In case discom does better, it can retain one half of the additional revenues. Thus, for every stolen unit recovered below 40 per cent, discom can retain Rs 2.04 as its profit even though it had paid only Rs 1.32 as the purchase price.

For matching NDMC, discom must bring down its losses to 16 per cent, implying a reduction of 24 percentage points below the negotiated 40 per cent. The additional revenues, assuming a modest turnover of 5,000 million units, will be about Rs 500 crore, of which discom can appropriate Rs 250 crore as profits.

Under the ES Act, discom can retain up to 5 per cent of its reasonable return by way of excess profits, and the balance must go into a reserve fund. Overlooking this statutory ceiling, the Delhi government has allowed discom to appropriate even 400 per cent in profits, which means about Rs 300 crore against a statutory ceiling of Rs 5 crore. If this ceiling had to be increased, the Commission could do it by a reasoned order under Section 28(3). Many argue that the Delhi government's action in leaving the profits open-ended and also in linking them to lax performance standards is untenable.

Even the bids received were conditional and non-responsive. But the Delhi government entered into close-door negotiations with the bidder. A few hundred crores were added for expanding the subsidised supply to the bidder; and his risk of losses was also reduced by about Rs 250 crore through lowering of the threshold by 275 per cent. In addition, a new anti-theft law was promised so that thefts could be reduced and the bidder could appropriate half of the theft reduction in added profits. Such changes in bid conditions normally require a fresh opportunity for all the shortlisted bidders, as was recently done for privatisation of the national highway between Jaipur and Ajmer, where a different bidder made a lower bid.

The valuation of the assets of discom has also been questioned. The total equity of discom has been fixed at Rs 116 crore and the private bidder will acquire the vast network, real estate, and monopoly business by paying Rs 59 crore for 51 per cent of the equity. This valuation is neither based on audited accounts (Delhi Vidyut Board [DVB] accounts have not been audited for a decade) nor is there any inventory of assets. Moreover, the valuation was not done by an approved valuer, nor were the principles of valuation specified in the Central Government's disinvestment policy and procedures followed. In addition, post-valuation investments of DVB are to be gifted away without a price.

The terms of privatisation appear to be shrouded in secrecy. Even the Commission conceded that it was not privy to the terms of privatisation, though Section 11(1) (k) of DERA requires the Commission to regulate the entry into or exit from the power sector.

You could ask: What if discom did not perform? Well, it will simply hold up transco's payments, as in Orissa where more than Rs 1,000 crore of public money has been lost. But if discom remains at the negotiated level of 40 per cent losses after five years, the consumer tariffs will have to rise by over 50 per cent.

You could also ask why no one is voicing much opposition. It seems that the crimes of DVB are so overwhelming that people simply want to jump out of the fire to get rid of it. That they are heading straight into the proverbial frying pan is a fact that their blinkered vision is unable to perceive. That is what happened when Enron came to India.

POSTSCRIPT

For a princely sum of Rs 59 crore, the entire network, real estate, and business of the distribution company of central and east Delhi was sold to a private entity through what could well be described as a negotiated deal that short-changed the taxpayer and the consumer. If the report[1] of the Comptroller and Auditor General (CAG) is to be relied upon, the private entity made a huge killing through the undervaluation of assets.

In the years after privatisation, the distribution company may not have succeeded in curbing theft to the level prevailing in the adjoining NDMC areas, but it has found ways of overcharging consumers through manipulated meters.

---

[1] Report of the Comptroller and Auditor General (CAG) on Government of NCT of Delhi (2004).

According to a report of the Delhi government,[2] more than 80 per cent of the meters deliver excessive readings beyond 2.5 per cent of what is due. In 2007–08 alone, this could have meant undue gains of well over Rs 30 crore. The story is not very different for the distribution company of south Delhi. The performance of the distribution company of north Delhi, however, is said to be comparatively better.

If we go beyond the official admissions relating to manipulated meters, there is a much larger issue relating to short-changing of the ordinary consumer and the public exchequer. The widespread resentment relating to the sharp rise in electricity bills after the private companies took over suggests that the private distribution companies have collected significantly larger payments over the years, but these do not seem to be adequately reflected in their revenues. There seems to be no mechanism or regulatory oversight to provide comfort to the consumers that the accounting of revenue collection and transmission and distribution (T&D) losses is credible. These doubts cannot be brushed aside in view of the recent government reports[3] relating to a huge under-reporting of revenues by a telecom licensee. Thus, how much is being siphoned out illegally is anybody's guess. In the absence of open access, the consumer cannot even choose another supplier and compel the incumbent monopoly to behave itself.

Indeed, the investments made in acquiring this power distribution company are like a gold mine. Equity owners, investment bankers, and business schools can hail these transactions as truly profitable. What price the consumer or the economy pays is a different matter.

[2] *The Times of India*, 23 March 2009.
[3] *The Hindu Business Line*, 7 December 2009.

26 Dabhol Revisited[*]

Do you know of an industry where private producers cannot sell to private consumers except through a state-owned middleman? Or any industry where producers can sell only to a state entity? Answer: the power sector. Despite economic reforms, the incumbent players have made sure that this premise remains unchanged. This is the theory that forms the epicentre of 'Dabholisation', as it allows government functionaries to continue to sign long-term power purchase agreements (PPAs) that were discarded in developed nations years ago. This arrangement enables incumbent players to retain their hegemony by frustrating the evolution of a market, thus perpetuating monopoly rents and the power to award contracts.

So whether it was opening up to private producers (such as Enron), or unbundling of the state electricity board as in Orissa, or the privatisation of distribution that is being attempted in Delhi, the liberty to buy and sell among producers and consumers has remained elusive. And unless this economic freedom is recognised and granted—even if in stages—power reforms will continue to beat around the bush and get nowhere. It is competition, not privatisation, that is the engine of economic reforms.

In a game that allows players to double up as umpires, the expectation of a fair outcome is unrealistic. In power sector reforms, the

* Originally published in *Hindustan Times*, 2 July 2002.

incumbent government functionaries and monopolistic entities are indeed players as well as umpires. Independent expertise or advocacy that would help build opinion in the larger interests of the economy is scarce. It is this configuration that allows the creation of private monopolies that would not only suit the prospective investors but also enable government functionaries to continue to sign PPAs and retain control. The proposition that consumer choice and competition will bring efficiency and price gains is yet to acquire its rightful place in the debate on power reforms. The bogey of theft is virtually being used for scaring the common man into yielding his economic freedom and choice in favour of private monopolies. This does not augur well for the economy as a whole.

In the rest of India, governments have shied away from increasing tariffs for fear of popular backlash. In Delhi, however, the government has issued directions to the regulator to increase tariffs for providing 'attractive' returns to chosen private investors. Be it Dabhol or the ongoing privatisation in Delhi, when it comes to attracting private investors, governments somehow manage to display abundant political will that would otherwise do a lot of good if applied to governance of the power sector.

This author had publicly spelt out the excessively high and unlawful profits that consumers would have to pay to private monopolies for supply of electricity in Delhi. Through item-wise calculation, it was brought out that these assured profits would be more than double of what the normal laws allow for distribution companies in India, such as in Mumbai, Kolkata, Ahmedabad, Surat, and Greater Noida. Also, honest consumers will continue to pay for the high level of thefts, as even after five years these monopolies will charge for transmission and distribution (T&D) losses of 34 per cent; and in case they bring them down, they will keep one half of the recovered stolen property in added profits, an arrangement unheard of. Delhiites will thus pay tariffs that would easily be the highest in India.

A consumer would legitimately expect that competition will bring services of international standards. A discom (distribution company) in Argentina reduced its T&D losses from 26 per cent to 8 in six years;

and in Peru, they were down from 20 to 10 per cent in four years. In Mumbai, BSES and BEST post losses of about 11 per cent while Ahmedabad and Surat lose 15 per cent and 14 per cent, respectively. In Delhi, NDMC (New Delhi Municipal Council) losses are 16 per cent. So it is only fair to expect that in five years' time, private discoms in Delhi will bring down losses to about 10 per cent—and not 34 per cent as negotiated by the Delhi government. How long should consumers pay for thefts as well as excessive returns to discoms?

The bidding process in Delhi seems vitiated as large concessions were granted to favoured bidders during post-bid close-door negotiations. Such concessions are offered to all the shortlisted bidders who are expected to compete on the basis of revised terms. This is normal procedure that was also recently adopted for privatising the Jaipur–Ajmer national highway. The Delhi privatisation is now a negotiated bilateral deal and not a competitive bid.

Consumers could somehow live with these deals if only they had the freedom to choose a competitor. We know that if Dabhol had to sell its produce in a competitive market, it could never have extracted such exploitative returns. Similarly, in the arrangement contemplated for Delhi, the privatised discoms will command a monopoly status.

The integrity of the privatisation process in Delhi is open to doubt on other counts too. For example, the valuation flouts the Centre's disinvestment manual and has lowered the value by over Rs 700 crore for the benefit of chosen bidders. The Delhi Vidyut Board (DVB) does not have a register of assets, so no one knows what exactly is being transacted. Nor does it have audited accounts for a decade. The situation in many other states is not very different. These are basic issues of governance that need to be addressed sooner than later. Diverting attention through half-baked reforms will bring a replay of the failures of the 1990s.

Then there is Orissa, the only state where privatisation of distribution occurred after independence.[1] A foreign company has packed

---

[1] Delhi was the only other case where privatisation of distribution was undertaken subsequently in 2002.

off after losing all its investment while the domestic company that remains is more than bankrupt. The T&D losses, after three years of privatisation, are about 47 per cent; political interference coupled with lack of police cooperation is cited as the principal reason for continued thefts. What if the same phenomenon occurs in Delhi? In the absence of political will, can private companies check rampant theft? And if the political will exists, can there be thefts of this order in the DVB? Or are we conceding that private discoms will have police personnel on their payroll for enforcing the law? There are indeed strong arguments for privatisation such as competition, efficiency, and price gains. But Delhi seems the first case of privatisation which has theft reduction as the main objective.

Whenever universally respected principles are perverted, bizarre consequences surface. For example, private discoms in Delhi will buy power at Rs 1.48 per unit from the state-owned Transco, but will sell at an average tariff of Rs 4.16 to the consumer. A bulk consumer like Delhi Metro Rail will pay Rs 4.80. Imagine a private discom pocketing Rs 3 per unit for simply carrying electricity for, say, 10 km. The new rules make sure that Delhi Metro will have no option but to buy from these private monopolies, which means that commuters will subsidise private discoms by about Rs 75 crore a year. Similarly, the government's own Jal Board will pay Rs 6.52 while the municipal corporation will shell out Rs 6.95 for street lighting to the private discoms.

Imagine the price and service you would have got if cellphones were provided by a monopoly; and remember how you benefited from a 60 per cent cut in long-distance charges the moment competition came. The world over, the rationale for restructuring of telecom and power sectors lay in competition. However much the Delhi government waxes eloquent about privatisation, competition is the most important issue it should have addressed. Instead, its power minister says competition will take about 11 years to come. If Delhi is going ahead this way, the fate of power reforms in the rest of India is anybody's guess.

POSTSCRIPT

So frustrated were Delhi's consumers with the state-owned DVB that whatever they got from the private monopolies was regarded by many as a great relief. The fact remains that the Comptroller and Auditor General (CAG)[2] had reported that undue gains of about Rs 3,500 crore were granted to the private distribution companies at taxpayers' expense by lowering the value of assets artificially. Works in progress valued at about Rs 1,788 crore and grid assets and transformers valued at about Rs 1,700 crore were not taken into account while computing the total cost of assets. It was further estimated by the CAG that if similar terms had been provided to DVB, it could have earned about Rs 4,100 crore over five years. In particular, the manner in which the terms of privatisation were changed after the bids were received created a strong suspicion of rent-seeking and crony capitalism.

As pointed out earlier, despite nine years of privatisation, the distribution companies remain private monopolies and not a single consumer has been able to opt for competing suppliers. T&D losses continued to be high—they were 33 per cent in 2006–07, well above the national average of 28.65 per cent—and the consumers had to bear this burden. Though these losses have slowly declined in subsequent years, there is little assurance against exaggeration of these losses by the distribution companies in order to siphon out revenues. In addition, the Delhi government has admitted that over 80 per cent of the consumer meters have been overcharging well beyond the permissible limits.[3] Where all this money has gone is a mystery that needs to be unravelled, as the increased payments by consumers do not seem to have reduced the high level of commercial losses that continue to be claimed by the privatised distribution companies in order to justify higher consumer tariffs.

While the rest can be a matter of debate, the stark fact that continues to stare us in the face is that no state in India has thought of replicating the Delhi model over the past nine years. In effect, this was one step forward that actually took us two steps backwards.

---

[2] Report of the Comptroller and Auditor General (CAG) on Government of NCT of Delhi (2004).

[3] *The Times of India*, 23 March 2009.

27 Missing Assets and the Power Game*

'Where have all DVB's assets gone...', you could well sing about the Delhi Vidyut Board (DVB) as the Bombay Suburban Electricity Supply and Tata Power took over its three distribution companies on 1 July 2002. Over Rs 1,000 crore worth of assets seem to have disappeared between one set of accounts and the other. That DVB accounts have not been audited for a decade is another matter.

To protect public funds, the Constitution has created an elaborate structure. It requires the Comptroller and Auditor General of India (CAG) to audit the annual accounts of public entities such as DVB. The audited accounts with the CAG report are to be placed before the legislative assembly for ensuring accountability of the elected government. And, of course, there is the judiciary as the custodian of rule of law. In addition, a regulatory commission has been set up under the Delhi Electricity Reforms Act, 2001 (DERA). Then there is the Central Vigilance Commission (CVC) and Lokayukta to act as watchdogs.

Yet, if public assets disappear, a citizen could well say in frustration that there is a failure of the constitutional machinery. In Delhi, about 55 per cent of the power bought by DVB is lost in the so-called transmission and distribution (T&D) losses. Not more than an estimated 15 per cent are technical losses and the rest is plain theft, some of

* Originally published in *The Indian Express*, 2 July 2002.

it in collusion with DVB employees. So if 40 per cent of the power supplied gets stolen, you are virtually living in a lawless jungle; this failure should normally have spurred some response from the government. But what you see is an attempt to escape lawlessness through the privatisation route.

Even if privatisation was happening for the wrong reasons, it could have been supported in larger public interest. But here much seems wrong; and an example is the case of vanishing assets aimed at reducing the price to be paid by private bidders for acquiring the power distribution companies. The Delhi Electricity Regulatory Commission had, after a public hearing, determined the gross fixed assets of DVB at Rs 3,841 crore in its order of 23 May 2001. In addition, capitalised works were valued at Rs 484 crore while works in progress were valued at Rs 1,078 crore. This added up to Rs 5,303 crore as the closing balance on 31 March 2002. Assuming that a modest Rs 100 crore would have been incurred as capital expenditure in the three months that followed, the total gross fixed assets would be Rs 5,403 crore as on 1 July—when DVB was restructured and split into five companies.

As against DVB's capital assets of Rs 5,403 crore, the gross fixed assets included in the Transfer Scheme notified by the Delhi government on 20 November 2001 aggregate Rs 4,263 crore only. This includes Rs 650 crore and Rs 510 crore of the transmission and generating companies, respectively; the remaining Rs 3,103 crore have been allocated to the three distribution companies that are being privatised. A gaping hole of Rs 1,140 crore is apparent between the two sets of figures—one approved by the Regulatory Commission and the other notified by the Delhi government.

Where have assets worth Rs 1,140 crore gone is a mystery. DVB argues that it followed the 'business valuation' method for determining the transfer price of its assets. That, however, cannot explain this disappearance from its account books. The only way books can be cleaned up is by writing off these assets in the prescribed manner. DVB should have made a 'dying declaration' and come clean on this issue before it was extinguished. Yet another blow to the exchequer was administered by a further reduction of Rs 743 crore in terms of accumulated depreciation. The value of these companies was thus reduced from Rs 3,103 crore to Rs 2,360 crore. As a result, private bidders would acquire 51 per cent of the equity of distribution companies by paying only Rs 481 crore for the vast network, real estate, and monopoly business with a revenue potential of over Rs 7,000 crore per annum.

'Business valuation' relates the value of an asset to the present value of expected future cash flows. It expresses the present value of a business as a function of its future cash-earning capacity. The future cash flow streams are discounted to the present value at an appropriate discount rate. Obviously, the valuation done on this basis cannot be further reduced by accumulated depreciation of the past as that is irrelevant to the net present value of future cash streams. Significantly too, the benefit of reduction in capital costs will not flow to consumers. The Regulatory Commission had hiked the consumer tariff by a hefty 22 per cent in May 2001, and one of the components of this tariff was the capital cost. Though the capital cost has been substantially reduced under the Transfer Scheme, consumer tariffs will remain unaltered.

Whichever way you look at it, public assets of more than Rs 1,000 crore seem to be vanishing between the Commission's order and Delhi government's notification. The public exchequer is also set to lose another Rs 743 crore to private companies in the guise of accumulated depreciation. Will all this happen with impunity or will any of the statutory authorities prevent it?

POSTSCRIPT

The huge reduction in the valuation of public assets evidently led to windfall gains for select private entities, for whom some of the bidding conditions were also relaxed after the bids had been received. By wrongly deducting the accumulated depreciation from the valuation determined through the business valuation model, an undue gain of Rs 743 crore was provided to the private distribution companies. In addition, a significant proportion of valuable public assets, including works in progress, was not taken into account while computing the total value of assets to be transferred to the private entities. Moreover, the manner in which the valuation was undertaken lacked transparency, as the details of valuation and the methodology adopted were never made public— they remained with the consultants whose manner of selection and appointment was also questioned by the CAG.

The author had pointed out these flaws repeatedly during the process of privatisation. As such, the government clearly had the opportunity to address these issues in a responsible manner. However, it went ahead without much caution or due diligence, only to be told later by the CAG[1] that it had caused a loss of about Rs 3,500 crore to the public exchequer by ignoring the valuation of certain assets. The CAG has also asserted that a surplus of over Rs 4,100 crore could have been earned by the state-owned DVB over a period of five years, if comparable conditions had been provided. This report of CAG was considered by the Public Accounts Committee (PAC) of the Delhi Legislative Assembly. While endorsing the said findings of CAG, the PAC[2] recommended an investigation by the Central Bureau of Investigation (CBI) into the alleged role of officers in conducting these transactions. So far, neither has any investigation been initiated nor has anyone been held accountable in any manner.

[1] Report of the Comptroller and Auditor General (CAG) on Government of NCT of Delhi (2004).

[2] Report of the Public Accounts Committee (PAC) of the Delhi Legislative Assembly on privatisation of electricity distribution in Delhi (2006).

28   Do Away with Monopolies*

Several pieces published by me in 2002 highlighted the pitfalls of the Delhi model of power reforms. Sadly though, these pieces have been more than vindicated. Unprecedented in recent memory, the otherwise business-like Delhiites came out on the streets to compel the Delhi government to roll back the tariff hike in July 2005.

People's will prevailed and any residual notions about the success of power reforms in Delhi were buried. Diehard supporters of these 'reforms' continue to underscore some marginal gains that represent slow incremental growth. They seem out of sync with a resurgent India.

Reducing losses from 51 per cent to 43 per cent over a period of three years cannot count for much, by any standards. Remember, transmission and distribution (T&D) losses of 40 per cent mean that while consuming 60 units, you also pay for 40 units lost, thus paying 66 per cent extra.

Recurrent tariff revisions, inadequate quality improvement, and alleged overbilling have offended the people at large, and rightly so. What ails the Delhi model? First and foremost, the Delhi model rests on conversion of state monopolies into private monopolies.

An international expert refers to such monopolies as an invention of the devil. Political dictatorships and economic monopolies

* Originally published in *The Times of India*, 6 October 2005.

disempower the citizen; they violate fundamental rights; they can never succeed.

Moreover, the Electricity Act, 2003, entitles consumers to choose from among competing suppliers of electricity, and mandates distribution companies (discoms) to provide 'open access' to their wires for transmitting electricity on payment of regulated wheeling charges.

Competition and choice must be introduced as early as possible. Second, the regulatory commission plays a pivotal role in consumer protection. All states have set up three-member commissions as per law. In Delhi, however, the Regulatory Commission had a chairman but no members for five years. Now it has two members but no chairman.

The person chosen to be the first chairman had no experience in law and finance; his skills were primarily technical. The results were, therefore, predictable. Third, the Regulatory Commission was bound by law to prescribe the standards of performance and to require defaulting Discoms to pay compensation to consumers.

Providing guaranteed profits without any service obligations is totally unacceptable. Unfortunately, the mandatory provisions of law have been followed in their breach, thanks to the Regulatory Commission. That the state government watched in silence is of equal concern.

If the bottled water you buy turns out to be adulterated, you can claim compensation. But not so for electricity supply in Delhi where the licensees are not constrained by any checks or balances. In the absence of a civilised remedy, the citizens simply took to the streets.

Fourth, Delhi citizens are crying foul that their bills have ballooned. Discoms, however, say that their losses have declined only by about 8 per cent in three years. So where has all the additional money recovered from consumers gone? Has the Regulatory Commission any clue as to who is making false claims?

Fifth, the Comptroller and Auditor General has flagged several grave irregularities that led to undue gains for the Discoms. It is also an admitted fact that the terms of privatisation were negotiated in favour of chosen single bidders even after their bids were rejected.

Implicit in the deal was a recurrent rise in tariffs, which was indeed predicted. This has compromised the credibility of the entire reform process in the public mind. Sixth, none of the principal players, including the consultants, had any experience or domain knowledge pertaining to successful privatisation of electricity distribution.

Nor did they do the necessary homework required for this complex task. Their approach was rather cavalier and entirely at the expense of citizens. Seventh, reforms are meant for the people; they need to be people-friendly or else they would fail. Initially, people welcomed private Discoms because the incumbent Delhi Vidyut Board (DVB) was anathema.

But after three years of privatisation, Delhi's citizens have revealed their mind in no uncertain terms. Their frustration cannot be overlooked. This episode is an example of poorly designed reforms, leading inevitably to accusations of mala fides or incompetence.

Either way, they distract attention from the core issue of how best to move forward. Privatisation in Orissa was carried out in 1997. It is generally regarded as having been a failure that scared away others. The Delhi episode could also hurt power reforms all over again.

Governance by trial and error imposes a heavy toll on credibility of reforms. We cannot afford to fail; the world is watching India. Even at this stage, the government can take measures to protect the future. First, consumer choice should be introduced immediately through open access to the distribution networks. Second, tariffs should be frozen for five years, except for adjustments to reflect changes in fuel price; discoms should earn their profits by reducing T&D losses. Third, performance standards should be laid down and enforced for consumer protection. Fourth, an eminent judge should head the Regulatory Commission for restoring its credibility. The Delhi government and its citizens can live happily thereafter, with true Bhagidari.

POSTSCRIPT

As pointed out earlier, privatisation of electricity distribution companies in Delhi has, quite predictably, produced sub-optimal outcomes as the governance model and industry structure were patently flawed. The taxpayers have lost several thousand crores of rupees by the transfer of valuable public assets at distress prices in a manner that lacked transparency and fair play.

The private companies are able to get guaranteed returns of a high order even as their quality of supply remains unsatisfactory. Compared to the erstwhile state-owned DVB, their services are certainly better. But compared to private distribution companies in Mumbai, Ahmedabad, and Surat, their quality of supply and performance standards have been much poorer and so are their T&D losses. Consumer tariffs of the private companies have also risen by about 50 per cent (between 2001–02 and 2007–08) as compared to DVB tariffs.

Widespread overcharging of consumers through manipulated meters is a proven malpractice. Power outages are not uncommon, especially during the summer months. Despite the mandatory provisions of the Electricity Act, 2003, open access has not been introduced for enabling bulk consumers to buy from competing suppliers. No one should have expected any better from private monopolies. That the Government of Delhi should have actively enabled these sub-optimal outcomes suggests failures of governance coupled with lack of accountability.

V
At the Crossroads

29 Infrastructure at Crossroads[*]

Although the economic liberalisation of the 1990s unleashed the growth potential of the Indian economy, its infrastructure sectors have remained shackled. The contrast presented by an unprecedented growth in manufacturing and services as compared to the dismal performance of the infrastructure sectors tells a story of inadequate reforms in policies and institutions that will continue to cast their spell in the years to come. The public sector controls most of the physical infrastructure in India. Together with inadequate spending, the inefficiency of the public sector has contributed to the infrastructure deficit. Attempts to induct private investment have been faint-hearted, and have typically led to sub-optimal outcomes encumbered with undue exploitation of the user and the public exchequer. The issue is whether the public sector will be able to improve its delivery, and whether private investment will play an important role in meeting the infrastructure needs of the Indian economy as it resumes its rapid growth trajectory after the interregnum caused by the global economic slowdown.

The infrastructure deficit could well become a binding constraint on India's high growth trajectory. During the Tenth Five Year Plan

* Originally published in Shankar Acharya and Rakesh Mohan (eds), 2010, *India's Economy—Performance and Challenges: Essays in Honour of Montek Singh Ahluwalia*, New Delhi: Oxford University Press, pp. 245–84.

(2002–07), about 5 per cent of gross domestic product (GDP) was invested in infrastructure (see Figure 29.1) compared to over 9 per cent in China and other East Asian economies. To bridge this gap, the Eleventh Five Year Plan (2007–12) assigns a high priority to infrastructure and envisages a total investment of about Rs 20,562 billion (US$ 514 billion)[1] as against an investment of about Rs 8,715 billion (US$ 218 billion) in the Tenth Plan, a jump of 2.4 times that will increase the share of infrastructure to 9 per cent of GDP by the terminal year of the Eleventh Plan. Though the anticipated investment in infrastructure during 2007–08 has risen to about 6 per cent of GDP, the target of 9 per cent represents a long haul. More so, because private investment is expected to rise from about Rs 1,722 billion in the Tenth Plan to Rs 6,196 billion in the Eleventh Plan, or an increase of 3.6 times. The challenges presented by such a quantum jump in private investment are enormous, especially since they require the commercial orientation of the policy instruments and a transparent and effective regulatory regime.

This essay attempts an overview of the key infrastructure sectors. It deals with the state of each of the major infrastructure sectors and the role played by the public sector. It also analyses the nature and extent of private participation, and examines some specific instances from the standpoint of governance and economic justification. The conclusions point heavily towards the need for improved governance.

POWER

The most important of all infrastructure sectors is power. From education and health to manufacturing and services, nothing can function efficiently without a reliable and affordable supply of power. Yet, this is one sector which has not been able to keep pace with the growth of the economy in the post-1991 period of liberalisation. For example, the shortage of electricity during peak hours has increased from 12.2 per cent in the first year of the Tenth Plan (2002–03) to 16.6 per cent

---

[1] The conversion rate used for this essay is Rs 40 = US$ 1.

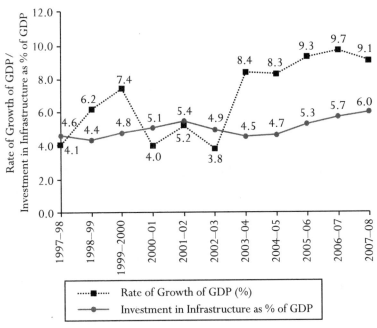

FIGURE 29.1   Investment in Infrastructure

Source: Planning Commission.

by the first year of the Eleventh Plan (2007–08). The commercial losses of power utilities have also increased from Rs 214 billion in 2002–03 to Rs 288 billion in 2006–07 (see Figure 29.2). The target of adding 41,110 MW of generating capacity during the Tenth Plan period fell short by 48 per cent and only 21,080 MW was added. The electricity industry has continued to be almost entirely in the public sector. About 88 per cent of the generating capacity and virtually all of transmission assets are in the public sector, while distribution is controlled by state-owned monopolies, except in Orissa, Delhi, Mumbai, Ahmedabad, and Surat, where these have been replaced by private monopolies.

The monopoly of state utilities has, in fact, been the most significant factor that has constrained the growth of the power sector. The incumbents have prevented any meaningful reform, and efforts to attract private investment have yielded little result. Of the total power produced, over 30 per cent vanishes in transmission and

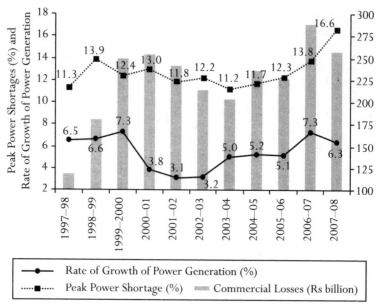

FIGURE 29.2   Power Deficit

Sources: Planning Commission, Central Electricity Authority, and Economic Surveys of Finance Ministry.

distribution (T&D) losses, much of which is plain theft. Besides raising consumer tariffs, this has also created strong vested interests that have erected barriers to reforms. Uneconomic tariffs for agriculture and household segments have only compounded the problems. Significant central assistance has been provided to the states under the Accelerated Power Development and Reform Programme (APDRP), but its design has not been able to incentivise any significant improvement in the performance of state utilities.

In the absence of a credible market, the power utilities continue to represent the 'single buyer' model, which implies that a producer of power can only sell to these utilities. Since most of these utilities are not perceived as creditworthy, private investment during the past decade has fallen far short of expectations. As a result, much of the capacity addition continues to take place in the public sector where losses can be transferred to the exchequer. Be it public investment or private, every additional MW of generating capacity created means an annual loss of about Rs 10 million for the power utilities, which suggests structural distortions in the sector as a whole.

By way of reform, several states have unbundled their state electricity boards (SEBs) into generation, transmission, and distribution companies respectively on the pattern followed in developed countries. However, they have perpetuated an industry structure based on an interconnected chain of monopolies that nullifies the basic purpose of unbundling, which is to introduce competition in the generation and supply of electricity. As a result, unbundling has failed to produce the expected outcomes. In the case of privatisation of electricity distribution in Orissa (1998) and Delhi (2002), the substitution of public monopolies by private monopolies has denied the gains associated with competition in terms of reduction in prices and improvement in the quality of services, as witnessed in India's telecom sector after it was opened to competition or when power utilities were required to provide open access in countries like the UK.

Private Investment in the Power Sector

Private investment in the power sector has been elusive for about two decades of economic liberalisation in India. Scores of private investors had lined up in the mid-1990s to set up generating stations as independent power producers (IPPs). On offer were typically negotiated deals with fairly high tariffs. Given the shortage of power and the prevailing mood in favour of economic liberalisation, there was considerable support for these deals, which also included projects based on naphtha, a highly uneconomic fuel for power generation. The motto of the day was 'costly power is better than no power'. However, most of these deals remained stillborn for want of payment security since the sole purchasers of power were the loss-making SEBs. To kickstart the process of investment, the Central Government agreed to extend sovereign counter-guarantees in support of state guarantees to eight IPPs for protection against payment default by the respective SEBs.

The Dabhol Power Company (DPC) of Enron was the first IPP to receive a sovereign counter-guarantee for its power purchase agreement (PPA) with the Maharashtra SEB. The project was cleared by the Central Electricity Authority and recommended by the Ministry of Power to the Ministry of Finance, which extended a counter-guarantee, albeit conditional and restricted in scope. During construction, the PPA was rescinded by the Maharashtra SEB in 1997 since the tariff was regarded as unaffordable by a new government that had assumed office after the commencement of construction. However, it was restored a year later on renegotiated terms that did not reduce tariffs but allowed DPC to build a capacity of 2,184 MW as against the earlier commitment for 695 MW. When the IPP actually started delivering about 740 MW of power in May 1999, the tariffs were simply unaffordable for the SEB. The PPA was rescinded yet again and the project remained shut for over five years. The private promoters took recourse to international arbitration at London under the omnibus provisions of the Bilateral Investment Protection Agreements (BIPAs) that offered much greater compensation compared to the sovereign counter-guarantee. Following an out-of-court settlement, the project was bought over and completed by two Central Government undertakings, National Thermal Power Corporation (NTPC) and Gas Authority of India Ltd (GAIL). In the entire process, the Indian economy lost a few billion dollars in the form of an idling asset and the production foregone, besides the damage to investor sentiment.

While dealing with Enron, the Ministry of Finance got sensitised to the underlying issues in such deals and decided to scrutinise the PPAs of the remaining seven projects eligible for counter-guarantees. Four of these fell under the weight of their own contradictions at different stages of the process. The three that remained were subjected to renegotiation which led to a significant reduction in tariffs. This sanitisation helped in warding off impending 'Enrons', besides improving the terms of three projects that have since been producing power (about 225 MW each) for almost a decade. In sum, of the eight IPPs selected for sovereign guarantees, only three succeeded, of which one got commissioned without a counter-guarantee. In the meanwhile, many other sponsors failed in tying up the finances required for setting up their respective projects without sovereign guarantees. As a result, the private investment that actually materialised was a small fraction of what was expected or needed.

In the distribution segment, following the unbundling of the Orissa SEB with assistance from the World Bank, its four distribution companies were privatised in 1998. One of these was won by a foreign company that could not survive for long in the local environment, and eventually ceded its business to an official administrator. The remaining three are being operated by an Indian company which functions as a private monopoly. A decade after privatisation, T&D losses in Orissa continue to exceed 45 per cent. During the initial years, the state-owned trading company that supplied bulk power to the distribution companies accumulated huge losses as the latter were unable to pay, especially because the retail tariffs were inadequate for absorbing the high T&D losses. However, this was reversed following the enactment of the Electricity Act in 2003 when the surplus power in Orissa began to be sold to other states at exorbitant prices. This form of power trading has been widely questioned as it compels consumers of other states to subsidise the consumers in Orissa. This practice has also enabled the Orissa regulator to avoid any tariff revision or rationalisation while the T&D losses remain above 40 per cent. The lure of trading has also ensured that a majority of rural households in Orissa remain without access to electricity. The Orissa experiment can by no standards be regarded as successful.

The next round of privatisation occurred in Delhi which privatised its distribution companies in 2002. Though T&D losses have come down from 46 per cent to about 30 per cent in the five years that followed, the quality of supply has improved only marginally while tariffs have gone up significantly. By way of contrast, T&D losses in cities like Mumbai, Ahmedabad, and Surat—where the distribution companies are privately owned—are 10.8 per cent, 10.4 per cent, and 6 per cent, respectively. The distribution companies in Delhi continue to function as private monopolies with all their attendant ills.

The Comptroller and Auditor General as well as the Public Accounts Committee of the Delhi Legislative Assembly have found serious flaws in the process of privatisation, including undue gains of several billion rupees to the private monopolies at the expense of the exchequer. These deals are also facing judicial review. Nevertheless, the quality of services provided by the erstwhile Electricity Board has left such adverse memories that, despite the aforesaid drawbacks, a fairly large number of consumers continue to support this privatisation.

As a measure of reform, the government enacted the Electricity Act in 2003. The new law replicated the reform model followed in developed countries, and required all distribution companies to provide open access to their networks for enabling bulk consumers to buy from competing suppliers, thus creating competition in the generation and supply of electricity. Bulk consumers in the developed world have enjoyed such choice for several years now, beginning with the UK that introduced competition as far back as 1990. Open access has also been extended to household consumers in several cities of developed countries. For example, a household in London can choose from among 12 competing suppliers while continuing to use the network of the area distribution company for transmitting electricity. In contrast, barriers erected by incumbent monopolies have ensured that not a single consumer across India can exercise such choice even six years after the enactment of the Electricity Act. It could well be argued that if open access had been allowed, investors would have set up additional capacity for sale to bulk consumers, thus alleviating the power shortage. This was more than demonstrated in the case of the telecom sector where access to consumers has galvanised the flow of private investment.

The only visible impact of the new law is the growth in 'trading', which is often a synonym for selling bulk power, at over three times the cost of generation. In the absence of access to bulk consumers, all trading is restricted to the sale of bulk power to a handful of state-owned utilities which bear the impact of high prices either in the form of commercial losses or by passing the burden on to consumers through an increase in the average tariffs. During 2008–09, about

46 billion units were traded at an average price of Rs 6.4 per unit. The total amount paid for this traded power was about Rs 300 billion, which constituted about 20 per cent of the total power purchase cost of all distribution companies and about 8 per cent of power in terms of volume. As a result, commercial losses of distribution utilities have increased from Rs 271 billion in 2006–07 to about Rs 526 billion in 2008–09.

While the government and the people at large are generally sensitive to profiteering in any essential service, this exploitation in the form of 'trading' is somehow continuing since its impact on the consumer is being diffused through the utilities. These transactions have also flourished because the governments of power-surplus states have created barriers that compel deficit states to buy at high prices. Of late, some power-deficit states have responded by imposing restrictions on 'export' of electricity in order to contain shortages and minimise high-cost imports. In effect, a common national market guaranteed by the Constitution of India for all goods and services does not seem to exist for electricity. As the volumes of such trading grow, they will only add to distortions in the power sector while the entrenched beneficiaries may become increasingly difficult to dislodge.

The persistent shortage of electricity has prompted some private players to set up capacity in the hope of making quick returns through 'trading' with state-owned utilities. They expect the utilities to buy at high prices in order to ward off popular unrest arising from outages. This arrangement eminently suits the 'merchant producers' who cannot hope to recover such high prices from direct sales to bulk consumers. It also suits the utilities as their monopoly remains unchallenged. However, as a consequence, the average consumer tariffs of utilities will rise, but mainly for the benefit of private producers who would exploit a regulated industry through the back door. There seems little prospect of a real market in the generation and supply of electricity as long as producers and traders of electricity must sell to a handful of state-owned utilities. In the absence of access to creditworthy consumers in the market, prospective investors will continue to hesitate in making investments. Conversely, consumers will continue to be deprived of access to competing suppliers of electricity that could help in alleviating shortages and improving the quality of supply.

A closer look at the roll-out of Ultra Mega Power Projects (UMPPs) of 4,000 MW each also raises some issues. Of the four projects bid out so far, two are based on imported coal while the other two will use domestic coal to be procured from dedicated mines. In particular, the dedicated coal mines offer possibilities of rent-seeking through a post-bid diversion of coal since its cost is significantly lower than the administered price prevailing in the market. In the case of one of the UMPPs, the diversion of coal has already been allowed by the government, causing an unsuccessful bidder to challenge the same in a court of law. Apparently, the bid process and project structure of UMPPs was such that only a few Indian corporates were able to participate, even though some foreign companies had an enormous interest in the Indian power sector. This has led to criticism by some that the project structure itself was tweaked towards this end. That the same bidder won three of the four UMPPs can only add to these doubts. In any case, it would be interesting to watch these projects unfold, especially as there are hardly any examples of such 4,000 MW power projects elsewhere in the world.

The power sector in India continues to be a maze of political economy issues. The incumbent state utilities, government-owned corporations, and a handful of private corporates seem to perpetuate well-entrenched interests that wield significant influence over policy-making. Thus, the anarchy in India's power sector will continue to be a drag on its growth prospects for several years to come. Setting the power sector in order would constitute one of the toughest challenges for the new government that assumed office in May 2009.

HIGHWAYS

The highways sector in India has suffered from prolonged neglect. The network of national highways extends over 70,548 km and carries about 40 per cent of the total traffic. Of these, about 12,053 km (that is, 17 per cent) has been four-laned so far, 37,646 km is two-laned, and the remaining 20,849 km is single-laned. The total length of expressways across India is only 183 km. State highways cover a length of 1,37,000 km, of which 71 per cent are single-laned roads while the rest are two-laned, barring some small sections of four-laned roads. A large programme of investment is necessary for augmenting this network to sustain a growing economy like India.

The highway sector got a boost in 1998 when the government imposed a cess on motor fuels, which provides about Rs 140 billion per annum, one-half of which is reserved for national highways. This resource, though substantial, was nevertheless inadequate for funding a national programme of reasonable proportions. In fact, these funds were meant to leverage private investment in national highways through a framework of public–private partnership (PPP) that was approved by the Union Cabinet in 1997. Indifferent to the potential of private participation for expanding the highways programme, the National Highways Authority of India (NHAI) continued with its construction contracts—and that too of an over-engineered variety. For example, NHAI routinely built four-lane highways even where the projected traffic justified only two-lane highways for the next decade. As a result, the programme costs increased significantly with a corresponding reduction in coverage.

During the Ninth Plan, a programme for four-laning 7,498 km of two-lane national highways was initiated, mostly for the Golden Quadrilateral connecting Delhi, Mumbai, Chennai, and Kolkata. Four-laning of 6,647 km on the east–west and north–south axis was added during the Tenth Plan (2002–07). While these two programmes were to upgrade 14,145 km, the remaining 56,403 km continued to be neglected. The investment target for the Tenth Plan period was Rs 740 billion. However, the achievement was only Rs 528 billion (at 2006–07 prices). In the case of state roads, the target and achievement were Rs 726 billion and Rs 677 billion, respectively. Private investment in the highway sector as a whole was only Rs 70 billion.

Highway projects in the public sector have typically suffered from large time and cost overruns. A comparison between the projects undertaken by NHAI and the PPP projects suggests that NHAI has taken more than twice the time compared to PPP projects, and the cost to the exchequer has been more than double as compared to the contracted costs at the time of project commencement. The structure of construction contracts is prone to corruption, and the in-house collection of tolls suffers from significant pilferage. NHAI has also attracted criticism from the World Bank in connection with some of its Bank-financed projects. To reverse these trends and to augment the resources for investment, the Committee on Infrastructure (chaired by the Prime Minister) approved a Rs 2,200 billion plan in 2005 which relied on the PPP approach for over 75 per cent of the investment. However, the award of PPP projects has met with stiff resistance from NHAI and, as a result, only a modest beginning has been made so far. It should be evident that without a substantive reform of this sector (including the restructuring of NHAI and state agencies), Indian roads will continue to be unsafe and congested.

Private Investment in the Road Sector

The first significant PPP project in the road sector was the NOIDA Toll Bridge, which was awarded by the local authority through negotiations in 1997. The same company later secured several other state highway projects on similar negotiated terms, which compromised user interests and the public exchequer. The sub-optimal outcomes of these projects have been described subsequently in a section on the conflict of interests.

Much to its credit, the Central Government has adhered to open competitive bidding for the award of all its highway projects. However, the first eight concessions for the construction of bypasses in the mid-1990s were poorly structured. Though the Cabinet subsequently approved a policy framework in 1997, it was not until 2002 that the first toll road project was awarded for a 94-km section (Jaipur–Kishangarh) on the Delhi–Mumbai highway. The six-laning of this two-lane highway was completed in a record 23 months and it operates as one of the best highways in the country. Though some other projects awarded thereafter have performed reasonably well, resistance from

NHAI has delayed a large programme that was otherwise feasible. As a result, less than 20 per cent of the year-to-year targets set by the government for the award of PPP projects have been achieved during the past three years.

Some of the significant deficiencies that have affected PPP projects of NHAI include over-engineering, delay in land acquisition, and a change in scope subsequent to the award of projects. For example, the Delhi–Gurgaon expressway was delayed by over two years due to significant changes in the scope of work, such as the addition of elevated road sections. These deficiencies could well entitle the concessionaires to seek large compensation from NHAI because in PPP projects, the compensation is not confined to additional costs alone; it is also payable for foregone profits. The Delhi–Gurgaon expressway also illustrates the phenomenon of over-engineering in the form of eight-lane flyovers crossing two-lane roads whereas flyovers/underpasses are usually built for smaller roads. In other words, there are eight-lane flyovers on this expressway instead of two-lane flyovers/underpasses on the state roads crossing the expressway.

The Central Government has since adopted a Model Concession Agreement (MCA) and other standardised documents for awarding PPP projects. However, there has been resistance to the process of standardisation. Much of the opposition has come from incumbent officials as also from construction contractors who prefer the earlier arrangements. Nevertheless, a large PPP programme of about Rs 1,750 billion is on the anvil. The way its delivery takes place will determine the evolution of the highways sector.

AIRPORTS

Air transport has undergone a significant transformation over the last five years. Air traffic was projected at 259 million passengers for the Tenth Plan (2002–07). However, it turned out to be 24 per cent higher, at 321 million. The opening of the skies to competition brought in new airlines, better services, and lower fares in the backdrop of a robust growth of the economy. This has, indeed, been a success story that has demonstrated the role of competition in accelerating investment and improving air services. However, public investment in airport infrastructure was only Rs 38 billion against a target of Rs 67 billion (at 2006–07 prices) for the Tenth Plan. Thus, traffic increased by 24 per cent as compared to the anticipated level while investment fell short by 43 per cent of the investment target.

Despite the phenomenal rise in air traffic and revenue generation, reform in terms of a better organisation and management of public sector airports by the Airports Authority of India (AAI) has remained dormant. In particular, there has been a consensus for a long time on the need to separate the Air Traffic Control (ATC) functions from AAI so that they can be upgraded and professionalised. However, AAI regards the ATC as a cash cow for funding its construction projects, and has managed to stall its separation for the past several years.

A large programme of public sector investment was initiated in the latter part of the Tenth Plan. However, this focused more on high-cost terminal buildings and less on airside development such as the improvement of runways, taxiways, and navigation services. AAI is also building very large and expensive terminal buildings at Kolkata and Chennai, although this could have been done through private investment on the lines of the four other metro airports. The construction of opulent and over-engineered terminal buildings that go well beyond the standards prevailing in developed countries borders on wasteful use of public funds, especially since 25 out of the 35 non-metro airports currently make losses. This clearly reflects an 'expenditure culture' that would add significantly to the losses of AAI. The lack of commercial orientation and accountability that characterise the functioning of AAI is bound to push up airport charges in an environment where airlines are trying to reduce costs in order to attract more traffic.

Private Investment in Airport Sector

The record of attracting private investment in airports is quite impressive. Four of India's largest airports—Delhi, Mumbai, Bengaluru, and Hyderabad—have all been transferred to private sector entities through long-term concessions. Prior to these concessions, each of these airports was congested and inefficient. Thus, these new airports will be a welcome change for airport users who can soon hope to see world-class standards—these are already visible at the Bengaluru and Hyderabad airports. However, some issues that are likely to emerge as implementation unfolds are identified subsequently.

In the case of Bengaluru and Hyderabad, even though these airports fell in the jurisdiction of the Central Government, the respective state governments conducted a sub-optimal process for selection of project sponsors without adequately defining the terms of the proposed contracts. Subsequently, the respective concession agreements were drafted and negotiated between the Central Government and the selected project sponsors. As a result, these were in the nature of negotiated contracts which were not entirely fair or balanced from the perspective of the government or the users. First, there was no mechanism for controlling the capital and operational costs of these airports. Thus, project sponsors were free to gold-plate costs and pass them on to the users through tariffs to be determined on a 'cost plus' basis. Second, almost all the airport income was allocated to the project sponsors. While competitive bidding ensured that 46 per cent of the airport revenues in the case of Delhi airport and 38 per cent in the case of Mumbai airport were to be paid to AAI, the negotiated sharing in the case of Hyderabad and Bengaluru was fixed at 4 per cent.

User charges for the Hyderabad airport have since been revised on an ad hoc basis, and passengers who were only paying Rs 200 per trip in the past, are now paying Rs 575—a three-fold increase. User charges for Bengaluru have also been increased from Rs 200 to Rs 460. In the case of international passengers, the fee has been hiked from Rs 200 to Rs 1,000 and Rs 1,070 per passenger for Hyderabad and Bengaluru airports, respectively. A significant rise in user charges, lack of oversight on costs, a low revenue share of 4 per cent, and other negotiated terms remain issues of concern. It can, however, be argued that the greenfield airports at Hyderabad and Bengaluru cannot be compared with the brownfield projects at Delhi and Mumbai. In the absence of competitive bidding, however, the loss to users and the public exchequer is anybody's guess.

The new airports at Bengaluru and Hyderabad are located at a distance of about 40 km from their respective cities. On their completion, the government closed the existing airports to provide monopoly to the new airports even though the existing airports had a fairly large capacity that could have continued to provide low-cost services to domestic air travellers. The numerous examples of cities having more than one airport did not persuade the authorities to allow two competing airports to function. As was to be expected, the closure of the existing airports led to a great deal of public criticism, besides several court cases. Thus, the time and costs associated with commuting to the new airports, coupled with a sharp increase in user charges for the recovery of uncapped costs, has been a double jeopardy for users. As for the respective concessionaires, they will benefit not only from airport business but also from the large real estate potential of these airports.

Concessions for the Delhi and Mumbai airports were finalised and bid out after much debate within the government. The initial proposal to allow the construction of large commercial buildings on about 250 acres of airport land was dropped after a close scrutiny of applicable laws which only permit hotels and passenger-oriented real estate development. This helped retain the focus on airport business that could otherwise have been relegated to a lower priority in view of the astronomical returns on the commercial use of real estate. However, the concession agreements for Delhi and Mumbai airports are flawed in respect of costs and user charges. There seems to be no provision for review and the control of capital and operational costs which have a direct bearing on user charges. Recent reports[2] suggest that the actual capital costs for the redevelopment of the Delhi airport are more than twice the costs estimated at the time of award, and Mumbai may follow suit. While the airport terminals may certainly come up

[2] *The Mint*, 25 September 2010.

as impressive structures, they would lead to significantly higher user charges based on a 'cost plus' regime.

In the case of Delhi and Mumbai airports, there is also an effort to undermine AAI's share in the revenues of these airports. For example, the concessionaire of Delhi airport has been allowed to take large deposits against future rentals of real estate, and also exclude these inflows from the computation of revenue sharing with AAI. Similarly, an additional airport development fee of Rs 200 per domestic passenger and Rs 1,300 per international passenger, which was recently levied on users of the Delhi airport, has also been excluded from revenue sharing. In the case of Mumbai also, a similar additional fee of Rs 100 for domestic passengers and Rs 600 for international passengers has been levied. Such redefining of revenues would evidently provide unanticipated gains to the concessionaire while causing a corresponding loss to the exchequer in a manner that was not contemplated in the contract. In effect, this could be viewed as a post-bid capital subsidy.

The award process for Delhi and Mumbai airports was also controversial. The international consultants of the government had pre-qualified and shortlisted only two of the bidders who would have got one airport each. However, their evaluation was questioned, reviewed, and ultimately discarded. The government subsequently lowered the bar in order to shortlist four bidders for each airport, and the bids that finally succeeded were very competitive. This modified selection process was generally regarded as transparent and also upheld by the Supreme Court.

The Delhi and Mumbai airports were certainly very attractive from the perspective of investors across the world. However, foreign airport companies did not participate except through an equity stake of about 10 per cent in the respective consortia led by Indian companies. This minority stake was virtually a necessary condition for pre-qualifying Indian companies who had no airport-related experience of their own. The bid process may have looked more credible if some foreign companies had also participated as lead bidders. Their absence raises the issue of whether the terms of these projects were so structured that only domestic players having the confidence of managing the 'environment' would participate. The fact that the concessionaires have been able to secure some post-bid concessions may only add to the discomfort of potential foreign investors. Though some of the post-bid concessions have been justified as responses to the global financial meltdown, their integration into the contractual and tariff framework would pose a serious challenge.

PORTS

Congestion at ports increased substantially during the Tenth Plan (2002–07) period since demand escalated and capacity addition fell far short of the target. The projection for cargo movement during the terminal year of the Tenth Plan was 565 MMT while the actual performance was 636 MMT, which meant an increase of 13 per cent over what was anticipated. While cargo movement increased by 214 MMT during the Tenth Plan—that is, from 422 MMT in the first year to 636 MMT in the last year—the capacity addition was only 161 MMT, implying that capacity addition fell short of the growth in cargo.

The Central Government owns and operates 12 major ports, which accounted for 80 per cent of the cargo handled during the Ninth Five Year Plan. This predominant role of the Central Government is in sharp contrast to the practice in developed countries where ports are typically controlled by local or city governments. Moreover, the organisational structure of major ports, which are run through Port Trusts, is generally regarded as antiquated. There have been several moves in the past towards their corporatisation. However, concerns arising out of industrial relations have prevented any worthwhile reform of these Trusts despite the economy's growing reliance on the growth and competitiveness of exports. Judged by efficiency parameters such as 'turn-around' time and productivity, Indian ports continue to fare poorly compared to Western and East Asian ports.

Efforts to promote capacity addition through private participation have made limited headway owing to resistance from the incumbents.

As a result, the plan to build 54 new terminals through PPP has progressed slowly. The low productivity of major ports, coupled with their inability to expand, has enhanced the opportunities for state governments to enable new private ports such as Gangavaram, Mundhra, and Pipavav to come up. Nevertheless, the major ports handled 72 per cent of the total cargo in 2007–08. Since the bulk of the capacity continues to rest with the major ports, there is urgent need for their reform and restructuring.

Private Investment in the Port Sector

Private investment in the port sector has not only been limited but also flawed. The first PPP project was a container terminal at Jawaharlal Nehru Port Trust (JNPT) in Mumbai. Bids were invited on the basis of the highest royalty per container that the concessionaire would pay to the Port Trust over a 30-year period, while tariffs would be determined periodically by a statutory regulator. The selected concessionaire got its first tariff order in November 2000 on the basis of low traffic projections. This meant that the costs were spread over a low number of containers, thus leading to a high tariff per unit. Through what appeared to be a regulatory capture, the concessionaire succeeded in stalling any tariff revision for four years despite an increase of about 85 per cent in its traffic. As a result, it managed to recover a return of over 100 per cent per annum on its equity. The irony of this episode was that though the rate of return was meant to be regulated, the actual profits were so high that this terminal came to be regarded as one of the most profitable port ventures anywhere in the world.

The concession for the container terminal at Tuticorin Port was also similarly flawed. The concessionaire got a high ad hoc tariff fixed in the first year (1999), and then adopted various means—including judicial intervention—to prevent any downward revision. In 2006, the tariff determined by the regulator was about one-half of what was actually being charged. Through court interventions, this downward revision has been stalled yet again, and the concessionaire is thus able to recover annual returns of over 100 per cent on its equity. Despite these examples, the Port Trusts for Mumbai, Chennai, New Mangalore, and JN Port have awarded four more terminals based on a similar framework.

All the concessions awarded prior to 2008 stipulated that tariff shall be determined by the regulator on a 'cost plus' basis which would include a specified return on capital. On the other hand, a bidder was free to win a concession by offering a revenue share that could exceed the regulated return. The arithmetic simply did not add up as several successful bidders offered a revenue share that was far greater than their regulated return, and implied recurring losses which could only be made up through manipulation and regulatory capture. For example, in the case of a container terminal at Chennai, the concessionaire will pay 46 per cent of its total revenues to the Port Trust, and this will be well beyond the regulated return on its equity. Conceptually, a 'rate of return' regulation is not compatible with bidding for revenue share. Thus, the tariff structure was flawed in any case. This has inevitably led to the subversion of the entire tariff regime through fraudulent practices. After several years of debate and much opposition from entrenched interests, the government has finally decided to substitute 'cost plus' tariffs by pre-determined tariff caps to be notified prior to bidding.

Private participation has made little headway in major ports. Against a target of 44 terminals, not more than seven have been awarded during the four years from 2005–06 to 2008–09. The Port Trusts as well as the existing concessionaires are all too willing to postpone expansion in order to minimise competition and enhance monopoly rents. In the process, the major ports remain synonymous with inefficiency, congestion, and high costs. A great deal of policy-related work has been accomplished in the recent years, and it is possible to turn the situation around by improving the organisational structure and functioning of Port Trusts as well as by rolling out PPP projects based on standardised documents and processes. The stage is set for a quantum jump but much will depend on how the new government elected in May 2009 plays out its role.

RAILWAYS

India is, perhaps, the only major economy which has not yet corporatised its railways; neither has it permitted the privatisation of any segment of rail operations. Thus, the Indian Railways function as a government monopoly with little incentive for efficiency and cost reduction. As a result, its organisational structure, management practices, and technology base have not been modernised. Over time, the railways have steadily lost their market share to the road sector, despite the comparative cost and environmental advantages that it possesses. The length of railway routes in India is almost equal to that of China. However, the railways in China carry about 47 per cent of the total goods traffic while the Indian Railways carry just about 36 per cent.

The expansion and modernisation of the Indian Railways over the decades was slow for want of resources, and also because its political economy did not encourage a commercial outlook. Populist pressures perpetuated uneconomic passenger fares, coupled with excessive freight charges that resulted in goods traffic getting diverted to roads, leaving little surplus for augmentation of the railway network and rolling stock. Thus, much of the railway system suffers from neglect and old technology. In fact, the 'Report of an Expert Group on Restructuring of Railways' (2001) brought out that the railways were heading towards bankruptcy. However, this trend was reversed through a reorientation in commercial policies, aided substantially by the robust growth of the Indian economy. As a result, the railways have earned significant profits during the Tenth Plan (2002–07) period. However, many of these policies are reversible and do not provide an assurance of sustained improvement since the organisational structure and management practices of the railways have virtually remained unchanged.

The projections for freight and passenger traffic in the terminal year of the Tenth Plan were 624 MT and 5,885 million, respectively. However, the actuals were 728 MT and 6,352 million, implying an increase of 17 per cent and 8 per cent, respectively, as compared to

the anticipated volumes. Such rapid growth would require accelerated capacity addition and modernisation whereas the railways do not
seem equipped for meeting these challenges. This is likely to impose
a heavy burden on the Indian economy. The challenges of getting a
monolithic government-owned structure to reinvent itself can hardly
be overstated; yet, change is inevitable as its time has come. When and
how this change is initiated and managed will determine the future of
Indian Railways and its impact on the economy.

Private Investment in Railways

The railways have shown little inclination for private participation in
upgrading their infrastructure. They have only allowed some private
investment for augmenting their own asset base. For example, the
railways have enabled some private entities to finance and build railway tracks for improving connectivity to their respective destinations.
However, the operation of these tracks remains with the railways.
These initiatives have been restricted in scope and represent rent-
seeking in return for certain preferential services to the investors.

The only successful PPP initiative undertaken so far in the railways
sector is the introduction of competing private players in the ownership and operation of container trains (2006). There were serious
problems in introducing this scheme because the railways-owned Container Corporation (CONCOR) was the incumbent monopoly that
obstructed any competition. Though this scheme has shown encouraging results since its introduction, several associated measures, such
as setting up of common logistic parks, have been withheld in order
to perpetuate CONCOR's primacy. In February 2008, the Minister
of Railways announced several PPP initiatives aggregating Rs 1,000
billion. However, there is little evidence to suggest that the railway
bureaucracy is inclined to move meaningfully in that direction.

The railways spent three years trying to attract private investment
for production, supply, and maintenance of about 2,000 state-of-
the-art diesel and electric locomotives under a long-term contract.
Incumbent resistance accompanied by manipulation of the contract

structure led to acrimonious debates within the government until a transparent structure was evolved. Just when international firms were ready with their bids, the process was aborted in a knee-jerk reaction prior to the general elections of 2009, when it was decided to set up these units as government factories. It can only be hoped that the obviously inefficient option of setting up government factories will not be pursued after the elections in May 2009.[3]

The Dedicated Freight Corridor (DFC)—a flagship project approved in 2007 for connecting Delhi–Mumbai and Ludhiana–Kolkata, with an estimated investment of about Rs 500 billion—was to be implemented partly through an independent government company and partly through PPP. Over 2007–09, the option of private participation has been abandoned, and the DFC Corporation is functioning like an extended arm of the Ministry of Railways, virtually oblivious of any commercial principles. The progress so far suggests that this prestigious project will also suffer from the usual cost and time overruns. Moreover, it remains to be seen how the railways will finance DFC, and several other ambitious projects, without recourse to private participation.

Metro Rail

Urban transport has suffered from continued neglect over several decades, both in terms of inadequate investments as well as lack of planning. While cities have been largely confined to inadequate bus services, the smaller towns usually lack any form of public transport. Of late, the capital-intensive mass rapid transport system (metro rail) is emerging as the preferred mode for the larger cities.

Besides a small section in Kolkata, the only metro rail project currently in operation is the Delhi Metro which represents an extraordinary example of project management in the public sector. However, it is quite unique in character and may not, therefore, be amenable

---

[3] The Government reversed its decision to set up government-owned manufacturing plants and commenced the process of private participation in 2010.

to replication. Its CEO is an outstanding project manager who has been given an unprecedented tenure of over 10 years, unknown to any other public sector entity in India. The equity of this company is held equally by the Central Government and the Government of Delhi, which means that neither exercises direct control in the way it is normally exercised over other public enterprises, thus giving unparalleled freedom and authority to the CEO. Above all, the first phase of Delhi Metro has received about Rs 100 billion from the government at an average interest of less than 1.2 per cent per annum. It has also received large tax waivers that imply substantial subsidies. In addition, about half of its operational costs are being met out of sale or leasing of real estate which has been generously provided by the government.

The Bangalore Metro project, which is being constructed on the lines of the Delhi Metro, is likely to demonstrate some of the inadequacies of the Delhi model. To begin with, its construction is already delayed as, among other reasons, its CEO has been changed frequently and the successive incumbents have not been able to demonstrate the project management skills that enabled the Delhi Metro to succeed. The Bangalore Metro also lacks real estate in proportions similar to the Delhi Metro. The interference of the state government and other local authorities is yet another issue. As time and cost overruns surface, the project is likely to face serious difficulties in financing its capital costs. When completed, operational losses may pose a constant challenge, especially because neither the Central Government nor the state government may be willing to bail it out as neither would own and control the project. The whole approach does not seem to be well thought out in terms of the governance model as well as its financial viability. Yet, Kolkata and Chennai also plan to go the same way as Bangalore.

On the other hand, Mumbai and Hyderabad have adopted the PPP model and their respective concessions have since been awarded. However, the Hyderabad Metro project has hit an air pocket as the selected project sponsor was charged with corporate fraud that led to a take-over by another firm. It appears that the project may have to undergo a fresh bid process.[4] Since all projects other than Delhi are yet to be implemented, the sector as a whole is in transition and much will depend on how these projects unfold.

TELECOM

The telecom sector in India is regarded as a success story of international dimensions. In the midst of 'command and control' operation of other infrastructure sectors, telecom went into a different trajectory and delivered truly extraordinary outcomes. Telephone density increased from 4.29 per cent (that is, 4.29 per cent of Indians owned phones) in the first year of the Tenth Plan (2002–03) to 18.31 per cent by the first year of the Eleventh Plan (2007–08), reflecting an annual growth rate of about 34 per cent, which is comparable with China. This phenomenal growth can be attributed mainly to the introduction of competition coupled with quantum improvements in technology, both of which have led to the rapid expansion of networks and a reduction in tariffs that are among the lowest in the world. It is a success story that deserves to be celebrated.

Investments in the public sector actually declined from Rs 888 billion in the Ninth Plan to Rs 452 billion (at 2006–07 prices) in the Tenth Plan. Though the target for public investment during the Tenth Plan was Rs 836 billion, actual investment fell short by 46 per cent. However, the total investment expanded to Rs 996 billion, largely because of a sharp increase in private investment that rose from about Rs 148 billion in the Ninth Plan to Rs 537 billion in the Tenth Plan. The expansion in telecom services was clearly driven by the private sector, with the public sector contributing only about one-fourth of the growth.

From the political economy perspective, the telecom revolution occurred not because governance in this sector was materially different from others, but because mobile telephony was virtually non-existent

[4] The bid process of the Hyderabad Metro Rail Project was annulled and the project was successfully bid out again and awarded in August 2010.

in the public sector, and the space that the private sector entered was virtually vacant and thus did not present much resistance from the incumbents. Moreover, the investment and technology required for a major roll out of mobile services seemed beyond the reach of public sector enterprises. Around the same time, interested corporates managed to exercise sufficient influence over the policymakers to enable private investment in an orderly manner. The opening up of the telecom sector has demonstrated yet again that competition can enable large inflows of investment at lower costs and with improved services. The expansion of this sector was clearly a boon for the Indian economy and the ordinary consumer.

Private Investment in Telecom Sector

Private investment in the telecom sector during the Tenth Plan period was about Rs 553 billion (at 2006–07 prices), and it exceeded the public sector investment of Rs 452 billion by over 20 per cent. In contrast, no other sector could attract even one-third of its total investment from the private sector. Much of the private investment was in mobile telephony which began in 1994 with the auctioning of licences that remained still-born until their migration to a revenue share arrangement in 1999. The competition that followed has led to a phenomenal growth in this sector. Nevertheless, the award of additional licences, and the allocation of spectrum and preferential treatment to certain licensees have created serious controversies from time to time.

In one particular case, an influential corporate used its fixed phone licence, which had an element of limited mobility in it for 'last mile connectivity' (that is, instead of laying cables to each household, a firm could, from a central location in a colony, connect each house in a wireless manner), to provide full-fledged mobile services across the country. This was subsequently regularised in 2003 on payment of an ad hoc penalty which was a fraction of what the company gained by way of market capitalisation through providing these, till then, illegal services. This was seen as a major concession that helped it to pole-vault over its other competitors. More recently, the award of licences in 2008 at a price discovered through an auction way back in 2001 (when the mobile market was hardly developed) has attracted a great deal of controversy. Critics have argued that, considering the market value of these licences, the public exchequer has lost about Rs 500 billion, which is equal to 1 per cent of India's GDP. In sum, the role of the Central Government as a licensor of service providers, who are otherwise regulated by an independent regulator, has often led to criticism. Nevertheless, competition in this sector has been quite intense and, as a result, the consumer and the economy have benefited significantly from private participation.

CONFLICTS OF INTEREST IN
PRIVATE PARTICIPATION

The mindset within the government is still in the public sector mould of the past when virtually everything was controlled by the state, and when issues could be resolved at any stage of a project without much concern about the winners or losers, since they all belonged to the state. However, private participation belongs to a different world which revolves around contracts between public and private entities that may have adversarial interests since the primary goal of the state is welfare while that of a private entity is profit. Thus, it is critical that the respective roles of public and private entities dealing with PPP contracts are clearly defined and adequately enforced. In the process, conflicts of interest must be carefully identified and addressed in order to avoid sub-optimal and unintended outcomes. There is abundant evidence to establish that the lack of clarity on this account has resulted in several flawed projects, causing substantial losses to the exchequer and the user.

A classic example of the conflict of interest emerges from a case study of the NOIDA Toll Bridge (see www.infrastructure.gov.in). A private infrastructure company—which began as an adviser to the project authority (NOIDA)—not only helped itself with the concession but also doubled up as a lender to the concessionaire. Its project was over-designed on the basis of unrealistic traffic projections, which justified high-cost structures. Moreover, the concession agreement did not stipulate any oversight by the authority in respect of costs. Above all, a return of 20 per cent was guaranteed for the entire capital cost, and even the project debt qualified for the same return. This unusual arbitrage of about 9 per cent on the entire project debt—which constituted 70 per cent of the project cost—raised the equity returns to over 40 per cent. Further, all losses or foregone profits were to be added every year to the capital costs and also qualify for a similar return of 20 per cent, which would be recovered by extension of the concession period. As events unfolded, the project was completed in February 2001 at a cost of Rs 4 billion; however, by March 2006, the concessionaire had revised the capital cost to Rs 9.5 billion by adding its foregone profits, all of which would qualify for a guaranteed return of 20 per cent. It has also claimed an extended concession period of 70 years as against the 30-year period specified in the concession agreement. In addition, it has also demanded real estate rights over large tracts of land.

In the case of NOIDA Toll Bridge, combining the role of adviser, concessionaire, and lender into one entity was a predictable recipe for disaster. Yet, it passed off without challenge in any forum of governance. Similar examples include the Baroda–Halol highway (Gujarat), the Ahmedabad–Mehsana highway (Gujarat), the Chennai–Puducherry highway (Tamil Nadu), and about 1,053 km of state highways in Rajasthan. This malady is by no means confined to road projects. The same approach has also been followed for the Tirupur water supply project in Tamil Nadu.

The company that played the roles of adviser, investor, and lender in the aforementioned projects also has a virtual monopoly over advisory assignments across sectors. Its modus operandi is to form joint venture (JV) companies with government entities where its equity stake of 50 per cent enables these JV companies to function as private entities while the remaining 50 per cent, which is held by the government, creates a misguided perception that these are government companies entitled to a preferential treatment. Several central ministries and state governments have formed such JVs for structuring and awarding their respective PPP projects. One particular subsidiary of this company has advisory assignments for over 500 PPP projects of different public entities. Performing advisory services on the one hand, and acting as an investor or lender on the other hand, constitutes an obvious conflict of interest that would never be allowed in developed countries.

There are other examples of such conflicts of interest. A leading law firm was the government's adviser in a large airport project. It was also the legal adviser of one of the prospective bidders. Soon after the project was awarded, it became the legal adviser of the selected bidder and tendered advice on matters connected with the same project. In the case of some other advisory firms where prospective investors own a significant equity stake, a conflict of interest arises when such investors bid for a project where the firm was an adviser.

Sub-optimal outcomes arising out of conflicts of interest have gone unchecked due to a weak contractual framework as well as the lack of awareness and resolve among policymakers to identify and contain the actual or potential damage to the exchequer as well as to the users of infrastructure projects. In 2005, to lend transparency to the entire architecture for PPP projects, the Central Government decided to streamline and standardise the processes and documents relating to infrastructure projects. Many such processes and documents have since been applied; however, they tend to attract much resistance from the beneficiaries of past practices. As the dust settles down, this new framework should bring about a significant improvement in the quality and cost of infrastructure.

CONFLICT WITH EXTERNAL DEVELOPMENT AGENCIES

A significant part of the funding for infrastructure projects over the past few decades has come from the World Bank, Asian Development Bank, and bilateral donors. All of them typically lend to the government, which implies that the projects would have to be in the public sector. From the lenders' perspective, this helps enlarge their portfolios and enables safer delivery of projects. On the Indian side, the incumbent ministries tend to welcome such external assistance as it helps them to retain these projects in the command and control mode.

Though external development agencies support private participation as a measure of reform, their loan portfolios are yet to reflect their policy prescriptions. In the meanwhile, several projects that could well have attracted private participation have actually been implemented in the public sector, which is often the subject matter of sharp criticism by these very agencies. In that sense, loans from international development agencies for financing public sector projects are not necessarily in the best interests of the economy and, in any case, do not conform to their own philosophical approach.

CONCLUSIONS

The description of the state of infrastructure in India presents a dismal picture. Yet, it offers enormous opportunities as well as hope. While the government has taken several reform initiatives, under-investment and inadequate governance seem to have perpetuated the infrastructure deficit. On the one hand, public sector inefficiencies and malfunctioning continue to act as significant constraints; on the other hand, private participation faces stiff incumbent resistance and is also prone to crony capitalism. The failures of governance have not only prevented the public sector from performing well, they have also vitiated private investment. In either case, the key problem areas lie in governance, which seems to be in transition. Some of the conclusions that emerge from this essay are summarised as follows.

Rise in Infrastructure Deficit

This essay demonstrates that the robust growth of the economy has created a greater demand for infrastructure services than that anticipated in the Tenth Plan (2002–07). In the power, telecom, highways, railways, airports, and ports sectors, the growth in actual demand outpaced all projections. On the other hand, the public sector could not meet the investment targets even though they were based on a lower projection of demand. As a result, the infrastructure deficit increased over the years—except in the case of telecom where the markets seem to have bridged the demand–supply gap with considerable ease.

No assessment has been made of the loss of employment, productivity, incomes, and quality of life on account of endemic power cuts and the persistent congestion on roads, railways, ports, and airports. No doubt it would be significant by any measure. Moreover, the investment foregone in infrastructure sectors could be of the order of about 4 per cent of GDP per annum, which by itself would have added significantly to economic growth. Though the government has made plans to ramp up investment in infrastructure to a level of 9 per cent of GDP by the terminal year of the Eleventh Plan (that is, 2011–12), it has not been able to initiate the required measures owing to constraints arising from the political economy of infrastructure sectors. As a result, the infrastructure deficit is unlikely to decline over the Eleventh Plan period.

Expenditure Culture

The wasteful use of public resources for building high-cost infrastructure projects is often driven by the desire of incumbents to preside over ever-larger contracts. For example, NHAI managed to corner almost all of the sectoral budgetary allocations for the development of the 14,500 km of national highways under its control, at an average cost exceeding Rs 60 million per km, while the state governments received an average of Rs 0.4 million per km per annum for the upkeep of the remaining 52,000 km of national highways. There is no doubt that the national highways entrusted to the state governments carry lower volumes of traffic. However, this discrimination in the allocation of resources primarily arose from the impulse to award larger construction contracts through NHAI even though its projects were most suited for private participation, which would actually have released public funds for the remaining network.

The DFC of Railways was eminently suited for private participation. However, the incumbents would much rather award construction contracts and spend the money themselves. The airport sector is no different. AAI is building large and expensive terminal buildings that would outshine their counterparts in developed countries. That these expensive structures would add to its losses and also push up user charges seems inevitable.

This story of over-engineering, excessive capital expenditure, cost overruns, endemic delays, and lack of financial viability is common across sectors. As a result, scarce resources are often misallocated and misutilised, leading to low productivity of investments in public sector projects. Viewed from this perspective, a shift to private participation would logically eliminate cost and time overruns, enhance investment, promote viable projects, ensure improved performance standards, and minimise leakages in revenue collection—this, of course, assumes that a fair and transparent framework would be enforced.

Lack of Accountability

The public sector has not only been inefficient in terms of time, costs, and quality of service, but has also virtually ceased to be accountable. While non-performance or the failure to achieve the agreed outcomes is rarely penalised, only departures from rule-based procedures and processes seem to get questioned. As a result, the focus is on adherence to procedures rather than on outcomes. For example, when only 21,080 MW of generating capacity was added during the Tenth Plan (2002–07) as against a target of 41,110 MW, no one was held accountable. In fact, targets in the power sector have been missed, Plan after Plan, and year after year. Similarly, in the case of national highways, the investment was only Rs 528 billion against a target of Rs 740 billion while its projects typically took about twice the time as compared to the contracted period, and the cost to the exchequer was more than double the contracted price. This story repeats itself virtually in all the sectors and projects. The hope that public sector entities would improve their performance significantly seems somewhat remote, and thus their enhanced targets for the Eleventh Plan (2007–12) may not be realised.

Failures of Regulation

The independent regulation of infrastructure services is crucial as they often constitute natural monopolies. For example, users of airport and port services have often been subjected to higher tariffs for want of credible regulation. On the other hand, users of toll roads are comparatively better off as much of the regulation is enshrined in the concession agreement itself. In telecom, competition alone has ensured consumer protection. As a matter of principle, where competition is possible, it provides the best guarantee for promoting user interests albeit with a light-handed regulation for ensuring that competition is free and fair. Where natural monopolies reside—such as in roads, ports, airports, and electricity distribution networks—the regulator must ensure non-discriminatory access, quality of service, and reasonable tariffs.

The failure of credible regulation is yet another facet of India's deficient infrastructure. Six years after the enactment of the Electricity Act, 2003, the regulatory commissions have singularly failed to introduce competition with a view to enabling the choice of suppliers to the consumers of electricity. This appalling failure is matched by the regulatory capture in the case of ports where regulated entities have managed to extract annual returns of over 100 per cent on their equity. The regulators in India have been created by statute, and are supposedly independent of government control. However, the near-complete absence of accountability, compounded by the lack of any overarching philosophy of regulation, does not bode well for the orderly growth of infrastructure in India. The Eleventh Five Year Plan spells out a strategy for the reform of regulation. However, its implementation in the face of opposition from the incumbents remains to be seen.

Contract Raj

The current scenario in infrastructure has many similarities with the 'licence raj' of the pre-1990s, when goods and services were either produced by the public sector through its 'commanding heights' or by private sector beneficiaries of 'licences' in a controlled market. While public sector inefficiencies and corruption took their own toll on the economy, the licensing of private enterprises became synonymous with crony capitalism, which kept competition at bay.

The abolition of licensing in the early 1990s changed all that, and the economy moved from the 'Hindu rate of growth' of 3–4 per cent to a robust 8–9 per cent per annum, which is what gave India a brand new global image.

The unprecedented growth in manufacturing and services has established the capacity and entrepreneurship of India, as a result of which it has begun to be recognised as an emerging economic superpower. However, in this whole process of transformation, not enough attention was paid to reform of the infrastructure sectors which have continued to remain predominantly in the public sector. From a political economy perspective, the loss of power and patronage following the de-licensing of industry has shifted the focus of politicians and bureaucrats to exercising control over infrastructure.

Incumbent public sector players have steadily expanded their operations, and remain unwilling to cede control in favour of private participation on a level playing field. For example, the move to invite private investment in the generation of electricity during the mid-1990s was restricted to the sale of power to state utilities under the 'single buyer' model. If only the producers had been allowed to sell directly to bulk consumers, a market would have evolved, as it did in developed countries, leading to the alleviation of power shortages. In contrast, when the technology revolution in mobile telephony persuaded the government to enable private entities to access telecom consumers directly, competition took over and eliminated all shortages.

In the highways sector, a beginning was made in the late 1990s to invite private participation in toll roads since budgetary allocations were inadequate. However, this was put on the backburner when the cess on motor fuels provided the resources for funding construction contracts exceeding Rs 750 billion. It has taken a great deal of time and effort to wean away the NHAI from its construction contracts with a view to awarding PPP projects that constitute the bulk of the Rs 2,200 billion five-year plan for the development of national highways. In the ports sector, the Port Trusts have successfully stalled any worthwhile private competition, thus preserving their monopoly rents. Thus, the plan to award about 50 PPP concessions for port terminals has progressed rather slowly. Other than the four metro airports that have gone the PPP way, construction contracts have expanded manifold at all the other airports. The railways have also remained wedded to their archaic form of contracts and, despite repeated policy pronouncements, PPP projects have made little headway. The metro rail systems for Bengaluru, Kolkata, and Chennai have also chosen the construction contract route, thus substituting potential private investment by budgetary expenditure. The story goes on.

Not only does the 'contract raj' enable the award of lucrative contracts, it also creates a fiefdom in the operation and control of infrastructure services. The structure of these public sector contracts typically leans towards a discretionary framework which is amenable to patronage and corruption that inevitably lead to time and cost overruns. Like the 'licence raj', it is extracting huge rents from the economy and thus affecting its growth. Just as the incumbent bureaucrats and other beneficiaries were not supportive of the de-licensing of industries, it is entirely predictable that they will not facilitate the liberalisation of the infrastructure sectors. The lessons of the transformation of the 1990s can well be applied to the reform of infrastructure sectors, if only the political will can be sufficiently demonstrated. In summary, the key issues lie in governance, and they directly relate to the opening up of these sectors to competitive private investment based on a level playing field and credible regulation. This is not to say that the role of public sector can be minimised. However, it should be required to compete with the private sector and provide improved services. Moreover, it should be enabled to undertake only viable projects that are self-sustaining, except in remote and rural areas where budgetary support may have to continue.

Rent-seeking

In the initial phase of private participation in different sectors, project sponsors were not selected through a competitive and transparent process. The project agreements were typically drafted by the respective beneficiaries, and then cursorily negotiated with the respective public entities. Several power projects and toll roads were built on this basis. As pressures grew in favour of a more transparent process of selection, project sponsors in the case of Hyderabad and Bengaluru airports were selected by the respective state governments through a sub-optimal form of competitive bidding, as the terms of the respective concession agreements were drafted and negotiated only after the concessionaires were selected. In the case of Delhi and Mumbai airports, the bidding process evolved further, and the concession agreements were finalised prior to bidding; however, they enabled the selected bidders to gold-plate costs and pass them on to the users, and also to find imaginative ways to redefine the contracts so as to reduce the amount to be shared with the government.

The malady of rent-seeking and crony capitalism runs across sectors. Concessions for port terminals have provided spectacular returns owing to faulty contracts, poor enforcement, and regulatory capture. Several highway concessions have created opportunities for rent-seeking in different ways. The way state-owned electricity distribution companies in Delhi were transferred to private entities has attracted the scathing criticism of audit authorities. The recent award of telecom licences at artificially low prices has attracted allegations of undue gains of about Rs 500 billion to favoured recipients. The examples can go on. Such deals are often justified in the name of expediency and development. At times, users suffering from the fatigue of low-quality public sector services even welcome the change. However, the key issue is whether development and growth can be ensured even while protecting user interests and the public exchequer in a reasonable manner. Private sector efficiency can be no justification for user exploitation since, sooner or later, it will cause a popular backlash and make it increasingly difficult for the government to engage in private participation. For example, seven years after privatisation of electricity distribution, Delhi has not been able to push for a similar approach in water distribution. Nor has a single state government shown any inclination so far to emulate the Delhi model of electricity reform.

The terms of pre-qualification documents and project contracts are often designed in a manner that compel the more credible and transparent bidders, especially creditworthy international companies, to stay away and leave the field to bidders who have greater capacity to 'manage' the political and bureaucratic environment. A close scrutiny of the outcomes in several cases establishes the intent and impact of such contracts. In summary, infrastructure projects are open to capture that inevitably leads to high-cost services. The consequent criticism and popular backlash have the potential of discrediting private investment and slowing down the growth of infrastructure. In a manner of speaking, it is necessary to protect infrastructure from the capitalists. The policy and contractual framework evolved by the government in recent years, coupled with increasing awareness, offers the hope of a bulwark against crony capitalism, and the promise of better services at economic costs. It could, perhaps, be a great experiment if it succeeds.

The Coalition Era

The coalition era, in which infrastructure portfolios are often divided like spoils, compounds the problems of governance and offers little elbow room for reform. For the same reason, crony capitalism and rent-seeking can continue wherever private participation is involved. Though the government has taken several well-meaning steps to facilitate competitive private participation in some infrastructure sectors, these are yet to stabilise. Much will depend on the ability of the Indian state to manage the political economy of infrastructure services. Following the comparatively strong mandate given to the Central Government after the elections of May 2009, there is hope that infrastructure sectors would see a quantum jump.

The Brighter Side

Much of this essay analyses the causes of lower-than-anticipated progress and also suggests the possible courses of action. On balance, however, it must be recognised that, in comparative terms, there has been significant progress during the past few years. First and foremost, the economy grew at a pace of about 9 per cent over a five-year period ending 2007–08. This was accompanied by a major push in infrastructure sectors. As compared to an investment of 4.5 per cent of GDP in the infrastructure sectors during 2003–04, the investment in 2007–08 increased to 6 per cent of GDP. Two world-class airports (at Bengaluru and Hyderabad) were commissioned in 2008, while those in Delhi and Mumbai are undergoing a complete makeover and will soon be able to compete with the best in the world. The growth in air travel has been around 20 per cent per annum in recent years. The growth in telecom has been truly remarkable, with tariffs among the lowest in the world. Private participation and expansion in the port sector have finally come to stay. And the railway sector has witnessed an unprecedented turnaround. Thus, there has been much progress all round. More important, the policies as well as the enabling framework that have evolved during recent years have the potential of achieving a very robust growth in infrastructure sectors as well as in the economy, the global financial crisis notwithstanding.

Despite the governance-related problems discussed in this essay, India's infrastructure is poised to make rapid strides in the years ahead. The pressure to improve infrastructure services is enormous, and the investment opportunities it offers will certainly result in much expansion. Thus, the next decade will see infrastructure sectors as the sunrise segments of the Indian economy. However, the central issue is whether India will build a high-cost and comparatively inefficient infrastructure comprising an initial spurt in growth which then later suffers from stagnation (like the phenomenon of middle income economies), or will it succeed in building a competitive and cost-efficient infrastructure that will not only be self-sustaining but also reinforce economic growth as a whole. The issues raised in this essay have no simple solutions as they involve complex processes of governance, with conflicting viewpoints, ideologies, and interests. However, there is no doubt that it is important to identify the issues and intensify the debate.

Governance is the Key

It is evident that the Indian economy is faced with a poorly performing public sector, which is characterised by inefficiency, lack of accountability, and corruption. Given its track record, simply allocating more funds will not yield the required infrastructure, in terms of both quantity and quality. Though the Eleventh Plan (2007–12) allocates twice the amount as compared to the Tenth Plan (2002–07), it is doubtful whether public sector entities will be able to deliver at that level. Even if they do, the remaining gap is rather large and thus private participation is inevitable. While recognising that there is no choice but to rely on PPPs for incremental investment, it is critical to weed out crony capitalism which must be regarded as the worst enemy of free and fair markets. If otherwise, the economy will carry the burden of an inefficient and corrupt public sector, on the one hand, and manipulated PPP projects, on the other hand, implying the worst of both worlds.

Over the past five years, the Central Government has created the policy framework and processes that can deliver PPP projects with speed and efficiency in a manner that would be regarded as fair, transparent, and competitive. However, vested interests within and outside the government pose a persistent opposition to the implementation of these policies. In particular, those responsible for implementing the new policies and fostering competition are also in charge of existing public sector operations. Unless there is a separation of the policy and oversight role from that of the ownership and operation of public sector entities, policy implementation will continue to suffer. It is of the utmost importance that the focus of top policymakers shifts to creating an enabling environment that will ensure a quick and diligent implementation of the policy framework that is already in place.

To conclude, there is an overwhelming demand for better infrastructure services, and their supply is possible through a better delivery of public sector projects and the greater role of private participation. Users and consumers across sectors have displayed their willingness to pay reasonable user charges if only better services are delivered. However, the state seems to have lost its ability to manage its public sector efficiently. Nor is it able to let in private participation on competitive terms. Thus, the key issue is the reform of governance in infrastructure sectors. To the researcher, this essay has attempted to offer insights into the processes and evolution of governance in infrastructure sectors; for the practitioner, it identifies the issues that need to be resolved for the Indian economy to grow at a robust pace.

POSTSCRIPT

This essay was published in 2010 and its conclusions continue to be relevant. It seems too early to write a postscript. However, the controversy relating to the award of telecom licences in 2008, which was estimated to have caused a loss of about Rs 500 billion to the exchequer, erupted into a major crisis for the Central Government after the Comptroller and Auditor General submitted its report to the Parliament. The report established wrong-doing on several counts and pegged the losses at a much higher level. This led to a furore in the Parliament and its functioning was stalled for several days, forcing the Telecom Minister to resign, followed by his arrest along with several private players and the then Telecom Secretary. Criminal proceedings are underway while the Supreme Court has assumed an oversight on the proceedings. This could well turn out to be a case of extraordinary corruption and rent-seeking in several ways. It also illustrates the demise of accountability in the civil services which acted as mute spectators—at times enablers—in the perpetuation of several frauds comprising this episode.

Epilogue
The Road Ahead

There is general agreement that the prevailing infrastructure deficit is one of the most critical constraints that must be overcome if growth is to forge ahead. The earlier chapters in this volume have focussed on a number of fundamental issues—institutional, legal, and financial—that shackle infrastructure development and which can only be resolved if the debate on reform is intensified and the support for change and reform enlarged.

Inflated costs, inadequate quantity, and poor quality of infrastructure assets are often a reflection of poor governance. Inadequacies in governance lead to a multiplicity of inefficiencies and also create room for corruption, which is increasingly being perceived as a major problem that must be addressed. This problem is common to projects in the public sector as well as in public–private partnerships (PPP), but it is particularly pressing in the latter category because the interface between the government and private entities naturally invites closer scrutiny. While lax treatment of a public sector service provider often passes off as an encouragement to inefficiency, the same behaviour towards a private sector provider invites suspicion of corruption. In either case, remedial action or any credible form of redressal seems to be wanting.

These considerations were reflected in recent developments where alleged scandals in telecom licencing, Commonwealth Games, the

Adarsh housing complex in Mumbai, land allotments in Karnataka, and so on, seem to have engulfed the entire nation in a heated debate in which the media, judiciary, Parliament, government, and political parties have all participated. As a result, the discourse on corruption has taken centre stage with several political leaders declaring their firm commitment to weeding out corruption from public life.

A notable development reflecting the concern with corruption was the declaration by the President of the ruling Congress Party, Smt. Sonia Gandhi, at the annual plenary session of the party held in December 2010, that her party would undertake effective measures to cleanse the system of corruption. These measures would include reform in the procurement of projects as well as in the allocation of natural resources. In pursuit of these announcements, the government has commenced extensive consultations with a view to identifying and implementing the requisite initiatives. It is time these matters are taken to their logical conclusion in order to restore public confidence and ensure some modicum of accountability in high political offices.

This chapter provides an overview of the nature of problems that the government faces and makes some suggestions for a way forward.

THE CONTEXT

The first four decades after independence witnessed the evolution of a strong and vibrant democracy in India. However, economic growth was accelerated only in the early 1990s when the 'licence raj' was dismantled as a relic of the socialist era. As part of economic liberalisation, industrial licensing was abolished; import tariffs were drastically reduced; and quantitative restrictions were eliminated. The stock markets were liberalised; controls on current account convertibility were removed; and foreign investments were encouraged. Within a span of two decades, India emerged as an economic powerhouse.

Reforms in Infrastructure

Much of the celebrated economic growth of the last two decades occurred due to the entrepreneurship that was unleashed by an open and competitive environment. This reflected cashing in on one-time gains from the removal of inefficient controls. However, for rapid growth to continue over an extended period, a modern and efficient infrastructure is crucial. Even in the 1990s, it was evident that the public sector did not have the resources for bridging the growing infrastructure deficit. This led to a plethora of policy announcements welcoming private investment, but with little success. The incumbent ministries were often seen as unwilling to let go of their fiefdoms and enable private entities to compete on a level playing field that would tend to diminish the possibilities of rent-seeking.

Serious problems can be discerned in every sector. For the past 18 years, capacity addition in the power sector has consistently fallen short of the targets by about half while the annual commercial losses of distribution companies have increased fifteen-fold compared to 1991–92. Though the pace of expansion in power capacity has improved in recent years, it continues to be well below the target. Moreover, the lack of progress in the distribution segment makes it difficult to believe that the power sector is on a viable track. The airports at Bengaluru, Hyderabad, Delhi, and Mumbai were developed through PPP, but further reform in this sector has been very slow. In the highways and port sectors, the award of PPP concessions has fallen short by over three quarters of their respective targets, year after year. The railway sector has seen the least reform. It continues to operate as a department-run enterprise with far too little economic or commercial motivation. These examples suggest that infrastructure reforms are incomplete and a great deal more needs to be done if performance is to be improved to a level that would sustain the growth target of 9 per cent per annum.

The Complexity of Infrastructure Reforms

Unshackling the entry of the private sector into manufacturing and services was certainly a bold departure from the past. However, far more challenging was the introduction of private participation in infrastructure. The latter is infinitely more complex because it relates to the delivery of public goods that are often monopolistic in character and traditionally provided by the government. Private entities cannot set up infrastructure projects on their own unless the government creates an enabling framework. This is far more complex than is normally anticipated.

The Barriers of Governance

Since the 1990s, the private sector has displayed a robust appetite for investment in infrastructure. Users have also displayed their willingness to pay a reasonable charge for improved services. The barrier that has stood between the matching of this demand with adequate supply is the governance of the infrastructure sector. In particular, the incumbent public entities have prevented competition and slowed down the roll-out of PPP concessions in order to preserve their turf. The key issue is when and how the conflicts of interest pervading the incumbent ministries will be overcome.

On several counts, India seems to have arrived. Investors across the globe want to partake in the opportunity that India offers. Its constitutional democracy based on the rule of law is among its greatest assets. It was gifted to this nation by some of the tallest men that history has known. Yet these undoubtedly positive factors are compromised by the fact that India is ranked high on various corruption indices. Though these indices are based on perceptions, most viewers are likely to conclude that they reflect an underlying reality. Reform of governance is, therefore, a critical issue. This is a subject by itself which goes well beyond the area of infrastructure, but the key governance issues relating to the infrastructure sector are outlined in the following sections.

PLAYERS CANNOT BE UMPIRES

For centuries, wise men have agreed that no man can be the judge of his own cause. Checks and balances need to be institutionalised as vital elements of good governance. Just as players cannot be umpires, a person having an interest in a cause cannot act as its arbiter. In the Western democracies, whenever conflicts of interest come to light, they are diligently eliminated and suitably penalised. A similar environment does not seem to have evolved in India. The success of reforms will be assured only if neutral umpires play a pivotal role.

Economic Liberalisation by Finance Ministry

The economic crisis of 1990 endowed the Finance Ministry with sufficient authority and opportunity to usher the celebrated reforms of the 1990s that may not have been normally acceptable to the incumbent ministries. The success of these reforms was in some measure an outcome of the fact that the umpire was different from the players. For example, industrial licensing was primarily the domain of the Industries Ministry, but the PMO and the Finance Ministry played a crucial role in demolition of the 'licence raj' in the early 1990s.

Telecom Reforms by PMO

The only infrastructure sector that has seen successful reform is telecom. The introduction of competition, coupled with a credible regime for interconnection among networks, led to a spectacular growth rate that was nearly the highest in the world. It also delivered user tariffs that are the lowest in the world. However, the reform strategy in the form of National Telecom Policy 1999 was devised by a Group of Ministers that managed to overcome the resistance from the Telecom Ministry with strong support from the Prime Minister's Office (PMO).

Role of the Committee on Infrastructure

The Committee on Infrastructure (CoI) was constituted in 2004 under the chairmanship of the Prime Minister. It provided a neutral platform that enabled an objective discourse on reform of the infrastructure sector, excluding the telecom and power sectors. An important outcome was the streamlining and standardisation of processes and documents that enhanced competition, ensured transparency, and reduced time and costs. As a result, India witnessed a large roll-out of PPP projects which have attracted unprecedented volumes of private investment. This has also received considerable recognition in India and abroad.

Players are Back as Umpires

With the closure of the first term of the Manmohan Singh Government in 2009, the Committee on Infrastructure lapsed too. It has since been replaced by the Cabinet Committee on Infrastructure (CCI) that functions like a normal committee of the Cabinet, where proposals are usually brought by the respective ministries. As a result, the initiative has reverted to the respective ministries. An illustration of the limitations of incumbent-led reforms is presented by the power sector where losses and shortages have only grown over the years.

Be it the economic liberalisation of the 1990s or the revolution in telephony or the CoI-led reforms, it appears that the reluctance of incumbent ministries had to be addressed by the Prime Minister either through the Finance Ministry or through various inter-ministerial fora. Where the ministries were left to their own devices, the outcomes were clearly sub-optimal. Yet the adoption of these obvious lessons would be constrained by the cares and compulsions of running a coalition government. Nevertheless, some way of resolving these problems would have to be found. Greater public awareness, coupled with a strong and committed leadership would also be necessary for restoring the fundamental principles of governance. A key institutional lesson is that the game cannot go on if players continue to act as umpires. Of course, the quality of players and umpires is also crucial.

ACCOUNTABILITY

It is self-evident that the absence of consequences often causes lax behaviour and wanton actions. It can lead to wrongful actions too. Most students would not study diligently if their job opportunities were not influenced by their grades. Farmers would toil much less if their crops were assured anyway. Factory workers would loiter if their output was not measured. Pilferage and corruption would flourish if delinquents went scot free. In all walks of life, progress occurs only if good behaviour is rewarded in a fair manner and bad behaviour is consistently punished. Unfortunately, over the years, this indisputable principle seems to have been lost sight of and accountability levels are far too low. Let us elaborate the different spheres where this is so.

Political Accountability

In Western democracies, persons holding high political office are not only held accountable, they also get penalised for their acts of omission and commission. In the US, for example, Illinois Governor Blagojevich was convicted for lying to Federal agencies and also removed from office in 2009. Similarly, Congressman Jefferson was sentenced to a 13-year jail term in 2009 after being convicted on bribery charges. In the UK, former MP David Chaytor was sentenced to 18 months of imprisonment in January 2011 for fraudulently claiming parliamentary expenses of £ 20,000.

In India, examples of fixing civil or criminal liability on persons holding high political office are conspicuous by their absence, notwith-standing the corruption that seems to pervade all walks of public life. For India to claim its rightful place among nations, this state of affairs would have to be altered with a sense of dedication and urgency.

The practice of evading accountability and circumventing the law has grown by leaps and bounds. The alleged scandal in the award of telecom licences in 2008 has brought these issues to the fore. The Report of the Comptroller and Auditor General (CAG), tabled in the Parliament in November 2010, has alleged that very large sums were lost to the exchequer because of under-pricing of spectrum allocation. The opposition parties were quick to seize this opportunity and created a storm that paralysed the entire winter session of the Parliament, be-sides sending the media into hysteria. Though the incumbent Telecom Minister did resign in this case, and has subsequently been arrested by the Central Bureau of Investigation (CBI), concern continues to be expressed that it may well take several years to fix individual liability, if at all.

In the past too, CAG reports have alleged several scams from time to time. For example, the CAG Report on the privatisation of electricity distribution alleged that the Delhi Government had doled out undue gains of several thousand crores of rupees to select private entities. This report was also endorsed by the Public Accounts Committee of the Delhi Legislative Assembly. Yet no one was ever brought to book.

Accountability of Civil Services

While much is written about political accountability, there is not enough focus on the accountability of the civil services. There is an all-pervading belief that the prevailing system allows little scope for judging merit and as a result, mediocre bureaucrats can easily rise to the top of the ladder simply by avoiding controversy. The preoccupation with avoiding controversy causes unwillingness to make difficult decisions which in turn leads to limited tangible results, but the resultant non-performance does not usually attract accountability. The net result of such an incentive structure is a signal that there is no need to perform.

Take the case of targets and achievements. The shortfall of about 50 per cent in the capacity addition target of the power sector for the Tenth Five Year Plan can be said to have caused considerable loss in growth and employment creation. The system is such that no one is held accountable even for such stark failures. Similar lack of accountability pervades the system in cases of repeated delays and cost overruns in implementing public sector projects. Each delay is explained but no one is held responsible.

In matters where decisions have to be taken under pressure from the political masters, the bureaucracy seems to have devised other means of avoiding accountability. By creating the committee system for decision-making, the officials have virtually absolved themselves of any direct responsibility. Though the committees are expected to debate issues, iron out differences and evolve consensus on matters of public interest, they sometimes tend to become tools for avoiding responsibility since a committee cannot be punished en masse.

In a culture where accountability is rarely fixed, bureaucrats often find it convenient to go along with their political masters even in cases that involve corrupt or unlawful acts. In all cases of wrong doing, it will be found that civil servants have either actively colluded or failed to speak up and looked the other way, thus acting as willing accomplices of corruption and wrongful deeds. Yet they seem to go unscathed. Consideration needs to be given to defining the action that civil servants should take when they perceive wrong doing, or should have perceived it. At the very least, they should be expected to place their reservations on record, not only on the files of their respective ministries, but also convey the same to the Cabinet Secretary.

The founding fathers of the Indian Constitution placed great reliance on the civil services. While advocating the constitutional provisions relating to civil services, Sardar Vallabhbhai Patel, in his address to the Constituent Assembly on 10 October 1949, said, 'You will not have a united India, if you do not have a good all India service which has the independence to speak out its mind ... The Constitution is meant to be worked by a ring of services which will keep the country intact.' Following these debates, the civil services were not only included in the Constitution, their independence was also guaranteed by providing constitutional safeguards against arbitrary penalties or removal. In addition, the Public Service Commissions were given a high constitutional status for ensuring free and fair recruitment in civil services.

The concept of permanent civil servants was borrowed from the Westminister model of governance that India chose to follow, as distinct from the appointment of top civil servants in the United States, who come and go with successive Presidents. The whole purpose was to create an independent civil services that would protect and promote the interests of the Republic of India. In retrospect, it does appear that the civil services have failed to perform their functions. If that be so, India might not need such a large and expensive civil services. It is time to rethink the role of the civil services and make them accountable for upholding the law and promoting the national interest. Failure to do so, whether through acts of commission or omission, must invoke stiff penalties, including possible imprisonment.

CONTRACT RAJ

The Licence Raj was characterised by excessive control and corruption, and its demolition led to the transformation of the Indian economy. The parallel of the erstwhile licence raj in the manufacturing sector is the 'contract raj' in the infrastructure sector where construction and operation of projects is governed by old-style conventional contracts which provide a great deal of control and discretion that tends to be synonymous with corruption and political clientelism.

Resistance to Reform in Contracting

A conventional contract implies measurement of all items of the construction works which are paid for on the basis of unit rates for each item. Additional quantities or new items can also be added during the course of construction. This inevitably leads to delays, collusion, and corruption, which in turn causes significant time and cost overruns. It also enables the oft-quoted contractor–engineer–politician nexus to flourish. By comparison, a turnkey contract transfers most of the construction risks to the contractor so as to ensure project completion without any time and cost overruns. While the turnkey approach is widely practised in the developed countries as well as in the private sector projects across countries, it remains a virtual outcast in the government departments in India.

It is interesting to note that although the Central Government had decided that the construction contracts for national highways and the dedicated freight corridor of Railways should follow the turnkey approach, which is also referred to as EPC (Engineering, Procurement and Construction), not a single turnkey contract has been awarded so far. In some cases, for example, the NHAI, the conventional 'item rate' contracts continue as before, but they are described as EPC contracts for public consumption.

PPP Concessions

A far superior mode of infrastructure provision is through the PPP approach where the construction, operation, and commercial risks are borne by a private entity, which is expected to provide the capital besides ushering in greater efficiencies and lower costs. The PPP approach also ensures optimal project selection and hence better allocation of scarce resources as compared to conventional contracts that are amenable to greater corruption and political cronyism. While the Central Government has adopted PPP as its preferred mode for the expansion of infrastructure sectors, and several PPP projects have also taken off, the roll-out of projects has been much slower than what was anticipated. Moreover, the award of PPP projects in the Central Government is based on standardised documents and processes that enable a speedy and transparent outcome. Yet, the progress in awarding concessions has consistently fallen short of the targets, as a result of which the infrastructure deficit has continued to persist.

The Commonwealth Games

The recently concluded Commonwealth Games in Delhi is yet another example where the failures of governance in ensuring the timely completion of the requisite facilities brought a great deal of embarrassment to the government. While the failings in this area are under investigation, some facts are worth noting. The only project which was completed well before the deadline was the Delhi airport which was developed through the PPP mode. The construction work for the Games Village was also completed in time through award of a turnkey contract that eliminated time and cost overruns. The oft-reported delays relating to the Village arose from the multiple contracts awarded for interior finishing which was not part of the turnkey contract. By contrast, all other project authorities resisted the PPP or even the turnkey approach and relied on the conventional contracts which inevitably suffered from time and cost overruns that have attracted enormous criticism.

Dismantling the Contract Raj

The Licence Raj was synonymous with command, control, patronage, rent-seeking, and corruption. Its demolition in the 1990s brought great improvement in the efficiency of the private sector. However, it should be a cause for concern that the focus of rent extraction may have shifted to the Contract Raj. Just as liberation from the Licence Raj unleashed entrepreneurship and growth in the manufacturing and services sectors, the next spurt of growth would require the dismantling of the Contract Raj that seems to be eating into the vitals of the Indian economy in the form of inadequate, inefficient, and costly infrastructure. Reform of the procurement of public works and services through competitive, fair, and transparent means would provide a quantum jump for inclusive growth.

Key Areas of Reform

The issues that have been discussed could be viewed as symptoms of a much larger malady. Yet conflicts of interest, lack of accountability, and the contract raj loom prominent in the governance of infrastructure. Resolving these would transform the sector. In addition, each segment of India's infrastructure has unique problems which stymie its resurgence. A brief summary follows, with particular attention to solutions.

POWER SECTOR

The mid-1990s witnessed over 100 foreign investors lining up to set up power generating stations. Not even 5 per cent succeeded, primarily because all power had to be sold to the State Electricity Boards (SEBs) that were generally regarded as bankrupt. The politicisation of SEBs over the years had led to unsustainable tariffs, weak managements, excessive pilferage, and rising losses. In 2003, the Central Government enacted the Electricity Act to create separate entities for generation, transmission, and distribution, respectively, with a view to enabling competition that would improve the services and reduce costs, besides accelerating the flow of investment. However, seven years have passed but competition remains conspicuous by its absence. The state governments have found ways to ensure that the supply of electricity to consumers remains a monopoly of the state-owned distribution companies.

It is evident that the unbundling of the SEBs has been pursued mechanically as an end in itself, though it was meant primarily as a means to enable competition. Despite the mandatory provisions of law, the incumbents have created barriers to the introduction of competition in supply to the consumers. To compound matters, the regulators have been manipulated by the producers and traders with a view to selling bulk electricity to the distribution companies at prices that are exorbitant by any standards. This has added significantly to the annual losses of distribution companies, which are likely to exceed Rs 60,000 crore in 2010–11—equal to about 1 per cent of GDP. According to the projections made by the Thirteenth Finance Commission, these losses would reach a level of Rs 1,16,000 crore in 2014–15.

Capacity addition in generation grew at a compounded annual growth rate (CAGR) of 3.11 per cent between 2000–01 and 2004–05. This increased to 4.56 per cent between 2004–05 and 2008–09, largely on account of the enabling framework created by the Electricity Act of 2003. However, this pace of acceleration in capacity addition is clearly inadequate for meeting the rising demand of a 9 per cent growth trajectory. As a result, peak shortages have increased from 11.3 per cent in 1997–98 to 13.3 per cent in 2009–10, despite the cumulative addition of about 79,000 MW of generation capacity during this period. Though the Act of 2003 is widely regarded as a piece of modern legislation that compares favourably with the first world, the actual governance of the power sector in India remains akin to the third world.

Opening up of Distribution Holds the Key

The rapid rise in the losses of distribution companies cannot be sustained for long and it may soon reach a flash point. For the past several years, much of these losses have been financed by bank loans that have been guaranteed by the respective state governments. Evidently, the banks cannot go on lending for much longer except at their own peril. As the realisation of bankruptcy of the distribution companies sinks in, investment in generation will tend to flee for want of creditworthy buyers. Unless the market is opened up and producers are allowed to sell directly to the bulk consumers of electricity, the current chain of monopolies will only perpetuate the existing shortages and profiteering.

Electricity being a concurrent subject under the Constitution, the Central Government has an overriding jurisdiction, and it needs to exert itself with a sense of urgency. Though several measures are needed to restore a semblance of order in the power sector, the single most critical reform is the introduction of open access and competition in the supply of electricity to consumers. This alone can turn around the power sector within a comparatively short period of time. The Central Government needs to adopt a proactive role in persuading the states to follow the law on open access. At the very least, the states that fail to respond should cease to get the ongoing central assistance which is linked to power reforms. In particular, the Central Government should earmark part of its discretionary quota of power allocation for direct sale to bulk consumers. Of about 5,000 MW at its disposal, at least 2,500 MW could be earmarked for this purpose. Such a move will not only galvanise the power sector, it would also demonstrate the Centre's commitment to power reforms.

Many would argue that open access and competition are no panacea for the deep-rooted ills of the power sector, and that they can at best bring marginal improvements. The key issue here is to recognise the difference between a monopoly supply chain and an open competitive market. The former is characterised by shortages, inefficiencies, and higher costs while the latter signifies greater efficiencies, lower costs, and an equilibrium between demand and supply. Moreover, an open market would enable and encourage more investment and production, while the monopoly structure would continue to discourage the investors who remain hostage to the incumbent monopolies for their off-take and payments.

It is indeed a paradox that the enormous success of the demolition of 'licence raj' in the manufacturing sector has failed to persuade policymakers in the power sector to eliminate monopolies in supply of electricity. As in the case of the telecom sector, direct access to consumers will motivate the suppliers to add capacity for meeting the supply gap. This will ensure large volumes of private investment that will alleviate shortages, reduce tariffs, and improve efficiencies—the same way as it happened for mobile telephony. The law has already been enacted in 2003, and now it is only a matter of its implementation.

HIGHWAYS

Upgradation of the highway network requires investment on a large scale. Until recently, highways were only financed through budgetary expenditure which meant taxes or government borrowings. The critical issue is whether highways should be funded by the general tax payers or by the users of a particular highway. There is growing consensus that investment in highways should be sustained by user charges so that road projects become self-sustaining. This paradigm shift towards commercialisation of highway projects constitutes the foundation of the PPP approach.

Performance of NHAI

NHAI was created by law to function on business principles, which essentially means that it should break even on its costs and revenues. It could either borrow from the market and repay out of user charges, or award projects on PPP basis to private entities. Unfortunately, NHAI has not shown the dynamism needed to pursue either of these self-sustaining alternatives. For several years, it has avoided adoption of EPC (turnkey) contracts and has continued to rely on conventional contracts that typically take twice the anticipated time and suffer from cost overruns exceeding 50 per cent of the contracted costs. If interest during construction and the forgone toll revenues are taken into account, the impact of cost overruns would be much greater.

NHAI has adopted the PPP approach as this was more or less mandated by government policy. However, the pace of the highway development programme remains slow while certain aspects do not seem to reflect adequate sensitivity to commercial considerations that are critical for PPP. Moreover, there is a tendency to over-engineer projects, which increases the costs of the programme, which would ultimately face the hurdle of budgetary constraints. In addition, the delay in commencing collection of tolls in a large number of projects has led to a significant loss of revenues over the years. Pilferage in collection of toll revenues is also a serious problem. In addition, the Ministry of Road Transport and Highways has recently made significant concessions in the toll rates, which were already very low by international standards. Increasing the project costs, on the one hand, while neglecting resource mobilization, on the other hand, has jeopardised the financial health of NHAI. These handicaps are often compounded by allegations of corruption, manipulation, and cartelisation, some of which are under investigation.

During a period of 10 years from 1995–96 to 2004–05, NHAI awarded PPP projects for a total of about 890 km representing less than 2 per cent of its network. Following the interventions of the Committee on Infrastructure, it was recognised that large volumes of private investment would be necessary for funding a credible programme of highway development. In pursuit of this objective, a model concession agreement was formulated to ensure a fair, transparent, and balanced framework for PPP in highways. Similarly, the bidding documents for pre-qualification and selection of bidders were also streamlined and standardised. As a result, in the five years between 2005–06 and 2009–10, it was possible to award PPP projects for a total of about 9,000 km. This is a quantum jump compared to past performance, but the fact remains that it is far short of the targets and the potential.

Restructure NHAI on Business Principles

The single-most important reform in the highway sector would be to enable NHAI to function on business principles. The budgetary assistance provided by the government should only be used for bridging the gap in the financial viability of its projects. In case it wants to upgrade the level of specifications and standards, it should raise its toll rates while carrying conviction with road users who should see value in paying more. The great advantage of a financially self-sustaining approach is that NHAI would be free from any hard budget constraints and could expand the road building programme exponentially. To enable this to happen, the government needs to restructure the NHAI so that it is able to function like one of the viable *Navaratna* public sector undertakings.

PPP in State Highways

The mantra of PPP in highways seems to be picking up in several states that have not only adopted the standardised documents and processes of the Central Government but also awarded more than 50 PPP projects while more than 100 projects are in various stages of formulation. These states include Andhra Pradesh, Bihar, Gujarat, Haryana, Madhya Pradesh, Maharashtra, Karnataka, and Rajasthan. The remaining states also need to be encouraged to adopt the PPP route.

PORTS

The major ports in India function through their respective Port Trusts which do not have adequate capacity, commercial flexibility, and functional delegation. Moreover, they are controlled by the Central Government, whereas ports in the developed world are usually accountable to the local government. There have been several moves over the past two decades to corporatise these Port Trusts, but to no avail. During the past ten years, traffic volumes have grown by a CAGR of about 6.5 per cent while capacity addition took place at a rate of about 6.2 per cent per annum. As a result, congestion has increased even while large volumes of cargo have been diverted from the major ports to the state sector ports.

In 1997, the PPP mode was introduced for building and operating port terminals through concessions to be awarded by the Port Trusts. However, between 1997–98 and 2007–08, only 15 PPP concessions for port terminals were awarded, and these were based on a sub-optimal framework that has promoted user exploitation, rent-seeking, and litigation. Thanks to the initiative of the Committee on Infrastructure, a distorted 'cost plus' tariff structure was replaced by a predictable and competitive tariff regime. Moreover, a model concession agreement was formulated for providing a fair, balanced, and transparent framework for private participation, besides the standardisation of bid documents for pre-qualification and selection of bidders.

Even after the rationalisation and standardisation of documents and processes was completed, the roll out of projects has continued to be inadequate, primarily on account of the resistance of incumbent Port Trusts who have awarded PPP concessions for less than 15 per cent of their annual targets, year after year. Though 2009–10 witnessed some acceleration and 8 PPP projects were awarded during the year, they constitute a small proportion of the targets as well as the potential. The key challenge, therefore, lies in ensuring that the incumbent Port Trusts award more PPP projects to address the prevailing congestion.

Private Investment is the Key

The slow capacity addition at major ports has failed to keep pace with the increasing volumes of cargo, leading to a demand for alternative ports. In response, several maritime states have awarded concessions to private entities that have set up new ports. This has helped relieve congestion and also introduced an element of competition. Though the share of state ports has been rising, the major ports continue to play a dominant role and they need to be expanded to cope with the growing demand for port services. This expansion is best achieved through PPP, which is why it is necessary to accelerate the award of PPP projects for ensuring the much-needed capacity addition in the port sector.

The Port Trusts also need to be corporatised. There has been resistance to this initiative for the past several years, but it can be argued that governance and transparency would increase greatly if the major ports were not only corporatised but also privatised.

AIRPORTS

India can take pride in building world-class airports at Delhi, Mumbai, Bengaluru, and Hyderabad. These projects have clearly demonstrated the benefits of private sector efficiencies as compared to the airports operated by the Airports Authority of India (AAI). However, a closer scrutiny of these cases would suggest that the selection process and contract terms were wanting in several aspects. The existing concession framework, though comprehensive and balanced in most parts, could be viewed as sub-optimal in some parts. For example, there is little oversight or restraint in expending capital costs that directly raise the user charges. In the case of Delhi and Mumbai airports, some post-bid concessions have also been granted. These include the exclusion of certain receipts from the computation of revenue sharing between the AAI and the concessionaire, as a result of which the annual payments due to AAI would be reduced significantly.

A number of other airports are undergoing a complete makeover through the award of high-cost construction contracts that would inevitably lead to an upward revision of user charges. The existing arrangements for the operation and management of these airports would remain unchanged in the hands of AAI. The gains of the PPP approach at the four metro airports have obviously failed to move the incumbent AAI to cede control in favour of PPPs.

Enhance Private Participation

There are three critical reform initiatives that need to be pursued in the airport sector. The first and foremost is the induction of private participation in the operation and management of all airports, including those where new terminals have been built by AAI. This would ensure greater efficiency and quality of service, better utilisation of airport assets, and increase in non-aeronautical revenues that would help reduce the user charges.

Contain the User Charges

The second reform initiative relates to user charges. Though an independent regulatory commission has been set up, it is yet to find ways of controlling the spiralling capital and operating costs being claimed by the private sponsors and the AAI. World-class airports should mean efficient and cost-effective airports and not grandiose structures that fritter away scarce resources. The whole purpose of reform and modernisation is lost if the user is subjected to unjustified charges. While competition has led to a significant reduction in airfares, the monopolistic airports seem to be raising their charges steadily. Regulatory interventions aimed at reduction in user charges, especially those arising out of gold plating of costs, should be assigned a high priority.

Separation of ATC

The third reform initiative relates to the separation of Air Traffic Control (ATC) from AAI, in line with international best practices. A well-organised ATC is essential both for safety as well as for ensuring optimum utilisation of the airport infrastructure. A less proficient ATC implies a lower number of landing/take-off operations that would translate into a larger requirement of ground infrastructure for holding the aircrafts and passengers. It can be argued that since AAI diverts a large part of the ATC income for funding its construction contracts, it continues to starve the ATC of funds necessary for upgrading the communication and navigation services. Though several committees have suggested separation of ATC from AAI, the incumbent AAI has thus far managed to forestall any action in this direction.

RAILWAYS

The railways sector is the least reformed, functioning as a monolithic government department, unlike in any major economy including even China. Several reports on the functioning of railways have pointed out that in the absence of corporatisation, it displays an inadequate commercial perspective; operates an outdated network and rolling stock; suffers from huge over-staffing; recovers irrational and unsustainable passenger fares; and levies excessive freight charges that add to the costs of the economy. Private investment constitutes only 4 per cent of the total investment in railways during the Eleventh Five Year Plan as compared to over 80 per cent in the case of the telecom sector. As a result, the railways sector has steadily lost its market share in favour of roads and air travel. This has not only imposed large additional costs on the economy as a whole, but also degraded the environment.

Need for Basic Reforms

In the present institutional arrangement, there is little hope for reform, which is critical for achieving energy efficient transport and for the transition to a low carbon economy. The need for institutional reform in the railways has been articulated on many occasions. The Rakesh Mohan Committee made several recommendations a decade ago. The Eleventh Five Year Plan as well as its Mid-Term Appraisal have also emphasised the pressing need for such reforms. The Ministry of Railways has also recognised the need for several reform initiatives in its vision document released in February 2010. However, reforms have not been implemented nor has a road map been laid out. The monolithic government-run structure does not seem suited to cope with the changes that have transformed the rest of the economy. The problem is compounded by the colonial legacy of a separate Railway Budget that perpetuates a government within the government. In the absence of modernisation, the railways would continue to be a drag on the economy. This could well continue for years to come, until a serious crisis would precipitate the much-needed reform.

First and foremost, the railways need to be corporatised for functioning on business principles. Second, they need to rationalise their fare structure, which is currently encumbered by unsustainable populist impulses that lead to very low passenger fares and exceptionally high freight charges. Third, they need to attract private investment for providing competitive and efficient services. Fourth, they need to modernise their network and rolling stock in order to provide improved services that suffer from a lag of several decades as compared to the Western world and China. It is often argued that these are politically sensitive areas, but if that is so, a serious effort needs to be made for mobilising the necessary political support. For the reform of the railways can only be postponed at a huge cost to the economy.

REGULATION

Sound economic regulation is a pre-requisite for the orderly growth of infrastructure. It is necessary for assuring private investors of a level playing field against the incumbent public sector entities. It is also critical for protecting consumer interests in terms of user charges and the quality of service. The need for independent regulators was recognised in the late 1990s and sector-specific laws have since been enacted, but the evolution of regulatory structures has been very uneven.

The port regulator only fixes tariffs and does nothing else. The telecom regulator has the duty to make recommendations, but lacks the power to implement them. The petroleum regulator is still awaiting a government notification that would enable it to commence some of its important functions. The airport regulator may suffer from the baggage of PPP concessions already awarded for the four metro airports. The electricity regulators have comprehensive functions and powers, but seem to have suffered from regulatory capture leading to the perpetuation of monopolies, denial of choice to the consumers, and excessive profiteering by producers and traders. Evidently, there is a complete lack of any cogent philosophy in these regulatory institutions. As if to compound these inadequacies, the regulators have been made accountable to no one.

Need for Regulatory Reform

The government has declared its intent to undertake regulatory reforms that would include objective selection of the regulators who would be autonomous in their functioning and have powers to issue and enforce licences as well as a duty to enhance competition. They would be made accountable to the Parliament through an outcome-based review of their performance. Given the growing instances of regulatory capture and abdication, there is wide support for regulatory reforms through an overarching Regulatory Reform Bill. A discussion paper prepared by the Planning Commission has undergone extensive consultations with the concerned stakeholders and experts. It remains to be seen whether the proposals in this paper can be actually carried forward.

CONCLUSION

Building infrastructure primarily through budgetary resources is no longer feasible, not only because of the competing demands from social sectors, but also because the investment needs have grown multifold. As a result, most of the physical infrastructure would need to be financed by user charges. Commercialisation of infrastructure is, therefore, inevitable. Once this paradigm is accepted, private investment can supplement public investment on a fairly large scale.

The total investment in infrastructure was Rs 9,19,225 crore ($230 billion) during the Tenth Five Year Plan (2002–07), which is expected to rise to Rs 20,54,205 crore ($514 billion) during the Eleventh Plan (2007–12) and Rs 40,99,239 crore ($1025 billion) during the Twelfth Plan (2012–17)—all at 2006–07 prices. The share of private investment was about 24 per cent of the total investment during the Tenth Plan, which is likely to exceed 36 per cent during the ongoing Eleventh Plan and reach 50 per cent during the Twelfth Plan. This quantum jump and structural shift is predicated upon reinforcement and implementation of the enabling policy and regulatory framework. That brings governance into sharp focus.

Address the Incumbents

The enabling laws and policy framework are already in place. The requisite documents and processes have also been streamlined and standardised. Yet the delivery is far short of the potential. Incumbent mindset and conflicts of interest are the key challenges. They need to be addressed through effective inter-ministerial processes that would have to be clearly mandated by the government, and implemented by the Finance Ministry and the Planning Commission. Participation of other stakeholders such as users, investors, and lenders would also be necessary.

Build Affordable Infrastructure

The rationale of the reform process lies in the creation of adequate physical infrastructure at affordable costs. In the euphoria of building new projects, costs should not be overlooked, as high-cost infrastructure can compromise the competitiveness of the economy and also reduce its growth momentum. The effort to build world-class infrastructure must, therefore, ensure that infrastructure services are both cost-effective as well as affordable.

Expand the Support for Reforms

While the need for reforms in broad terms is widely accepted, actual implementation of reform initiatives is presently confined to a handful of policymakers. It is necessary to achieve a much wider ownership and support for systemic reforms in infrastructure. Unless this is done, the implementation of reforms would remain susceptible to pressure from vested interests. It is, therefore, necessary to enhance public awareness and participation so that reforms enjoy the support of a wider spectrum and are also seen as people friendly.

Enhance Accountability and Professionalism

Absence of accountability seems to be the root cause of corruption and inadequate delivery. It also marginalises the need for professionalism in the bureaucracy. Restoring accountability and professionalism are the key challenges of governance that need to be addressed with a sense of urgency—at least for the infrastructure sector.

Reinforce Due Diligence and Anticipation

Implementation by trial and error has been the bane of governance in India. Though some experimentation may be necessary in the process of evolution and development, it cannot be unleashed without sufficient diligence. In the past, several reform initiatives were not adequately thought through and led to instances of gaming, rent-seeking, and corruption. This has created legitimate suspicions about the integrity and underlying objectives of such initiatives. The inability to anticipate problems is often responsible for yielding to the vested interests that push for seemingly convincing options that may in fact be partisan. Where the quality of due diligence and anticipation is sound, it tends to run counter to the vested interests and is often labelled as negative or anti-development. For ensuring sustainable outcomes, it is necessary to recognise the role of due diligence and anticipation in the governance of the infrastructure sector.

Outcomes are Predictable

The essays in this volume demonstrate that governance of infrastructure is not rocket science. The issues and options are usually quite clear and the consequences of following any particular course are also quite predictable. For reasons described in this chapter, public interest is often compromised, thus imposing a heavy burden on the economy and the common man. Good governance is the key to avoiding these predictable failures. And that can only flow from the fountain-head of the government, the complexities of the Indian polity notwithstanding.

Bibliography

Acharya, Shankar and Rakesh Mohan (eds), *India's Economy—Performance and Challenges: Essays in Honour of Montek Singh Ahluwalia*. New Delhi: Oxford University Press, 2010.

Address by the Prime Minister at the Conference on 'Building Infrastructure: Challenges and Opportunities', October 2006, available at http://infrastructure.gov.in

Address by the Prime Minister at the Conference on 'Building Infrastructure: Challenges and Opportunities', Vigyan Bhawan, Delhi, 23 March 2010.

Bharat Nirman, *A Business Plan for Rural Infrastructure, 2005–09*, available at http://bharatnirman.gov.in

The Business Standard—India 2008. New Delhi: Business Standard Books, 2008.

Central Electricity Regulatory Commission, Quarterly Reports on Trading, October–December 2008, available at http://www.cercind.gov.in

Central Electricity Authority, 'Power Scenario at a Glance', January 2009, available at http://cea.nic.in

—————, 'Monthly Review of the Power Sector', June 2010, available at http://cea.nic.in

Chawla, Divya (Planning Commission, Secretariat for Infrastructure), 'Commercial Use of Land at Delhi and Mumbai Airports: An Analysis of the Question of Law and Public Policy', August 2010, available at http://infrastructure.gov.in/

Government of National Capital Territory of Delhi, Delhi Metro Rail Corporation Ltd., *Annual Report, 2008–09*, available at http://delhimetrorail.com

Government of India, 'Report of the IMG on Simplification of Customs Procedures in Air Cargo and Airports', April 2006, available at http://infrastructure.gov.in

——————, 'Financing Infrastructure Projects through the India Infrastructure Finance Company', May 2006, available at http://infrastructure.gov.in

——————, 'Financing Support to Public Private Partnerships in Infrastructure', May 2006, available at http://infrastructure.gov.in

Government of India, 'Formulation, Appraisal and Approval of Public Private Partnerships Projects', May 2006, available at http://infrastructure.gov.in

——————, 'Report of the Committee of Secretaries—Road Rail Connectivity of Major Ports', May 2006, available at http://infrastructure.gov.in

——————, 'Report of the Core Group—Financing of the National Highway Development Programme', May 2006, available at http://infrastructure.gov.in

——————, 'Report of the Task Force—The Delhi–Mumbai and Delhi–Howrah Freight Corridors', May 2006, available at http://infrastructure.gov.in

——————, 'Report of the Task Force—Financing Plan for Airports', July 2006, available at http://infrastructure.gov.in

——————, 'Report of the Committee on Road Safety and Traffic Management', February 2007, available at http://infrastructure.gov.in

——————, 'Manual of Specifications and Standards for Two-laning of Highways', May 2007, available at http://infrastructure.gov.in

——————, 'Model Concession Agreement for PPP in Container Train Operations', June 2007, available at http://infrastructure.gov.in

——————, 'Report of the Task Force—Financing Plan for Ports', July 2007, available at http://infrastructure.gov.in

——————, 'Report of the Task Force—Tariff Setting and Bidding Parameters for PPP Projects in Major Ports', August 2007, available at http://infrastructure.gov.in

——————, 'Guidelines for PPP—Request for Proposal', November 2007, available at http://infrastructure.gov.in

——————, 'Guidelines for PPP—Request for Qualification', December 2007, available at http://infrastructure.gov.in

——————, *Eleventh Five Year Plan 2007–2012*, 2008, available at http://planningcommission.nic.in

——————, 'Manual of Specifications and Standards for Four-laning of Highways', March 2008, available at http://infrastructure.gov.in

——————, 'Report of Inter-Ministerial Committee—Restructuring of National Highway Authority of India', March 2008, available at http://infrastructure.gov.in

——————, 'Projections in the Eleventh Five Year Plan—Investment in Infrastructure', August 2008, available at http://infrastructure.gov.in

_____, 'Approach to Regulation of Infrastructure', September 2008, available at http://infrastructure.gov.in

_____, 'Model Concession Agreement for PPP in Urban Rail Systems', January 2009, available at http://infrastructure.gov.in

Government of India, 'Report of the IMG on Norms and Standards for Capacity of Airport Terminals', January 2009, available at http://infrastructure.gov.in

_____, 'Report of the Task Force on Measures for Operationalising Open Access in the Power Sector', January 2009, available at http://infrastructure.gov.in

_____, 'Draft Regulatory Reform Bill', April 2009, available at http://infrastructure.gov.in

_____, 'Model Concession Agreement for PPP in National Highways', April 2009, available at http://infrastructure.gov.in

_____, 'Model Concession Agreement for PPP in Non-metro Airports', April 2009, available at http://infrastructure.gov.in

_____, 'Model Concession Agreement for PPP in Operation and Maintenance of Highways', April 2009, available at http://infrastructure.gov.in

_____, 'Model Concession Agreement for PPP in Ports', April 2009, available at http://infrastructure.gov.in

_____, 'Model Concession Agreement for PPP in State Highways', April 2009, available at http://infrastructure.gov.in

_____, 'Model Procurement-cum-Maintenance Agreement for Locomotives', April 2009, available at http://infrastructure.gov.in

_____, 'Report of the IMG on Customs Procedures and Functioning of Container Freight Station and Ports', April 2009, available at http://infrastructure.gov.in

_____, 'Report of the IMG on Reducing Dwell Time of Cargo at Ports', April 2009, available at http://infrastructure.gov.in

_____, 'Model Request for Proposal (RFP) for Selection of Technical Consultants', May 2009, available at http://infrastructure.gov.in

_____, 'Frequently Asked Questions (FAQs) on Model RFQ Document', May 2009, available at http://infrastructure.gov.in

_____, 'Report of the Committee of Secretaries on Review of Toll Policy for National Highways', May 2009, available at http://infrastructure.gov.in

_____, 'Model Concession Agreement for PPP in Redevelopment of Railway Stations', May 2009, available at http://infrastructure.gov.in

_____, 'Model Concession Agreement for PPP in Greenfield Airports', May 2009, available at http://infrastructure.gov.in

_____, 'Selection of Consultants: Best Practices', May 2009, available at http://infrastructure.gov.in

_____, 'Guidelines for Monitoring of PPP Projects', May 2009, available at http://infrastructure.gov.in

_____, 'Private Investment in Infrastructure', May 2009, available at http://infrastructure.gov.in

Government of India, 'Guidelines for Establishing Joint Ventures in Infrastructure', July 2009, available at http://infrastructure.gov.in

_____, 'Model Request for Proposal (RFP) for Selection of Legal Advisors', July 2009, available at http://infrastructure.gov.in

_____, 'Model Request for Proposal (RFP) for Selection of Transmission Consultants', July 2009, available at http://infrastructure.gov.in

_____, Ministry of Communication and IT, Department of Telecommunication, *Annual Report, 2009–10*, available at http://dot.gov.in

_____, Ministry of Power, *Annual Report, 2009–10*, available at http://www.powermin.nic.in

_____, Ministry of Railways, *Annual Report, 2009–10*, available at http://indianrailways.gov.in

_____, Ministry of Road Transport and Highways, *Annual Report, 2009–10*, available at http://morth.nic.in

_____, Ministry of Shipping, *Annual Report, 2009–10*, available at http://shipping.gov.in

_____, 'Compendium of PPP Projects', March 2010, available at http://infrastructure.gov.in

_____, 'Investment in Infrastructure during the Eleventh Five Year Plan', March 2010, available at http://infrastructure.gov.in

_____, 'Model Request for Proposal (RFP) for Selection of Financial Consultants-cum-Transaction Advisers', April 2010, available at http://infrastructure.gov.in

_____, 'Compendium of PPP Projects in State Highways', July 2010, available at http://infrastructure.gov.in

_____, 'Model Transmission Agreement for PPP in Transmission Systems', August 2010, available at http://infrastructure.gov.in

_____, Ministry of Civil Aviation, *Annual Report*, various years, available at http://civilaviation.nic.in

_____, *India Infrastructure Report*, published on behalf of the Ministry of Finance by National Council of Applied Economic Research (NCAER), June 1996.

Indian Ports Association, 'Private Participation', 2008, available at http://ipa.nic.in

The Indian Railways Report 2001: Policy Imperatives for Reinvention and Growth, Report of Expert Group on Railways, National Council of Applied Economic Research (NCAER), January 2001.

Investment Commission, 'Opportunities in the World's Largest Democracy', 2008, available at http://investmentcommission.in

Kuhad, Prateek (Planning Commission, Secretariat for Infrastructure), 'Bidding Process for the Delhi and Mumbai Airports: A Case Study', August 2010, available at http://infrastructure.gov.in/

Morris, Sebastian, Ajay Pandey, G. Raghuram, and Rachna Gangwar (Indian Institute of Management Ahmedabad), 'Introducing Competition in Container Movement by Rail: A Case Study', December 2009, available at http://infrastructure.gov.in

National Highway Authority of India, *Annual Report, 2005–06*, available at http://nhai.org

Pandey, Ajay, Sebastian Morris, and G. Raghuram (Indian Institute of Management Ahmedabad), 'Structuring PPPs in Aviation Sector: Case of Delhi and Mumbai Airport Privatisation', July 2010, available at http://infrastructure.gov.in

Pargal, Sheoli (Planning Commission, Secretariat for the Committee on Infrastructure), 'Concession for the Delhi–Noida Bridge: A Case Study', August 2007, available at http://infrastructure.gov.in

Salhotra, Bharat (Planning Commission, Secretariat for the Committee on Infrastructure), 'Concession for Nhava Sheva International Container Terminal: A Case Study', November 2007, available at http://infrastructure.gov.in

Telecom Regulatory Authority of India, *Annual Report, 2008–09*, available at http://trai.gov.in

World Bank, Proceedings of the Annual Bank Conference on Development Economics (ABCDE), National Council of Applied Economic Research (NCAER), 2003.

UB.S
175840
20-1-12